THE BRITISH AIRWAYS STORY:
STRUGGLE FOR TAKE-OFF

The privatisation of British Airways was first
announced in 1979 but has been postponed
almost annually for half a decade. The state
airline has had to overcome a string of set-backs,
culminating in an epic legal battle to resolve BA's
relations with Sir Freddie Laker in the aftermath
of the February 1982 collapse of Laker Airways.

THE BRITISH AIRWAYS STORY combines the
story of an already celebrated lawsuit with a
narrative of the tumultuous events inside BA as
it prepared itself for the private sector. Written
by a former *Financial Times* journalist, now a
management consultant, it offers a balanced,
informative and compelling analysis of the
British Airways story.

About the Author

Duncan Campbell-Smith was educated at
Stratford-upon-Avon Grammar School and
Merton College, Oxford, where he got a First in
Modern History in 1972. He spent some years
working in finance on Wall Street and in the City
before studying and travelling widely in the
Arab world. He joined the *Financial Times* in 1979
as a writer on Middle Eastern business and
banking affairs, then moved to the financial staff
in 1981. He was a Lex columnist on the paper
for two years. He joined McKinsey, the
international management consultants, in 1985,
and now works in the firm's London office. He is
married to a painter and has one son.

THE BRITISH AIRWAYS STORY:

Struggle for Take-Off

Duncan Campbell-Smith

CORONET BOOKS
Hodder and Stoughton

To My Mother

Copyright © 1986 Duncan Campbell-Smith

First published in Great Britain in 1986
by Coronet Books

British Library C.I.P.

Campbell-Smith, Duncan
  The British Airways Story.
  1. British Airways—History
  I. Title
  387.7'065'41   HE9843.B7

  ISBN 0 340 39495 1

Printed and bound in Great Britain for
Hodder and Stoughton Paperbacks, a
division of Hodder and Stoughton Ltd.,
Mill Road, Dunton Green, Sevenoaks,
Kent (Editorial Office: 47 Bedford
Square, London, WC1B 3DP) by
Cox and Wyman Ltd,
Cardiff Road, Reading.

Contents

Acknowledgements

This book was written in a brief interval between leaving the *Financial Times* and joining McKinsey last autumn: I am hugely indebted to both of them for making that possible. The FT was generous enough to leave me with a sabbatical intact, while my colleagues-to-be at McKinsey's London office responded with positive enthusiasm to a plea for a personal computer – without which the time constraints would have been overwhelming.

I should like to thank all those participants in the events I have tried to describe who gave me their time and assistance – sometimes with misgivings but almost always with courtesy and patience – so that I could at least have every chance to record a faithful version of the story. A few, and they will know who they are, will be only too pleased to see their names omitted here. But it would, anyway, be impractical to attempt a list of the many people whose views and recollections allowed me to assemble even this highly selective account of what happened to British Airways over the years covered by the book.

As a non-lawyer, though, left struggling sometimes to grasp all the prickly legal issues which confronted the airline, I need to acknowledge one particular source of assistance rather more precisely – namely, all those lawyers in Washington and London who did their best more than once to help me understand what was at stake. Since the settlement of the Laker litigation, I have received especially invaluable help from Douglas E. Rosenthal and Leonard N. Bebchick.

Amongst individuals not directly involved in it, I am grateful to Sir Edmund Dell and to Professor John Quelch of Harvard Business School for alerting me to important aspects of the BA story. I must also thank my literary agent Felicity Bryan for helping to launch me off on the book in the first place. And special thanks are due to Howard Davies and Peter Stothard for reading it in manuscript and offering numerous helpful criticisms.

Above all, my deepest thanks go to my wife Anne-Catherine for her encouragement and her forebearance in providing – despite all the subversive efforts of an eighteen-month-old son – what amounted to laboratory conditions for authorship.

1

Speedbird or Dodo?

Privatisation is a buzz word in contemporary British politics. But in 1979, it was a novel term to describe a relatively new-fangled notion – or, as many thought, an ugly name for an unlikely policy. Few people really supposed that sweeping denationalisation amongst Britain's state-owned industries was much more than a forlorn Tory hope.

British Leyland, British Steel, British Shipbuilders . . . the very presence of the 'British' label seemed to announce: 'Here lie dwindling markets, losses piled on pre-tax losses, chronic overmanning and odious comparisons with Japanese or German competitors . . .'

British Airways looked different.

The state airline had a prominent and secure position in a generally prosperous global market which it was notoriously difficult for outsiders to break into – as Sir Freddie Laker spent most of the seventies discovering. BA enjoyed far more autonomy than the general run of UK nationalised industries. And above all, it made profits.

In short, the Tories decided in 1979 to privatise BA by selling at least half of the Government's ownership off to the private sector. Alas, it was less than two years before critics of the airline began to spin a familiar tale. Rumours of gross incompetence and inefficiency were circulating widely by the summer of 1981. They culminated in a twelve-page indictment of the airline's

1

management which effectively torpedoed what remained of any credibility for a sale of BA shares in the foreseeable future.

No one ever identified the authors behind 'A Minority Report', as the twelve pages were entitled. What they revealed, though, about BA in August 1981 left no doubt the authors were burrowing on an inside track. Their 'Moles' Report', as it was known, made electric reading. Its strictures, well-founded or not, were sharp and to the point:

'If you want a glass of milk, go and buy a cow' was the airline management's guiding philosophy.

The BA board had reacted to crisis on all sides by talking over and over again about whether or not executive directors should go on having the use of corporation chauffeurs.

Its policies had resulted in a 'peasant class' of travel on BA's European flights, repackaged catering arrangements which amounted to 'doggy-bag specials' and a general subservience to trade union pressure which had the management running to the pilots' union headquarters for routine meetings.

And the financial consequences, with about one-fifth of the flag-carrier's international routes losing money, had 'brought the airline to its knees'.

Or so said the moles. BA's board rejected the report as malicious and ill-informed. But it was given extensive coverage by Fleet Street and copies were widely circulated in Whitehall and Westminster.

And so ended the first attempt to sell off shares in BA.

It was a more serious setback even than was realised at the time. For within six months, another shock had resounded round the airline world: Freddie's Laker Airways had gone bust. Its collapse was going to produce infinitely more malicious and ill-informed reports about BA – and an obstacle to the sale of BA shares which might have been avoided but for the business woes of 1979–81.

But all of this lay far ahead when the idea of selling off

BA first saw the light. Britain's flag-carrying airline was going to be the flagship of Tory privatisation. It was big, highly visible – even a touch romantic. It looked the ideal candidate, in fact, for one of the most fundamental political changes planned by Mrs Thatcher and her new Ministers in the aftermath of their election victory in May 1979. They had signalled their privatisation policy long before the election. It had been set out formally in the Tory manifesto. No time was to be lost in beginning the long-awaited struggle to roll back the frontiers of the state. The Government's Economic Policy Committee met late in July to pick the first targets.

The National Enterprise Board's ragbag portfolio offered some easy pickings. But they were hardly likely to make much of a stir. Some larger companies like British Aerospace or Cable & Wireless were candidates. But was the sale of either of these really going to sound like three blasts of the trumpet before the walls of the public sector?

Hardly. British Aerospace was relatively small and was anyway busy building parts for civil airliners which would continue to need public subsidies. Cable & Wireless had no operations in the UK, so few people outside the City had ever heard of it. Something more bracing was required. If it were not so big and complex, British Telecom might almost have filled the bill . . . but it was a public service, which rather complicated matters.

Thus came about that on 20 July in a thinly attended House of Commons, John Nott, the greenhorn Trade Secretary, proclaimed the Government's intention to sell 'a substantial minority holding' in British Airways. There was a gratifying furore, with alarm, shock and dismay expressed on the Opposition benches. It was 'nothing short of aerial piracy', said Labour Party critics, 'the most outrageous piece of looting'. That was more like the required response.

Taking the initiative with BA also allowed the new Government to set a reasonably straightforward course for the civil service. Privatisation represented virgin territory for Whitehall. Senior Tories, most notably Sir Keith Joseph, had been working on the policy's political implications for a long time ahead of the election and had shared their views with several prominent industrialists. But there was not much on the civil servants' files. Fixing BA as the target meant they could be set to work on the finite task of preparing immediate legislation. BA was a statutory corporation and there would need to be a Civil Aviation Bill to change it into a Companies Act animal suitable for private investors.

What private investors might think about the deal had already been the subject of speculation in the City of London for a few months. Nott invited merchant bankers Hill Samuel to manage the preparations for the sale, though the passage of the Bill would itself preclude any flotation until the autumn of 1980 at the very earliest.

So much for the constitutional aspect and the market context, two of the three items which made up BA's initial privatisation agenda. Item number three, awaiting the convenience of the politicians, was the suitability for sale of the public asset itself. Would British Airways fly?

And on this last count, as things turned out, the new Government could hardly have chosen a more disastrous pioneer for its privatisation policy. What followed, as a result, were two years of almost unmitigated embarrassment for the Buy The Flag brigade, as the advocates of a BA sale were inevitably branded ('Fly the flag' was a recently adopted BA advertising slogan). And when BA finally set out with an aggressive plan to put all the embarrassment behind it, the airline was to fly slap into the biggest controversy in the international aviation industry since 1945.

The chances of selling any shares in BA began to recede publicly almost from the very week of Nott's announcement. First the sale date was postponed until the autumn of 1981, then, in the midsummer of '81, it was shelved indefinitely. The potential marketability of the airline was, by then, of less interest to anyone than the immediate prospect of its total financial collapse.

It all came as a most unpleasant surprise. To anyone visiting BA's headquarters on the perimeter of London's Heathrow Airport back in 1979, it must have seemed inconceivable that this huge organisation was in fact teetering on the edge of chaos. The Shell and BP fuel stations, the engineering sheds and jet-engine test bays, the rows of crowded check-in counters and information desks, the blue-and-white fuselages of BA's planes roaring over the rooftops every few minutes – all the paraphernalia of the modern airline on its home base looked and sounded as much a part of Heathrow as the very smell of the place. Even to those who spent every working day of their lives in the HQ offices of Speedbird House or in BA's fleet maintenance hangars, the notion of any abrupt change for the worse would surely have seemed fantastical. Was this not, after all, a nationalised industry?

It was indeed. But in 1979 the struggle to change that status was about to begin – the struggle for take-off as a commercial company fit to compete in the private sector.

Sir Frank McFadzean, BA's chairman at the time of the election, had been one of the businessmen most privy to Sir Keith Joseph's privatisation plans. He had been enthusiastic about the opportunities opening up for the airline as a consequence of its growing autonomy. Concorde's acquisition costs were to be written off, for example, and BA given more scope to buy the aircraft it wanted. (It had already, in 1978, bought Boeing 737s instead of the 1-11s which British Aerospace had been pressing it to take as the replacement for its ageing Tridents.)

Indeed, Sir Frank had got himself into a spot of bother back in April for lending his public support to the idea of a BA share sell-off. One prominent left-wing MP called it 'the depth of disloyalty' and urged the chairman's dismissal. As it was, Sir Frank resigned anyway within a few weeks of Mrs Thatcher's arrival. After a heart attack in 1977, he had been only a part-time chairman. Now he made way for the older man – Ross Stainton, at sixty-five a year older than McFadzean and one of many executives at the top of BA who had spent virtually all of his working life with the company or one of its antecedents. Stainton was replaced as chief executive by Roy Watts and a succession of management changes followed all the way down the line.

The new men smothered Nott's announcement with faint praise. They welcomed assurances that there would be no attempt to hive off BA assets, as the Heath Government had tried to do, and looked forward to discussions 'in order to come to a view'. But their reservations were plain to see. Ostensibly, their caution sprang from uncertainty about the outlook for international airlines generally. Not unreasonably, they argued that a sale in such circumstances might necessitate a low price for the airline – City commentators were already suggesting its total value in a sale might be around £300m., only three or four times its 1979 net earnings. They feared this might rebound adversely on BA in its commercial dealings and they worried about its possible impact on the morale of employees.

It was a cogent argument, expertly backed up by merchant bankers S. G. Warburg – BA's own advisers – and in all probability was lent a measure of discreet support by not a few civil servants in the Aviation Division, too. The Government gave every sign of regarding BA's response as so much shilly-shallying in the face of its bold political initiative. What Nott and his advisers did not appreciate – but the BA management suspected only too strongly – was that changes in BA's operating environment were at that very moment wreaking havoc with its internal budgets.

The widely respected Roy Watts and his senior colleagues had concluded a daring and comprehensive plan for the airline's future just the previous autumn. Entitled

'BA Marketing Strategy: An Internal Appreciation', it was being disseminated amongst all BA staff at the time of Nott's bombshell. The essence of the plan was a blueprint for what BA was to look like in 1986; but suddenly, many of the plan's key assumptions were starting to look a little odd – and odder with every week that passed. Intense government and Whitehall scrutiny of it could not have come at a more delicate moment.

The 1978 plan implied three main lines of change. First, the airline was going to spend £2.4bn. replacing all its noisy and old-fashioned VC-10s, Tridents and Boeing 707s. A shiny new fleet was to emerge, built around the Lockheed TriStar and Boeing 737s, 757s and Jumbo 747s. (Hostile critics of the privatisation plan were not slow to suggest that it was a desperate, government-inspired remedy aimed eventually at ridding the Public Sector Borrowing Requirement (PSBR) of the burden of funding this investment programme.)

Second, new productivity was going to be achieved by restricting BA's workforce to its current level of 57,500 in the face of steady traffic growth. There was no denying that the airline was ridiculously overmanned. But if the same number of employees could be handling 30m. travellers by 1986 instead of 16m. – flying in 200 aircraft instead of 194, thanks to the latest wide-bodied designs – then the prospective gains would be impressive.

And third, BA was going to pull some clever tricks with its schedules. The world's airline industry in 1979 was alert as never before to subtle categorisations of passenger traffic. The Watts Plan envisaged nothing less than a radical change of competitive tack by BA in its global marketplace. Leisure passengers would rise from 66 to 80 per cent of the total and BA would aim to make more money by selling cheaper tickets to ensure fuller aircraft.

The plan was a formidable intellectual exercise. It was coherent, detailed and internally consistent. But it relied on a string of predictions. As early as September of that year, it was clear these were horribly awry. In fact, disaster loomed. The second OPEC oil price rise was sending the airline's fuel bill through the roof. The international economy was slithering into recession, making a nonsense of most traffic projections. BA's attempt to move a little away from the business traveller was threatening to confuse its market image. And overhead costs were spiralling out of control.

The impact of BA's results remained unclear just long enough to leave John Nott's sale announcement sounding credible . . . for a week or two. Seven days later, it was revealed that operating profits in the year to March 1979 had fallen short of budget by nearly 25 per cent. After another seven days came public confirmation that BA's fuel bill looked like rising from £270m. in 1978–9 to at least £400m. in 1979–80.

By early September, Watts was writing to all employees to warn of a serious downturn in profits for the current year. He had originally hoped that profits before tax and interest might be around £157m. Now the forecast had to be cut to £100m. In January 1980 it was cut again, to £35m. BA was in a tailspin.

Symptoms of the decline were everywhere. Close behind the profits downturn – by the end of the year 1979–80, the actual pre-tax figure emerged at just £1m. – there followed a very public cash crisis. Far from building a new fleet, there was suddenly talk of jumbos having to be sold. The impact on morale within the airline was disastrous. Strikes began to plague its operations. With seventeen trade unions at BA, there was never any shortage of contentious issues to spark off industrial action. But much of the discontent was unmistakably spontaneous. There was uproar, for instance, when the British Airways motif was repainted on the side of the fleet, to leave just 'British' in its place. It would save a lot of paint, joked the directors. BA stood for Bloody Awful, said the wags, so the word 'Airways' was redundant anyway. As for the Speedbird on the side of the fuselage, a dodo would be more appropriate.

At the management level, morale at Speedbird House slumped disastrously. Discontent expressed itself in furtively circulated memoranda sniping at the executive board. Occasionally, sniping gave way to a regular broadside. 'BA Marketing Strategy: An Internal Appreciation,' for example, was really nothing of the kind: it deprecated every strand of the Watts 'holiday airline strategy'.

The strategy itself was quickly grounded for revision. New plans were rolled out for discussion. And there was plenty of that: every armchair strategist in the country was hard at work on a fresh start for BA. No one, though, seemed to have anything sensible to say about the £2.4m. investment programme. It had looked ambitious enough when management was still assuming that £1.5bn. would come from the airline's own cash-flow. With BA notching up pre-tax losses by the autumn of 1980, the programme was becoming an embarrassment.

The airline had a million problems, but three stood out a mile.

Fuel costs were rising traumatically. One US cent on the price of a gallon of jet fuel translated into an additional bill of about £5m. for BA. It was no wonder that profit forecasts had begun to look academic, with fuel prices doubling in 1979 alone. In the year ending March 1981, fuel accounted for 30 per cent of BA's total costs. The second OPEC oil shock had catapulted BA – like all other airlines in the world – into a completely new environment.

Every airline management faced the problem of how to lift fares anything like fast enough to keep profit margins intact. In this crisis, adaptability was not proving BA's strongest suit. This, of course, had much to do with its second big problem: in a word, flab. It was not just that BA looked about 25 per cent overmanned, which it certainly was. The very structure of the airline was hopelessly overweight.

The 1974 amalgamation of BOAC with the domestic and European divisions of BEA had produced a hybrid racked with management demarcation squabbles. The competitive advantages sought through the merger had been hopelessly defeated by the lack of a unifying corporate culture. It was a classic example of a textbook malady. 'Any treatment of strategic relationships among business units must confront the difficulties of actually achieving them or horizontal strategies will fail,' as Michael Porter has written. '. . . Cooperation can prove very difficult to achieve if business units have differing cultures.'*

BA had differing cultures in spades. Ever since the days of the original Imperial Airways, the forebear of BOAC, the intercontinental crews had been inclined to cast a patronising eye on short-haul crews in Europe. BEA men regarded BOAC as stuffy, snobbish and uncommercial. It was a bizarre extension of the English passion for subtle class distinctions: BOAC was the public school airline, remembered a Whitehall adviser in 1983, BEA was the grammar school airline. The clash between them plagued the affairs of both.

Thus, management could see the need for redundancies as well as anyone else. Stories were ten a penny about hundreds of surplus pilots sitting at home on full pay. But interdivisional hostility seemed to sap the board's resolve. Swingeing reductions in the workforce were somehow always superseded by one judicious pruning scheme or another. To get round the problem, the Watts Plan had put its faith in a fast-growing market: BA would hold its ground, while the consumer caught up. But as the 1979–81 recession struck home, the consumer headed in the opposite direction. Passenger numbers were actually falling.

Enter problem number three. Gerry Draper, BA's commercial director, occupied one of the hottest seats to be found anywhere in British business. For his airline was encountering a whole new style of competition. It

* Michael E. Porter, *Competitive Advantage: Creating and Sustaining Superior Performance* (1985).

was not emerging a conspicuous winner in this contest, either, and its market share on several critical routes was slipping badly. It was being given the elbow by a novel consumerism on the one hand and deregulation on the other. Hard times were instilling a new sense of commercial priorities amongst BA's international rivals: many were busy cultivating a glossy new consumer image which the British flag-carrier, hit by repeated strikes and a well-publicised morale problem, was finding hard to emulate.

Catering, cabin service and maintenance efficiency all came in for criticism from the Civil Aviation Authority (CAA). A survey conducted by the International Airline Passengers Association in the summer of 1980 brought little comfort. BA was rated as the most preferred international airline by 19 per cent of the poll; but then, it was easily the biggest in the world. More revealing, to its critics anyway, was that nearly 33 per cent put BA at the very top of their list of airlines to be avoided at all costs – ahead, it was widely noted, of Aeroflot, Nigeria Airways and even teetotal Arab carriers.

As for the damage being inflicted by deregulation, there seemed no end to it. Domestic US airlines had been opened to chill gales of free market competition by President Carter's Airline Deregulation Act in 1978. But the philosophy was catching. Invitations from Britain's increasingly autonomous CAA for new route licence applications were drawing a formidable response from independent airlines like Britannia Airways and Dan Air, never mind British Caledonian.

And then there was Sir Freddie Laker. He actually applied in October 1979 for up to 666 additional European routes just to underline the point – though it needed no reinforcing by 1979 – that the independents would grab whatever share of BA's revenues was going.

Laker Airways, with its tiny walk-on Skytrain service from Gatwick to the US, symbolised the challenge. It was also the independent causing BA the most substantial damage. Since 1977, Laker had used cut-price fares to claw its way up to being one of the volume leaders amongst the dozens of international airlines flying the North Atlantic. In the process, it had decimated the profitability of what, a decade earlier, had been one of the most lucrative as well as one of the most prestigious of BA's routes anywhere round the globe. By 1980, when Freddie was given a licence to fly his planes from Gatwick to Miami, the spare capacity over the Atlantic was becoming a bad joke. Airline analysts were falling over themselves to calculate the equivalent number of completely empty jumbo jets crossing every day. (It was well over twenty and rising fast.)

BA struggled to get on terms with all its new adversaries. Its efforts, though, only worsened the financial situation. Concorde, for example, may have been a boon for the airline's market image; but insiders reckoned it was losing £300,000 a week – and that was only taking into account its running costs, since its capital cost had now been written off!

In the cut-fare stakes, BA's senior executives had done their best to reach a *modus vivendi* with Laker Airways. The CAA encouraged all scheduled British airlines to iron out pricing policies between themselves as far as possible. Some of the top men at BA – who were personally not unsympathetic to what Freddie was trying to do – had spent endless hours thrashing out detailed fare strategies with Freddie and his staff. They had tried to allow him a niche while containing the threat posed by low fares to the profitability of the Atlantic market. But they had succeeded better at the first task than the second. By the summer of 1980, Laker still had its niche and the fare strategies were leading BA's chiefs to talk publicly of their alarm at the pricing antics of 'soap-powder salesmen'.

Other European transatlantic carriers like KLM, Lufthansa and Swissair opted out of the fares battle. Not so BA: in July 1980 it unveiled a New York stand-by fare of

£84 (against £85 on the Skytrain). Next month, Laker cut to £78. The month after that, BA was down to £77 – and its North Atlantic losses were piling higher and higher. As, indeed, were losses across the whole spectrum of BA's mainstream operations. For the Government and its privatisation policy, the gathering misadventure was utterly galling.

It was also vaguely disconcerting. For as the pressure grew on BA to improve its performance in readiness for privatisation, so the squeeze seemed to be worsening for Freddie – that white knight in shining armour of British entrepreneurs. Could it really be the case that forcing ahead the privatisation of BA was less than wholly compatible with espousing the virtues of Mrs Thatcher's favourite businessman? (And what, for that matter, about Sir Adam Thomson and his private British Caledonian group?)

The irony was lurking; but the Prime Minister and her Cabinet colleagues seemed hardly yet aware of it . . .

The earliest warnings of danger ahead referred only to the situation within BA. The City cautioned that political tides and airline economic cycles did not necessarily move together. BA's executives pleaded for a prudent postponement. Commons debates over the Aviation Bill – particularly in its committee stage – produced umpteen telling points against a rapid sale. But John Nott pushed the Bill ahead through the first half of 1980 with more and more explicit references to a sale date around the autumn of 1981. Accountants Ernst & Whinney were even set to work preparing the Long Form: the document which the Stock Exchange requires for every new share sale and which it demands must be both comprehensive and fully up-to-date.

By October, the Civil Aviation Act 1980 was on the books. The BA board and its powers under 1977 legislation could in due course be dissolved to make way for British Airways Plc. The corporation's Public Dividend Capital of £180m. – that is, the quasi-preferential stock held by the Government in lieu of ordinary shareholders' equity – could be extinguished and replaced by shares with an aggregate nominal value of £180m., which would be held by the Secretary of State. A new capital structure could be established and the shares could be sold.

That, anyway, was the theory.

The Government, however, could see perfectly well what was happening in practice. Formal advice that a sale should be abandoned arrived from merchant bankers Hill Samuel in October 1980. By then, the Prime Minister herself had already intervened. What was needed, the Cabinet agreed, was a fresh start under fresh management – and a Hercules fit to clean out the airline's Augean stables. What no one could know – and not even the gloomiest Cassandra predicted – was that in BA's predicament lay the seeds of another, altogether subtler bar to privatisation which no solitary Hercules would prove able to move. And by the time the Government realised this, it was to be only too well aware of the irony of BA's dealings with Freddie.

2

Ready for Freddie

Sir Freddie Laker was doing one of the things he always did best: self-promotion. It was Wednesday, 3 February 1982, in the Flying Tigers' hangar at New York's John F. Kennedy Airport and Freddie was rehearsing in front of the cameras for a new TV commercial for Laker Airways. A telephone call came through for him from London.

One of his closest aides, Robin Flood, took the call and explained that the boss was busy. Could she take a message? Well, said one of Freddie's personal assistants at the other end, it was a slightly curious message but simple enough. The Midland Bank wanted to know if Freddie would be kind enough to drop in at its City headquarters as soon as he returned to Gatwick the next morning. No problem, said Mrs Flood. She knew Freddie's only pressing commitment the next day was a meeting with counsel in London over his pending third divorce and that was not until late afternoon. He could take his flight that evening, as already arranged, and be with the Midland – albeit a touch bleary-eyed – by 10.00 a.m. on Thursday.

Freddie finished his film session and was given the message. It sounded, he said, like the meeting he had been waiting for since early the previous summer. At last the banks were going to set the seal on eight months of desperately grinding negotiations to reorganise the finances of his airline. Laker Airways and its pioneering Skytrain operation over the North Atlantic had been knocked for six by sterling's sharp fall against the dollar since 1980. But Freddie had known all along that things would work out in the end. Just the previous Monday night, he had been taken out to Tramps nightclub in London and entertained by the bankers. Champagne had flowed all round. The restructuring deal was as good as done, all seemed agreed. Freddie had flown over to New York to make his commercial on the Tuesday, only stopping beneath the steps of his Concorde flight to let the world know he was off the ropes.

'I am flying high today and couldn't be more confident about the future,' Freddie told the press. His famous exuberance had returned and it struck everyone who met him when he arrived in New York. He seemed back to the old form of the seventies, when Skytrain had looked the most exciting innovation in civil aviation since the arrival of the jet. In fact, after seven traumatic months, Nemesis lay just around the corner. He owned 90 per cent of an airline business – his first wife, Joan, owned the rest – which, for all its fame and glory, had rested in March 1981 on shareholders' equity of rather less than £25m. It was now buried in debt.

Freddie had borrowed £228m. in 1980 to buy a fleet of DC-10 aircraft. This alone helped ensure that Laker Airways' debt exceeded its equity by around five to one by early 1981. Then, with almost unbelievable nerve, he had borrowed another £131m. from a group of banks led by the Midland to buy three of the new A-300 Airbus aircraft just coming off the production line in Toulouse.

It was less bold, perhaps, than foolhardy in the extreme. Freddie had been courting disaster, given the parlously depressed state of the international travel market at the time. What then made catastrophe well-nigh inevitable had been Laker Airways' failure to protect itself against the insidious accounting effects wrought by changing currency values. About two-thirds of its revenues were earned in pounds. When sterling had fallen abruptly against the dollar – which it did in

1981 – all those dollar borrowings had been magnified horribly, relative to the airline's earning power. In short, the net worth of Laker's balance sheet had simply evaporated.

The world's financial markets provide ample ways for a business to protect itself against this kind of blow. But Freddie had decided to accept the risk. Indeed, the banks had virtually forced him to do so, since – incredibly – Laker Airways had not been deemed creditworthy enough to be offered the currency cover available.

Once reality began to intrude, the going had been awfully tough. First the dollar's resurgence had blown an ugly hole in Laker Airways' accounts. Then, as urgent talks with the bankers had become public knowledge over the summer of 1981, the company's day-to-day business operations had begun to suffer: an accounting problem had turned in classic fashion into a cash-flow crisis.

By the end of October, the German and Austrian banks in the Midland loan syndicate had had enough. They argued for folding up the business there and then. And there was even worse to come. In October 1981, Pan American World Airways had launched a savage fares war on the North Atlantic. It halved the price of a ticket from Heathrow to New York and slashed fares on all other US destinations from London by up to 66 per cent. TWA and BA followed suit. The new schedules came into force on 1 November. On the morning of that day, the staff of Laker Airways' Skytrain service from Gatwick to New York arrived at their airport offices expecting some nasty surprises. For one thing, there was still a train strike running and Skytrain had been badly hit for weeks by the loss of its rail link with Victoria Station in Central London. But it was planes, not trains, which were the real worry on 1 November.

BA, Pan Am and TWA were all offering single economy fares to New York for around £124. That matched the cut-price level available on Skytrain, which offered only a stand-by walk-on service where the others were selling a prebookable return seat. Skytrain prices to other US cities had all been matched in the same way. The result was unmistakable. Skytrain's passenger list that morning had been cut to half its usual length . . . and it had stayed that way. Through January 1982, Skytrain had flown to New York with 60 per cent of its seats empty.

So, after eight torrid months, Freddie was not unnaturally elated at the prospect, as he saw it now, of a fresh start. Of course, things would have to be different in future – in his private life as well as his business affairs. His third marriage had broken under the strain of the crisis. His wife had suddenly left the family home in Sussex and flown off to Miami, taking Freddie's adored four-year-old son, Little Fred, with her. That was one item on Freddie's agenda for Thursday 4 February. The other, now scheduled by the Midland, promised hardly less traumatic changes.

As the founder of Skytrain and the kind of folk hero rarely encountered in modern British business, Freddie was surely going to find some aspects of the bankers' eventual solution hard to swallow. But he knew the alternative was bankruptcy. After months of brinkmanship and bluffing, he was ready to accommodate pretty well any solution they put to him. As he set out from Manhattan on the Wednesday evening, perhaps Freddie again ran over in his mind the details of the rescue envisaged earlier in the week. It was clear that he was going to have to sell his three Airbuses. It was thought that the aircraft's manufacturer, Airbus Industrie, would agree to the cancellation of options on another seven without the usual penalty.

As for Laker Airways' immediate cash-flow problems, presumably someone would suggest a way forward. The Clydesdale Bank, a Midland subsidiary, had already been paying the airline's staff and fuel bills for some weeks out of an extended overdraft facility. McDonnell Douglas, the US manufacturer of Freddie's DC-10s, had helped out with at least one interest instalment on the Midland Airbus loan during January – and there seemed a better than evens chance that Freddie's friends at McDonnell would come to his help soon in other, more substantial ways.

These included the prospect of a small cash injection, probably £4m. or so. Far more importantly, though, McDonnell appeared ready – along with General Electric of the US, manufacturers of the DC-10 engines – to facilitate a grand restructuring of the Laker Airways balance sheet. McDonnell and GE had guaranteed $46m. and $10m. respectively of the $228m. loan put together by the Export-Import Bank of the United States in 1980 to fund Freddie's purchase of his DC-10 fleet. The idea now was that they should convert all or most of these amounts into equity capital, for a stake in the business to be decided later.

In a bravura display of confidence at Heathrow on 2 February Freddie had treated such technical details in characteristically cavalier fashion. Relabelling debt as equity at this stage of the game would leave Laker Airways just as strapped for ready cash as it was before, contrary to the impression given by Freddie that the proposed rescue was about to spirit £60m. of new money out of thin air. But this little dash of hyperbole probably said more about Freddie's view of the press – which always verged on the unscrupulous – than about his grasp of the financial realities. The vital point, as he knew well enough, was that equity support from McDonnell would be almost bound to win him more time from the bankers. Freddie had cause, however, to be nervous about McDonnell's support.

It was not that he had any doubts about the sympathetic approach being taken by the St Louis-based company. Its top men had made no secret of their genuine regard for the maverick of the world airline industry. When a DC-10 crashed at Chicago in May 1979, killing all its 274 passengers, McDonnell had found itself at the centre of a storm of hostile publicity. All DC-10s in the world were grounded. The popular press had a field day advising readers how to avoid DC-10s in future. Freddie, as badly hit by the grounding order as any airline chief in the world, spoke out boldly in defence of the aircraft's manufacturer and publicly extolled the virtues of the DC-10.

John Brizendine, McDonnell's chief executive, and Sandy McDonnell, its chairman, did not forget this gesture. By 1981, many key figures in the company had close personal ties with Freddie. Now he was counting on their support for the rescue operation to succeed.

But sympathy and even cash subsidies were one thing, equity capital was quite another. The very idea was sending McDonnell's European airline customers into paroxysms of rage, as Freddie well knew. Shortly after arriving in New York on the 2nd, he had had a long telephone conversation with David Sedgewick, a senior vice-president of McDonnell. Sedgewick had just arrived back in London after dividing a hectic day between Zurich and Frankfurt. He had been visiting some big customers and he was a worried man. For five days, he told Freddie, McDonnell had been bombarded by Europe's leading airlines with talk of dire consequences if the company dared to come to the rescue of Laker Airways.

Now, as he waited at Kennedy Airport for the evening's Skytrain flight, Freddie sought reassurance again that his prospective equity partner was still committed to a shared future. He rang Sedgewick in London. Well, said Sedgewick, things were sticky because the CAA was still not satisfied with the rescue package as it stood. There remained a lot to be done. Freddie had never doubted that.

It was under a dreary winter sky that Freddie's plane came down to land at Gatwick the next morning, bitterly cold and with every sign of more snow on the way. When Freddie stepped on to the tarmac, he was immediately handed a message from his secretary. He was awaited at the Midland Bank and his solicitor, John Rowney, would meet him there. He sped off to the City.

The two men were shown to a conference room. A few minutes later George Gillespie, one of the senior members of the Midland team involved in the rescue talks, came in and sat facing them at the table. He regretted to have to inform Freddie, said Gillespie, that Laker Airways' overdraft facility with the Clydesdale Bank was being withdrawn that morning. There was no doubting the implication. Short of a miracle, Laker Airways was dead.

It could hardly have been more absurd. Freddie had just finished making a TV commercial for a campaign in the US with the copyline 'Are you ready for Freddie?' Yet here he was, apparently unprepared for the total collapse of his own company.

The Midland, though, was ready for Freddie.

The various parties to the rescue talks were brought into the meeting through the morning. Sedgewick himself turned up and Freddie rounded fiercely on him: why had he lied over the telephone? But Sedgewick insisted – as McDonnell has done ever since – that its cash support for Laker Airways remained on the table. It was just that, well, the money required (according to the CAA's calculations) to guarantee Freddie's safe passage through the rest of 1982 just did not look available: 'thus no chance for Freddie', as Sedgewick had actually noted in his private diary just two days earlier.

Without such a guarantee, those masterminding the rescue – most notably Ian McIntosh, a managing director of Samuel Montagu, the merchant banking subsidiary of the Midland – could see no way of reaching an agreement which would be acceptable to the Bank of England and the CAA, both of them by now closely involved and both of them acutely mindful of the disastrous collapse of Court Line eight years earlier. (The Court Line package-tour empire had collapsed without warning, in the

21

middle of a summer season. It left thousands of British holidaymakers stranded abroad as the company disappeared into liquidation.)

The Laker traffic figures for January were so gloomy and the bankers' projections for cash-flow over the coming months were so alarming that even Freddie had to concede a mere £4m. from McDonnell would only buy his airline a few more troubled weeks at best. He played desperately for more time. The Midland refused it; but Freddie talked long and hard enough to avoid receivership at least until the next day. The bank gave him until 9.00 a.m. on the Friday to find a new source of cash.

At lunchtime, he telephoned Iain Sproat, the junior Trade Minister in the Government. Freddie explained the situation and the two men pondered for a while the applicability of various statutory powers allowing the Government to bail out ailing companies. But it was no good and Sproat had to confess as much. In the afternoon, he told the Prime Minister of Freddie's predicament. Now the irony of pushing BA harder was beginning to look a little more conspicuous. Mrs Thatcher held an impromptu meeting with Cabinet colleagues to see what could be done. Nothing, they were advised by the Treasury. Mrs Thatcher reluctantly agreed.

There was time for just one more throw. Freddie telephoned Harry Goodman, boss of the Intasun tour company, to see if he might be interested in discussing the purchase of Laker Airways' holiday subsidiary. Goodman was in Spain; but he put the telephone down and flew straight back to Gatwick. It was midnight by the time he and Freddie sat down together, in the nearby Hilton Hotel. Their talk lasted a couple of hours before they agreed: no deal.

It was 4.30 a.m. and Freddie had had very little sleep since Wednesday morning. The filming session at the Flying Tigers' hangar seemed a long time ago. There was nothing more that could be done. He snatched a quick nap, then called the Laker directors who were not already there. The board convened at 8.00 a.m. Half an hour later, Freddie's solicitor telephoned Dennis Kitching, the head of Midland's corporate finance division, to say the airline was inviting Clydesdale to appoint a receiver within the hour.

Iain Sproat stood up in the House of Commons that afternoon to deliver one of the dozens of epitaphs voiced through the day. 'Sir Freddie is a very great man,' said the Minister, 'who has done wonderful things for passengers around the world . . .' No one in or out of the Government showed any inkling of the less than wonderful things his collapse was going to entail – for politicians, civil servants, lawyers and airline executives around the world . . . but most of all for BA. They were soon to find out.

3

Man with a Mission

Lord King of Wartnaby was once asked how, as a captain of industry, he sought to motivate his employees. 'Fear,' he replied.

John Leonard King is the man to practise what he preaches. Heavily built, with large, farmer's hands and a glaring eye, he has a formidable physical presence. It is lent just a hint of menace by the faintest of lisps and an outwardly languid manner.

Those deceived by the langour and the dry wit – and he can be very good company when he chooses – are liable for a shock. While still its new chairman, King flew to New York to meet BA's transatlantic employees. At a cocktail party in his honour, he met an attractive lady who introduced herself as the manager of the airline's US properties. 'And how many people do you have on your staff?' asked the chairman politely. Twenty, came the reply with breezy cheer – but there were regular meetings with the Speedbird staff either in London or New York, so they could all keep closely in touch. Ah yes indeed, said the chairman. All twenty-one were fired within the week.

King has chaired a long string of quangos and charities since the mid-seventies. He is treated with respect, and a little caution too, by those who know him well in public life. 'John King is a splendid, tough character', in the words of one senior Tory Minister, ' – but remember to sew up your pockets when he is coming to see you.'

His robust approach to life is best reflected in his passion for hunting. Aged sixty-three, much of his recreational energies now have to be confined to shooting, fishing and helping the British Field Sports Society Fighting Fund. Horses and riding, though, are his real love. He was a celebrated Master of Foxhounds for more than twenty years with the Duke of Rutland's Belvoir Hunt. Married since 1970 to the daughter of the 8th Viscount Galway, King in some ways presents the very picture of a landed Tory magnate.

But he is closer by far to Mrs Thatcher's vision of Toryism than this might suggest. Indeed, his combination of traditional Tory values with the plain-speaking individualism of a self-made industrial millionaire is a blend which might almost have served as Mrs Thatcher's ideal when the search began in earnest for the men to spearhead her assault on Britain's nationalised industries. (He admires Mrs Thatcher deeply 'for her forthrightness and her will and her objectives'.)

King was born in London but is most truly a Yorkshireman. His parents came from Yorkshire, as did his first wife. His first efforts were made there to set up his own business, just before and again after the war, and he formed a close friendship early on with another young Yorkshireman whose family was prominent in the horse world – James (now Lord) Hanson.

King's rise to industrial eminence is quickly told. He acquired a small Birmingham ball-bearings business in the late forties, built it from a Yorkshire base into one of the four UK leaders in its field by 1969 and then collected a handsome £3m. in cash on the sale of his personal stake when his company was taken over by Labour's Industrial Reorganisation Corporation: the Wilson Government insisted, against King's opposition, on rationalising the ball-bearings industry to keep out a foreign competitor. (King had wanted to sell out to SKF, the big Swedish industrial group.)

With a fortune in the bank, King then developed a

reputation as a man who got things done in business. He rescued two ailing companies and chaired Babcock International, the power-engineering group, through a decade of dynamic growth in the seventies. That earned him a knighthood in 1979. Meanwhile, he had begun to move into public life with a timely zeal for fighting back against Socialist designs on the private sector. ('I wondered whether one was grand enough for the Tories,' said King in 1983 to a perceptive interviewer who questioned his youthful political instincts. 'I was certainly too grand for the Labour Party. So I had a look at the Liberal Party, and when I discovered that it was nothing more than a convenient attitude of mind, I got on with being a Tory.')

Like McFadzean at BA, he was one of the industrialists close to the Tory planning process ahead of the 1979 general election. Soon afterwards, a row broke out over the new Government's intentions towards the National Enterprise Board. In a letter to the press which was widely read as a signpost to the future, King laid into the NEB for collecting 'an absurd hotch-potch' of investments. 'The NEB,' he concluded, 'should see itself as a reluctant provider of funds of last resort, charged with the normal duties of good husbandry, but nothing more.'

That November, as if to make clear the NEB's role in the new Government's scheme of things, Mrs Thatcher appointed King as its deputy chairman. (It was feared, after his letter, that he might be too much of a hot potato for the chairmanship itself.) He was also offered the chairmanship of the British Steel Corporation, which he declined.

So when, in the summer of 1980, the Department of Trade asked a firm of London head-hunters to produce a shortlist of candidates for the chairmanship of BA – a part-time position – no one in Whitehall was very surprised to see King's name on the list. He got the job in September 1980. Ross Stainton, the outgoing chairman, had been unwell for some time after a heart attack in 1979 and there had been months of speculation as to whether his successor would be an airline man or an outsider. The mounting insolvency crisis in the corporation settled that.

As for King's brief, that was clear, too: he had to knock the airline into shape for take-off to the private sector. And King needed no persuading on that score: rather the opposite. Privatisation was almost a precondition of his acceptance. Whether he appreciated the enormity of the job from the start seems doubtful. He assumed his post as chairman on 1 February 1981 and made a point in his first months of beginning meetings by asking senior managers when the airline would be ready for privatisation. But perhaps this was just for effect. The reality, anyway, is that his appointment was followed by a kind of phoney war.

King had warned that no one should expect immediate fireworks. He saw 'a steady job to be done', he said. For the most part, this seemed to consist of reorganising BA's main board. It was largely non-executive and even excluded, for example, Roger Moss, the finance director, who was confined to the subordinate executive board. The new chairman recruited a fair number of his personal cronies. These included the late Alex Dibbs, the deputy chairman of National Westminster Bank who had joined the NEB alongside King, and Bobby Henderson, the chairman of merchant bankers Kleinwort, Benson.

King himself, though, was rarely seen at either of BA's head offices at Victoria and Heathrow. He preferred to hover remotely over the airline from his chairman's office at Babcock & Wilcox's headquarters in St James's, with its horse drawings and foxhunting portraits. There were those amongst the senior managers of BA who began to doubt that he would ever really make much of an impression.

This was an error of judgement.

BA's formal results for the year to March 1981 surfaced the same week as the moles' 'Minority Report' of August that year. The figures caused a sensation. The airline had lost £141m. before tax. Repeated increases in its external borrowing limit had been taken up and total borrowings had risen to almost £800m., well over twice the size of BA's equity capital. The debt mountain was £500m. more than it had been two years earlier – and most of it was owed to banks, who were going to require cash repayments, let alone interest charges now running at around £100m. a year. Yet in 1980–81, BA had generated no net cash whatever. Nor would the airline be able to fall back on the kind of accounting adjustments which so often saved the bacon where a nationalised industry had borrowed from the taxpayer.

Announcing the debacle at a press conference, King hid his discomfort with the look of blank astonishment which has always served him well in moments of adversity. But he had also prepared a more substantial riposte. There would have to be changes, he warned, and 9,000 jobs would go in the next two years. Someone asked whether compulsory redundancies were planned. No, said King, they were ruled out – 'that is, just for this morning'.

In fact, almost all BA's employees were about to experience the thrills of being a postwar fox in the Duke of Rutland's country.

This began to dawn on the corporation in September. At a series of union meetings, a gaunt Roy Watts warned that redundancies might, after all, have to be compulsory. The high finances of the airline were lost on many employees; but everyone could understand the message that BA, according to someone's calculation, was now using a fleet of 174 jet aircraft to lose £200 a minute around the clock. It was going to have to stop, said Watts, and no one was left in any doubt that it was going to be painful. Indeed, there were emotional scenes, with BA girls openly in tears at the check-in counters at Heathrow and many senior managers expressing genuine dismay.

In the marketing department, there was particular consternation. On the North Atlantic route, the cheap fares game of cox-and-box with Laker Airways was going to have to be reappraised for a start. But it was more than just BA's pricing strategies which were due for a shake-up. A string of domestic and international routes were to be cut, the aircraft fleet pruned and eight aircraft servicing stations closed. The airline's all-cargo services and its staff training college were both summarily axed. During the rest of 1981 hardly a week passed without news of some further retraction or closure. The assets sale programme for the next twelve months was valued at £160m.

Many staff decided they had already had enough when pay rises were frozen and the pension scheme was cut back. Management wanted 9,000 redundancies by June 1982 and invited resignations by October 1981 in return for generous severance terms. A mite too generous, as it turned out. When the deadline was extended, the total number of applications rose to almost 16,000. There were many critics both inside and outside BA who sounded a note of alarm at such sweeping redundancies, executed so hastily.

Two principal problems undoubtedly caused some damage to the airline's operations. On the one hand, those keenest to take the money and run were often the more ambitious and resourceful employees whom BA could least afford to lose. Thus the 'right' people went and the 'wrong' people stayed, or so said the critics. (Management tried hard – causing some resentment in the process – to exclude from the scheme those who were preparing to leave anyway and those it deemed tougher to replace. But many must inevitably have slipped through the screening net.) On the other hand, the speed of the lay-offs allowed for too little planning. Some departments emerged woefully short of staff while in others the overmanning was scarcely affected at all.

Management lifted its redundancy target to 12,000 and ended up paying out £150m., which was half as much again as it had originally intended. Clearly, some things at BA were going to take a long time to change.

Some more senior members of the staff made a less happy exit. Roger Moss, the chief financial officer, had made an unfortunate initial impression on King. (He had presented the chairman with a BA budget in the time-honoured BA fashion – as though its approval by the board was simply a formality. King's reaction had been thunderous.) Early in March 1982, Moss was summoned to the chairman's office. He was unceremoniously told he was taking a month's leave of absence – and he would not be returning to his desk at the end of it.

The immediate reason for this abrupt departure was quickly apparent. The very next day, 5 March, King presented to his main board a pile of numbered documents: they were copies of a highly sensitive report on the airline just completed by accountants Price Waterhouse. The firm had been invited the previous October to make a thorough study of the corporation and its problems. What it had now produced was a 500-page analysis with thirty-one specific recommendations suggesting BA's quickest route to privatisation. Moss had always been an outspoken critic of what he saw as premature ambitions in the boardroom to sell off the airline. It was clear from this date onwards that there would be no room for doubters.

King was already a man with a mission. Now, by courtesy of Price Waterhouse, he had a concrete plan to boot.

In essence, the plan was threefold. First, throw every possible accounting disaster into the results for the year 1980–81, about to end. Second, retrench all possible overhead costs, cut the workforce back by another 12,000 to around 35,000 and decentralise BA's operations back into the three divisions (long-haul, short-haul and domestic) which had predated the unsuccessful 1970s merger. Third, rebuild the balance sheet by selling off various profitable subsidiaries – and, above all, by persuading the Treasury to inject £800m. or so of fresh Public Dividend Capital.

The projected result of these measures, said Price Waterhouse, would be pre-tax losses of about £250m. for 1981–2; but BA would be able to look forward to a profitable year in 1982–3 and the prospect of privatisation within two years.

Yes, but was the Government still a true believer after such an unremitting stream of gloom? Iain Sproat had done his utmost to sustain the impetus behind a sale. When he arrived at the Department in September 1981, Sproat simply refused to accept the view of officials that BA was a dead duck for at least the lifetime of the current parliament. But not everyone shared his enthusiasm. It was no secret that John Biffen, Nott's successor at the Trade Department, had been privately sceptical in January about the possibility of selling BA shares at all.

The setbacks endured by King in his first year as chairman had left outside observers confused about the Government's real intentions. Then, just days after King's first anniversary at the start of February, the whole picture was transformed. It was Sir Freddie Laker's first contribution to the privatisation story.

The Laker Airways collapse was exquisitely embarrassing for the Government. That lurking irony behind the BA sale plan was now glaringly exposed. It was not just that Freddie was a glamorous entrepreneur championed by the Tories for years past. It was the cruel contrast between the Cabinet's impotence to rescue Freddie and the virtual obligation on it to continue pouring millions by the week into the black hole that was BA's treasury.

On the very afternoon of Iain Sproat's appeal to Mrs Thatcher on Laker Airways' behalf, he had to put his name to a written parliamentary answer confirming yet another in a string of fresh borrowing limits for the flag-carrier. The situation troubled a number of other Cabinet Ministers as well as Sproat. One result of this was a top-level discussion, for the first time, about the feasibility of selling off the entire equity of BA rather than just a minority stake. The Government could not afford to risk appearing half-hearted about the sale after what had happened to Freddie! And there was another consequence: King would get all the support he needed for his sale plans – from the Prime Minister herself.

So it was that King went to 10 Downing Street on Maundy Thursday, 8 April 1982, with his Price Waterhouse plan, proverbially speaking, under his arm. General Galtieri's troops had invaded the Falkland Islands the week before; but Mrs Thatcher and the Trade Secretary gave BA's chairman their full attention. He got the clearance he wanted to launch a full-scale pre-privatisation blitz. After a run of false starts, this would be the clean break that was needed.

Meanwhile, Freddie Laker was talking a lot about his own future plans. Not all of them were going to prove quite as helpful to BA as his recent collapse.

4

Enter the Lawyers

Freddie was visiting his estranged wife and their son, Little Freddie, in Miami at the beginning of March 1982. As he had done countless times before, he asked the BA office manager in Miami for a first-class ticket home. Since his last trip, however, the world had changed for Freddie.

Top men in most of the world's airlines have reciprocal arrangements to pick up free first-class air tickets as and where they want them. When Laker Airways had passed into receivership, on 5 February 1982, Freddie had lost this entitlement – in theory, anyway. But by March Freddie was already proclaiming plans for a new 'People's Airline'. And this, as he told BA's Miami office, should have kept him on the free travel list.

There followed a frantic exchange between the office manager and BA's brass at Heathrow. It seemed there were going to be quite a few economy-class passengers on the same flight who had each paid a normal fare and then been asked for an additional £130 by BA. The normal fare, unhappily, had been paid to Laker Airways: they were among the 6,000 tour and charter passengers stranded abroad by the collapse.

BA was caused some embarrassment by the whole incident. In the end, Freddie got his free first-class ticket; but it was quickly made clear that it would be his last from BA.

In the crushing aftermath of the events of early February, Freddie had to endure a great many humiliations of that kind. He lost all his most glamorous possessions – including his famous 85-ton yacht, *Tutinella*, on the Riviera – to the posse of receivers who moved in and broke up Laker Airways: they wasted no time selling it off piecemeal, to recoup as much cash as possible for the Laker bankers who appointed them. He was stripped of his membership of Lloyd's of London and was cold-shouldered by many in the British travel industry who had idolised him in the past.

One man, though, went conspicuously out of his way to offer Freddie a public helping hand. The telephone rang the very first weekend of the receivership and it was Tiny Rowland, an old friend and the chief executive of Lonrho, the international trading group. If Freddie wanted a base to work from and assistance of any kind, said Rowland, he had only to ask. The offer was taken up – and it helped to keep Freddie so busy over the next few months that he must have had little time left (arguably, too little) to mourn his old group's passing. For Rowland gave him the wherewithal and some financial support to set up a new company – Laker II – which Freddie fanfared as the base of two new businesses: the People's Airline and, later, Skytrain Holidays. Rowland even promised publicly to reimburse the holders of £700,000 worth of defunct Laker Airways tickets.

This largesse was encouraged by the Government as well as the remarkable public reaction to Freddie's collapse. While 50,000 signatures were being presented to Downing Street and £70,000 donated to the Sir Freddie's Friendly Fund, Iain Sproat lunched with the Lonrho chief executive to offer the Government's blessing for whatever plans could be concocted to get Freddie back in business again.

Such plans certainly existed. Orion Royal Bank, the City of London subsidiary of one of Laker Airways' commercial bank creditors, was burning plenty of midnight oil in an attempt to mobilise fresh equity support for Freddie; a prospectus was circulating in the City and there even seemed a good chance, briefly, that Export-Import Bank of the United States, which had funded a DC-10 fleet for Freddie, might juggle papers around to leave the fleet with his new airline. But it all came to naught. Most of those at the centre of the action thought a rescue was doomed from the start. Even the charm and persuasiveness of Orion Royal Bank's Christopher Chataway could do nothing to effect a rescue, once it became clear what a financial shambles Laker Airways had become during its helter-skelter expansion.

This was not how Freddie saw the failure of the rescue. It fuelled his conviction that he had been ruthlessly taken apart by BA and the other big airlines who had been his competitors. They were conspiring against him now, as they had conspired against him all through Laker's troubled existence. And he made no bones about this view in public, either. 'These other people, the airlines, are there to destroy,' he told the press in March, 'they were the predators.'

If Freddie meant this only in the most general of senses, there was someone else closely involved in his stormy career as an airline boss since the sixties who suspected it might be nothing more than the truth – in the most legal, or rather illegal, of senses. Who suspected, that is, that Laker Airways had been harried and harrassed until it folded, the victim of some of the world's leading airlines hunting in a pack as predators of the sky. And BA, as he saw it, might well have been the foremost in the pack.

His name was Robert (Bob) Beckman, originally from Philadelphia but for many years now a well-known US lawyer on the Washington DC circuit specialising in aviation matters. Most US lawyers look indistinguishable from US accountants or US bankers: the same Brooks Brothers style of suit, sober tie and plain shirt. Beckman, by contrast, habitually looks dressed to kill, in his double-breasted suits and bright silk ties with breast handkerchiefs to match. He likes to cut a dash.

Beckman had worked for Freddie since 1967; but he was far more than just a legal adviser. Freddie had often referred to him teasingly as 'my expensive American lawyer'. In fact, the two were close friends of long standing and Beckman felt a profound emotional attachment to both Laker Airways and its chief.

In the first place, Beckman was and remains an ardent anglophile. Painstakingly patrician in his tastes, he is an active member of his local polo club in Potomac where he lives with an English wife, the daughter of a peer. The inimitable Freddie, with his cockney irreverence on the one hand and his 75-acre Epsom stud farm on the other, must have been Beckman's dream client.

Freddie's arrival in Washington had been the making of Beckman's career. The principal aspiration of all the two hundred or so aviation law attorneys on the DC circuit in the sixties and seventies was to become the leading outside counsel to at least one major airline. Beckman in the 1960s spent most of his time working on behalf of municipal authorities in the US on the bread-and-butter work of airline regulation. Laker Airways, in professional terms, was Beckman's ticket to the big-time.

Above all, however, Beckman's relationship with Freddie was a bond forged through years of shared adversity in the desperate struggle from 1971 to 1977 to put Skytrain in the air. His combination of shrewdness, industry and sheer dogged persistence had been indispensable to Freddie. Beckman helped him in 1970 to gain his first 402 Permit, the licence to fly charters into the US. He struggled with Freddie in the vain attempt to win a Skytrain licence in Washington during the beleaguered Nixon Administration. He stood by Freddie in the UK when the CAA in 1972 granted clearance for Skytrain – in 1975–6 when the Labour Government tried to rescind it. Freddie's contract to purchase his first DC-10 aircraft was negotiated in Beckman's office on Connecticut Avenue, one side of a small triangle of streets in the centre of the US capital where virtually every prominent law firm in the city can be found. And Beckman had been Freddie's right hand through all the legal shenanigans which had accompanied Skytrain's ultimately doomed bid for price leadership over the North Atlantic.

No one who knew this background could have been in any doubt that Beckman would react fiercely to the bankers' attempts to wind up Laker in February 1982. But he did a lot better than that. By June, the US lawyer came up with grounds for a civil suit to force BA and some of the world's other leading carriers to pay off Laker Airways' debts . . . and leave Freddie with money enough to start all over again. Preparing this suit cost Beckman and his partners in the firm of Beckman, Farmer & Kirstein months of hard work with no guarantee of any trial case at the end of it. Nor had Beckman, in February 1982, any firm evidence whatever for his suspicions. Freddie had deliberately kept him away from the refinancing efforts in 1981–2 so as to avoid being accused of indiscretion. ('What do I need you for?' Freddie had said when Beckman offered his help in the autumn of 1981. 'I've got the Bank of England working for me.')

Yet from the outset Beckman never wavered in his conviction that a grave injustice had been done. And he saw two grounds for believing that the courts would think so, too – one general and the other quite specific. Generally encouraging was the existence, in abundance, of prima-facie evidence that there had been high-jinks in high places at many stages of the Laker story. The airline had been terribly buffeted in the relentless sequence of North Atlantic tariff revisions since 1977. It had been badly let down at the end by the apparent withdrawal of a complex refunding exercise underpinned by McDonnell Douglas. Both episodes looked fishy in several respects.

Take the tariff revisions, for example. It was surely odd that BA, Pan Am and TWA had so often moved their fares simultaneously to identical levels. And if Laker had been operating on the finest of margins, how was it that the big carriers had been able – at a profit – to offer exactly comparable fares while serving up all the frills cut by Laker? If they had all done it by operating at a loss, was this not a good reason for supposing they had acted in concert? And it was a matter of record that the airlines had met together in recent years and discussed their transatlantic ticket prices.

As for McDonnell's change of heart, it was absolutely no secret that half the leading airlines of Europe seemed to have been in touch with each other on that occasion, all of them threatening McDonnell in remarkably similar language with serious commercial consequences were it to help bale out Laker.

What made all this so potentially explosive, as Beckman appreciated, was the impression it gave of an international cartel going about its usual business with a blatant disregard for everything that the American courts of the twentieth century had ever said about US antitrust law. And it had extended its operations into the land where big business cartels were simply anathema to the whole system.

Beckman understood perfectly well that behind this apparent clash of ethics there hung a long tale. The international airline business since the Second World War had been dominated in every aspect of its affairs by the International Air Transport Association (IATA), a self-proclaimed cartel. Yet US airlines had participated in the international industry throughout this period. The two had been reconciled for the greater part of the time by a special dispensation in US law and regulatory practice which gave the airlines immunity against antitrust prosecution. But – and this was the crux of the matter – this immunity had always been hedged with careful conditions. And over the 1977–82 years of Skytrain's existence, those conditions had assumed a positively Byzantine complexity.

The cause of the fresh complexity was simple: the Carter Administration had deregulated the US domestic industry and done everything in its power to minimise the antitrust immunity offered to any airline flying into US airports. The effect had been dire and multifaceted: IATA's unity had been shattered, foreign airlines had found themselves flying blind in a legal fog and foreign governments had been incensed by what they saw as an unacceptably high-handed approach to international affairs. And nowhere was the confusion worse, naturally enough, than on the North Atlantic routes between Heathrow and the US.

For Washington's aviation lawyers – many of whose professional practices were gravely threatened as a result of domestic deregulation – the antitrust issue on international routes was a source of endless, and usually lucrative, argument. There were times – to coin a familiar image – when it was as though they had been invited to play soccer on some giant pitch with no goal posts at all. Whenever the ball was booted over the goal line, the position of the posts would have to be decided by a mass conference of the players, with due regard for each and every detail of previous goals awarded (or, of course, disallowed).

In short, there appeared to Bob Beckman to be more than a fighting chance of proving that illicit big business practices had played more than a walk-on part in his client's tragic history. His steely determination to establish this, however, sprang from much more than a calculated assessment of the general legal background. There were always cynics in later years who maintained that Beckman was just a glorified ambulance-chaser – that curious genre of US attorney, turning others' misfortunes into a living by suing for damages on their behalf and taking a hefty cut of any winnings. But these critics mistook their man.

Beckman really believed that Laker had been picked off ruthlessly by the airlines cartel and he believed it with passion. Underlying this conviction was the consideration of at least one seminal experience from the past. For the cartel had undeniably ganged up on Laker once before. Back in 1974 – when Freddie had been awarded a Skytrain licence by the UK authorities but was still waiting vainly for a go-ahead from the Americans – BA, Pan Am, TWA and British Caledonian had agreed together to limit their aggregate capacity on the North Atlantic routes.

The first OPEC crisis had been followed by a staggering collapse in the market: charter traffic was down by 30 per cent and Pan Am, for one, was staring bankruptcy in the face. Intense negotiations had been concluded successfully at a meeting in the offices of the Civil Aviation Bureau (CAB) in Washington in the middle of September that year. (The recently restructured BA sent along its Western Routes Manager, Ossie Cochrane.) When the deal was announced, it emerged that the four carriers were only bound by its terms on condition that Laker's Skytrain remained grounded!

At this point, Beckman had used the Freedom of Information Act to obtain a transcript of the CAB meeting. It revealed a long and involved discussion amongst the four airlines – with a British Embassy official present – about the need to keep Laker Airways off the route. This looked to Beckman like a blatant own goal in the antitrust game and he promptly filed a civil suit explaining why. Meeting under the aegis of the CAB, he argued, meant immunity to antitrust for talks about capacity limitation. But this did not include immunity against antitrust charges of conspiring to keep Laker Airways out of business!

On that occasion, Beckman won hands down. The airlines filed for settlement immediately and abandoned their agreement for another which excluded any reference to Laker Airways. (In fact, BA and then the UK Government itself later tried to make up for the exclusion with blocking action of their own against Laker; but that is another story.)

Beckman was sure, in February 1982, that those same forces of intrigue and conspiracy had been at work again.

Hence the zeal with which he longed to set about the work of investigating the collapse. But on whose behalf?

Near the end of the month, he got a telephone call from a Mr Christopher Morris. The caller identified himself as the senior liquidation partner in the London offices of Touche Ross, one of the Big Eight international accountancy firms. Morris had been appointed the liquidator of Laker Airways and he was over in New York to look at Laker's US operations. He had just been advised by his New York colleagues to get in touch with Beckman. So could they arrange a mutually convenient meeting?

It was the first of a series of occasional talks between the two men over the spring and summer of 1982. Sometimes Freddie himself participated, though more often not. Gradually, Beckman prevailed on Morris to see that substantial grounds might exist for launching a civil antitrust suit against several of Laker's former competitors. And he was not just thinking of the US carriers. Beckman saw BA as a principal defendant. If successful, the suit might merit damages running into hundreds of millions of dollars . . .

In June 1982, he handed Morris a 150-page legal opinion setting down his case formally. It was agreed that Beckman should have the chance to put his case before a panel of Touche Ross's most senior men. The date fixed for the presentation was 10 November 1982.

5

Hijack at Heathrow

King strode out of 10 Downing Street in April 1982 like
John Peel with his hounds and his horn in the morning.

The Price Waterhouse team had recommended in its
report that late 1983 was really 'the earliest possible date
for privatisation'. But the accountants had also confessed
themselves 'enormously impressed with BA's strengths,
achievements and innovations . . . (especially) the
commitment and dedication of its management . . .' As
King had hoped and trusted she would, Mrs Thatcher
agreed that these remarks should be the cue for the
airline's future. A sale some time around September 1983
would be the firm goal. He would need two or three new
men in his team, who would demand more than the
usual nationalised industry salaries, King told the Prime
Minister; but if he had them, the job could be done. Mrs
Thatcher assured him of her fullest support.

So the chairman set off with a few more Peel-like view
halloos to waken the dead – or the merely sleeping –
around the management corridors of his airline's headquarters at Heathrow. The trauma of the previous
autumn, with its lay-offs and warnings of a new frugal-
ity, was quickly followed by further decisive action to
implement key areas of the Price Waterhouse Report.

Only the previous July, the board had gone out of its
way to deny that there would be any move back towards
the old BOAC/BEA days before the 1970s merger. But
this was no time for worrying too much about rigid

consistency. At the end of April, it was announced that the airline's operations would be decentralised into three divisions based on intercontinental, European and mainland/charter networks with effect from 1 May.

The grand merger had never looked like working and King knew it. But anyone who thought the decentralisation was simply a return to the old BOAC/BEA days was seriously mistaken. It was, rather, the vehicle which King wanted to use for the introduction of a far more commercial and internally competitive regime. The heads of the new operating divisions – who at first were to be the powerful Gerry Draper, and the younger Peter Hermon and Stephen Hanscombe respectively – had to know that their performances would be minutely compared. But the implicit rivalry was to extend all the way through the airline. No longer was it going to be a glorified amalgamation of the Home and Foreign Offices, a sort of civil service on wings. BA had to become a real business.

Another recommendation in the report referred to the sale of subsidiaries. This, too, was set in motion. Group companies with good records but no integral place in the BA structure had 'For Sale' notices conspicuously displayed to the City. Some, like International Aeradio, enjoyed virtual independence already and seized the initiative to arrange new partners or owners conducive to their business plans.

King's energy, however, was not watched without misgivings by everyone at BA. There were those who honestly doubted whether privatisation at this breakneck speed was a sensible course at all. And no doubt there were some, in Whitehall as well, who would have preferred a quieter life at almost any price. Against their opposition, open or otherwise, King determined to move quickly. It was not conspicuous to outside observers, but the process of decentralising the airline's operations had in some ways left even more power in the hands of the chairman and those immediately around him. For King,

Alex Dibbs and Bobby Henderson kept a tight central hold over all the airline's finances and planning, while day-to-day operations were left to the old executive hierarchy. It was almost as though there were two parallel managements in place by the end of June: Labour opposition jibes that BA had been hijacked were not so wide of the mark.

But what King needed now, as he had told Mrs Thatcher, were one or two more key recruits for his own team. Russell Reynolds, the international head-hunting firm which found Ian MacGregor for British Steel, had been given the task in the midsummer of 1981 of finding a new chief executive and a new finance director. But the search had so far been in vain. Now the need for a financial man, in particular, was growing urgent. The Price Waterhouse Report had even commented on it. (Recommendation No. 9: 'The absence of a finance director on the main board should be rectified.') Roger Moss's departure made the problem acute.

In the event, it was Moss's abrupt exit which led to the first of the critical appointments.

For Norman Gordon Edward Dunlop, until recently resident in Singapore, the call from Whitehall to enter the BA counting house must have been a moment to savour. He was stepping into a huge UK company on the brink of great things just at the moment when his former British employer, Commercial Union Assurance, was reeling in the face of catastrophic results which seemed to threaten its very survival.

Originally trained as an accountant by Thomson McLintock in Glasgow – 'anyone who goes through that and survives is going to be useful', as King would put it later – Gordon Dunlop had been CU's chief executive from 1972 to 1977. After a celebrated row in 1977, the board of CU had paid him £100,000 to go away. But the composite insurance giant's biggest problems in 1982 were still springing above all from huge loss-making operations in the US – and it was over strategy in the US that Dunlop and the CU board had parted company.

Indeed, the extent of Dunlop's responsibility for CU's calamitous decline over recent years – and the extent to which he had taken the rap for others on the CU board – was still a source of debate in the City when Dunlop arrived at BA. It even added a touch of controversy to his appointment. (CU's chairman Sir Francis Sandilands, as he then was, had justified Dunlop's golden handshake in 1978 on the grounds that he had had a well-paid job and was unlikely to find it easy to secure a similar one.) But the Scottish accountant had many powerful champions – including Alex Dibbs and Bobby Henderson, who had known him well during his gruelling years at CU's helm.

Dunlop had gone off to Singapore in 1979 and spent two busy and successful years there, reorganising the financial affairs of the local affiliate of the Inchcape shipping group. Since the spring of 1981, though, he had been looking for a suitable chance to return to the UK. As an old aerospace man himself – he had worked for De Havilland and Hawker Siddeley Aviation for eight years before joining CU – Dunlop had been watching events unfold at BA with intense interest. When he read in the press that Roger Moss had been fired, Dunlop wrote to King, on 14 April 1982, suggesting that he might have something to contribute to BA's future.

King did a bit of homework on Dunlop's background. Then he cabled back within days to Dunlop's home in Singapore and asked him to call round to St James's 'as soon as you arrive in London'. When they met, King was not much impressed by the cut of Dunlop's suit – but in every other respect, he knew very quickly that he had found the man he was looking for. After two long discussions with Dunlop, King sounded out his boardroom colleagues. Their reaction was unequivocal and King recommended Dunlop to his political masters. He had picked him as a no-nonsense character: and it would undeniably have been difficult to find anyone further removed than Dunlop from the popular archetype of Public Sector Man. It took Whitehall a full six weeks to review the choice. But at last his appointment was confirmed and Dunlop joined the airline. It was June 1982 and he was fifty-four.

The customary euphemism used of Dunlop by Fleet Street is that he is 'forceful'. With his rolling Perthshire accent, thickset frame and small, beady eyes he can certainly be that. He has, too, a disarming smile which can accompany bad news as well as good. But he is also imaginative, dynamic and extremely hardworking. 'Outstanding' is King's favourite epithet for Dunlop's ability. It was his tragic misfortune, say his protagonists, that his years at CU coincided with an era of grave crisis throughout the international insurance industry. As for his reputation for trenchancy, nothing in his record at BA has dispelled that.

Dunlop used his enforced six weeks' wait before joining the airline to prepare himself thoroughly for his first steps. He arrived displaying all the urgency of a receiver appointed to rescue what he could while there was still time – and the collapse in May of Braniff, the Texas-based international airline, coming so soon after Laker's crash, helped vest the new man with still greater authority.

Every year, the airline drew up a corporate plan covering the next five years which was submitted to Whitehall. Dunlop studied the plan, just completed, for the 1982–3 to 1986–7 period. Certainly it had made some adjustments for privatisation. (As the Comptroller & Auditor General noted in 1984, 'The Plan gave priority to achieving profitability as soon as possible, if necessary at the expense of larger but longer-term profits.')

Dunlop decided, however, that it was a long way short of being a blueprint for the commercial revolution which he and the chairman had in mind. They wanted *Ten Days that Shook the World*, not *Biggles Takes Charge*. The plan went in to Whitehall, but it was made clear that another would be on its way in due course, quite possibly very different.

Again, the new man refused to be rushed into setting new financial targets. The old ones had not spread much happiness. In the three years ending in March 1982, BA was supposed to have made a return – in current cost-accounting terms – of 6 per cent annually on its assets before taking account of interest and tax. In the event, it had scored a negative 5.2 per cent (and interest on its soaring debt, of course, had gone through the roof).

More than two years later, MPs on the Public Accounts Committee (PAC) cross-examined senior civil servants closely about these next months. 'There was a good deal of correspondence in the year in question,' they were told, 'as to what was desirable [by way of forecasts and economic assumptions]. The new members of the Board who came in thought that the basis of the planning [in earlier years] had been rather rigid and had not really been useful for decision-taking.'

No such shackles were going to impede Gordon Dunlop. The financial return for 1982–3, and for 1983–4 as it turned out, was only agreed with the Government at the tail-end of March 1983! (But then, it was set at 5.75 per cent and BA achieved 9.3 per cent for Dunlop's first year, so no one was really complaining.)

In short, the Government in mid-1982 had no profitability target for BA, no real corporate plan in front of it, very little idea of the computer modelling methods being used by the airline's treasury and little if any written outline of a long-term strategy. It was highly irregular – and undoubtedly a case of a desperate malady calling for desperate remedies. As the same PAC session in 1984 was to hear, BA was that summer 'in the process of making a major recovery from a virtually disastrous situation . . . [it was not regarded] as tidy administration but the situation was not tidy.' That was a masterly Whitehall understatement.

For any incoming finance director, the shambles at BA would have been a shock. For a Scottish accountant, it must have verged on the blasphemous. Dunlop's reaction had a sweeping impact.

First to feel it, naturally enough, were the accounting departments. Financial controls over whole areas of the airline's operations were simply nonexistent. The corporate treasury had no idea whether the relevant operations were unprofitable or not. Those found to be so, as controls were steadily imposed, were threatened with immediate curtailment. Numerous overseas routes disappeared, for example. Most were from Gatwick or provincial airports; but destinations from Calgary to Damascus were among the long-haul connections from Heathrow which received the chop. A question mark was even put over the domestic UK network in its entirety, with 7,000 jobs. (BA's various shuttle services alone were reckoned to be losing £60m. a year.) In the event, the network was heavily pruned: 650 staff on the Highlands and Islands operation were losing £5m. a year – there were 170 left in the year to March 1984 . . . and they made profits of £400,000.

In some areas, continued heavy spending was unavoidable; but savings were made where possible. The fleet of 757s still on order from Boeing remained integral to the airline's modernisation; but two of the nineteen were off-loaded to one of the UK holiday charter operators. Meanwhile, six Lockheed TriStars were put up for sale. (The Ministry of Defence took them before the end of the year.)

Above all, however, the overhaul of the accounting systems entailed a fresh approach to ticket pricing. Within weeks of his arrival, this had immersed Dunlop in one of the single most important events in the transformation of the airline – the battle with the bucket shops.

It was critical. It represented a public relations triumph for Dunlop: he took over at an early stage from the auditors who had been requested by King to examine ticket procedures. It was also a useful political tool for Dunlop inside BA, enabling him to assert his influence far beyond the financial department to others, notably marketing, where his intrusion was resented for many months. It signalled the final, total rejection of the Watts Plan of 1978 for BA's long-term future. And it led directly to the banishment of almost all the old, top-management hands from the pre-King era.

The single most important word in the 1978 Watts Plan was: volume. Watts and Gerry Draper, the commercial director, could see perfectly well that BA was burdened with an enormously inflated cost structure. But they believed the trade unions would resist demanning tooth and nail. (It was, after all, 1978–9 that saw the Callaghan Government's Winter of Discontent.) Any attempt at sweeping lay-offs, they decided, could break the airline. The alternative was to go for a higher volume of business whilst keeping the cost structure stable.

Most specifically, BA would fill the empty seats on its aircraft by an intensive use of discount pricing. Block bookings from travel agents would be rewarded with handsome discounts. BA would become the world's leading low-price airline operating at high volumes on the back of the projected explosion in passenger traffic over the years through to 1986.

But companies which opt for a suddenly inflated volume of business can face frightening control problems. Even Britain's successful supermarket retailers – the merchants of 'pile 'em high and sell 'em cheap' fame – found their resources stretched by the pursuit of cut-price, high-volume expansion in the 1970s. But at least (usually) they had the stringent financial control over inventories and sales to let them know exactly what was happening as their battle unfolded. BA simply got totally and horribly lost.

As the block sales went out to the travel agents, the airline had far too small a monitoring force to correlate the supply of empty seats on its aircraft with the demand for cut-price tickets. Instead of just selling off the empty seats – leaving as many as possible of each plane's passengers to pay normal fares – BA began in effect to replace full fares with discount fares. Worst of all, though, it really had no idea each day how many full fares were being displaced in this way. But it was certainly a sizeable proportion. One indication of this was the fact that travel agents who wanted to buy BA tickets direct from the airline were finding none left for sale – and were having to buy them instead from the bucket shop agents with the cut-price blocks!

By 1982, the whole market was in disarray. Not only was BA losing revenue – perhaps £20m. a year, perhaps £100m. – from the consequent underpricing of so many of its seats. The airline was even being taken to the cleaners directly by the bucket shops themselves. Commissions being paid to the travel agents were sky-rocketing to the point where they were arguably a bigger problem for BA than the discounts themselves.

Nor were commissions the only bone of contention between BA and the travel agents. For discounts were awarded on a kind of sale-or-return basis. If the bucket shop sold the ticket at the full price level, it kept the retail margin. If it sold at a discount level, it applied to BA for a rebate to make up the full retail margin. BA ordained the discount levels. Many bucket shops found they could sell the tickets for more than BA's hard-pressed pricing team dictated. So they would put a bit of cardboard between the carbon papers of the tickets, write out the actual (higher) price to the passenger, write the (lower) BA discount price on the copies returned to BA – and claim the maximum rebates just the same.

Not surprisingly, all this attracted considerable interest from the British police. What attracted the attention of King and Dunlop, however, was the size of the ticket rebates bill that BA was paying. The rebates went into a 'Special Promotional Costs' budget. It was

£110m. in 1981–2 and £125m. in 1982–3. They were both too expensive and too vague for Dunlop's new controls.

The time had come for some fundamental changes.

Just before Dunlop's arrival, Draper had in fact already acknowledged the failure of the whole volume strategy. He had brought in McKinsey, the international management consultants, who very quickly indicated that the required changes were reasonably obvious – but would need considerable resolution from top to bottom of the airline if they were to be successfully implemented.

Discounts and travel agents' commissions were fundamental to the old Watts Plan because it put a priority on maximising traffic volume. Many half-empty planes just could not be filled with 'standard' marketing techniques – even at the hands of Gerry Draper, whom everyone in the international industry regarded as one of its most effective salesmen anywhere. McKinsey recommended the alternative answer to the half-empty planes problem: cancel them. This would entail many route cut-backs. It would also help bring down the level of discount sales which were undermining BA's whole pricing structure. McKinsey further recommended stringent controls on escalating commission payments – which contravened IATA regulations but were everywhere rampant in the industry – so that BA could start ensuring it was getting value for money from its principal distributors.

In reality, King and Dunlop needed no consultants to point the way forward. Together, they provided the resolution to force through the measures. With the help of the marketing department – still smarting slightly at his apparently roving brief – Dunlop made it almost a personal campaign. By September, BA was employing private detectives to travel round the bucket shops buying up their stocks. There would be no more straining to fill up aircraft at any – and unknown – cost.

It was not just the products of the old strategy that

were to be discarded, however. Its exponents had to go, too.

Draper was asked to see the chairman in his office in St James's on 30 July. BA's commercial director had enjoyed far more power over the airline's affairs than his title perhaps suggested. He had been the dominant personality amongst its senior managers for some years. But Draper had made almost as bad an initial impression on King as had Roger Moss.

The writing appeared on the wall for Draper one day during a lunch with King at Speedbird House. It was during the Pope's visit to Britain early in the summer of 1982. He was tired, said King, of seeing the Pope descending all the time from a British Caledonian aircraft: why could it not have been a BA plane? 'Well, we quoted,' said Draper. King objected that he thought it would have been worthwhile, given the media exposure, to have set aside some money from the advertising budget if that was necessary to get the job. Draper demurred. 'It's swings and roundabouts,' he unwisely ventured. 'There are just as many people who would refuse to fly with us because we'd carried the Pope.' King glowered back at him over the lunch table. 'What?' he exclaimed. 'You mean the Paisley crowd?' There followed a long and painful silence.

On 31 July, it was announced that Draper, aged fifty-five, would be giving up his duties at the end of August.

Just one week later, the Hounslow tumbril clattered into St James's once again, this time carrying Stephen Wheatcroft, the sixty-year-old director of economic development. He lost his executive responsibilities on the spot.

Moss, Alan Ponsford (director of public relations), Draper, Wheatcroft . . . the *tricoteuses* of Fleet Street began to listen for the arrival of all the old guard.

At Speedbird House, meanwhile, Dunlop and the accountants were hard at work on two presentations which would sum up the passing of the old and the arrival of the new. The first was the profit-and-loss account for the year to March 1982. The second was Dunlop's promised financial plan, to be taken in Whitehall as an amendment to the May corporate plan.

BA had not done too badly on its trading account in 1981–2. Higher interest costs had not quite managed to wipe out the savings made from the reduction in the workforce: the airline had an operating surplus of £13m. against its £95m. loss the year before. But when the full results for 1981–2 were announced on 19 October, all eyes were on the after-tax figure. BA reported a jumbo-sized net loss of £545m.

For just as Price Waterhouse had recommended, the board had thrown in the proverbial kitchen sink. There were 1981–2 redundancy costs of £100m. There was a £208m. write-down of the value of the fleet, reducing future depreciation charges usefully. There was even £98m. to pay for another 7,000 redundancies – first publicised in July and due to cut the workforce further from 42,000 to 35,000 – which had yet to be effected. (BA's insistence on including this last figure had prompted a great deal of toing and froing between Heathrow and the auditors' offices in the City.)

Transferring the loss to reserves wiped out BA's meagre capital base and left it with negative equity of £257m. The airline, in short, was royally, supersonically, bust.

But all that, said Dunlop's plan, was the legacy of the past. (A past, as King bluntly put it on 19 October, when BA had been run 'as though money grew on trees'.) His new plan presented an airline able – in the Auditor General's words of 1984 – 'to operate as a limited liability company, wholly government-owned, but able to finance its future needs without government assistance.' In other words, the business was about to be turned through 180 degrees. In the space of a few years, BA had just run up debts of nearly £1 billion. Now it was going to generate enough cash over the period from 1983–4 to 1986–7, according to Dunlop's plan, to pay for capital expenditure on its airline fleet of more than £800m.!

Also that autumn, Dunlop decided that his own contribution was going to be the last of the various strategies, reports and plans which seemed to have accompanied BA's recent progress like confetti. So he dismissed the services of most of the consultants still working for the airline.

Most, but not all. Duncan Fraser & Partners was a firm of City actuarial partners with a very special task – and Dunlop kept them at it.

Even before he arrived at Speedbird House, Dunlop decided something would have to be done about BA's huge pension fund. He visited the airline's actuaries, R. Watson & Co., in Reigate and satisfied himself that the fund was generally in a healthy state. But it had one big technical problem: BA's pensions, true to the nationalised industry sector, were linked to an inflationary index. As Dunlop realised, the stockmarket's perception of this potential exposure to future hyperinflation might one day be disastrous to privatisation.

What made matters doubly difficult was that the deed of the index-linked scheme could not be closed. Drawn up in 1948, it was impossibly complicated – it had been amended countless times – and it contained a solvency clause, to be activated in the event of closure, which no one could understand.

Dunlop brought in Hugh Wynne-Griffiths, a partner of Duncan Fraser whom he had used in Singapore on Inchcape business. Wynne-Griffiths came up with a marvellously simple solution late in 1982. BA, he said, should begin a new private-sector-style scheme with indexation limited to 5 per cent. Employees could be invited to switch from one to the other. Those who so wished could remove their accumulated rights as cash, which BA would produce by selling underlying assets owned by the old scheme. The alternative would be for employees to invest their accumulated rights in the new scheme as additional years of service.

Some huge sums of money were involved. If everyone moved, BA would have to sell pension fund assets worth £300m. Perhaps this explains the delay in gaining Whitehall's approval for the substitution scheme the following year. (It was eventually launched – though not until March 1984.)

Rather more immediately, there were the results for the first half of 1982–3 to be considered. Scarcely a month after the publication of the calamitous 1981–2 accounts, BA appeared to have made a net profit of about £100m. in six months.

Wonderfully useful, accountants; but of course, there were still a few snags – and they were not confined to the accounts.

The reported profits had been helped considerably – as the Labour opposition pointed out at Westminster – by the size of the losses taken for the previous year. And as for Dunlop's plan, it presupposed a number of contentious measures. It was recommending, for example, that the Government should take responsibility for the repayment of about £800m. of BA's outstanding debt, in exchange for BA surrendering its bottomless tax losses. (Talks on this issue had in fact started between BA and Whitehall in October.)

And most perplexing of all in some ways, the BA board members remained in chronically pessimistic mood, however uplifting the contrast between their projections for the future and the misery they were leaving behind. They were almost a mirror image of their predecessors before 1981, who had offered nothing but optimism despite doom-laden statistics.

Nothing in BA's general attitude, however, was going to deflate Iain Sproat. He had been telling everyone who would listen since the summer that September 1983 was the target date for privatisation – in time to beat the next election, assuming a full five-year term for the current parliament. When the half-year's profit appeared on 8 November, he hailed it as 'almost miraculous'.

Yet within two weeks, the word around Whitehall was that privatisation in 1983 was a dead duck. The Sunday press lobby on 19 November was given a firm steer: September 1983 was no longer an operative date. More time, it seemed, was needed to build up a run of profits. In fact, privatisation would have to wait until after the next general election . . . much as Dunlop's predecessor, Roger Moss, had warned ten months earlier.

The key to the abrupt change of heart was the dispiriting flop of Britoil's privatisation in the third week of November 1982. That prompted everyone in Whitehall and the City to cast a much colder eye over BA's prospective track record.

Something else had happened in November, too. Very few people had heard about it by the 19th. But it was one day to constitute a sounder reason for delaying privatisation than even BA's stormy commercial record.

6

Hardball

'It is a street-smart, gutsy firm with few formalities, a top-notch staff, intelligent and innovative partners, and hot prospects for continued growth . . . It is intimidating, ill-mannered, informal, hungry, and aggressive . . . Touche Ross plays for keeps.'*

Beckman could hardly have ended up with a more suitable member of the Big Eight accountants with whom to launch his suit. But the Touche Ross involvement with Laker Airways did not start out as a mammoth undertaking – quite the contrary.

Christopher Morris, the forty-year-old head of its London liquidation department, was staying with friends in Fulham over 16–17 February 1982. He lives in the heart of London's stockbroker belt at Cobham in Surrey; but a train strike made it convenient to spend the night in town and his wife had joined him for dinner at his friends' home. The telephone rang and it was Bill Mackey wanting to have a few urgent words about the Laker affair.

Mackey was one of the two joint receivers who had been sent in by the Midland group eleven days earlier. The no-nonsense Scottish accountant had been catapulted to national fame overnight, his sepulchral features made instantly familiar by the hordes of Fleet Street photographers who had been dispatched to cover

*Mark Stevens, *The Big Eight: An Inside View of America's Eight Most Powerful and Influential Accounting Firms* (1981).

57

Laker's dismemberment. But after the initial onslaught on those Laker subsidiaries which were obviously disposable, like Arrowsmith Holidays, Mackey had run into a little technical difficulty.

Receivers are generally appointed by lenders to grab the assets of a company on the legal basis of a mortgage triggered off by default. This applied in the normal way to the task facing Mackey and the various other banks' receivers in connection with the English subsidiaries of Freddie's business empire. Unfortunately for them, however, the most valuable assets left behind by his collapse – including all the aircraft and their spares – were vested in the Laker Airways company proper, as opposed to Laker International or any of the other entities registered under English law. And Laker Airways had been registered by Freddie in Jersey – where the local Norman French law had never made any provision for mortgages.

This had not stopped the leading creditors from launching legal action in London to assert mortgage rights over the Laker Airways assets. Exim Bank, for example, had dispatched a lawyer and a loan officer from Washington to help their receivers begin the work of repossessing Laker Airways' DC-10s, now sitting in the slush beside Gatwick's runways. But it was quickly apparent to Bill Mackey that some dangerous conflicts of interest might emerge on the back of the distinction between English and Jersey law. Would all the unsecured creditors of Laker Airways, for example, be delighted to find the company stripped to the bone by secured creditors acting through receivers whom Jersey law did not recognise?

The protection of any Laker Airways' creditors, therefore, would properly have to fall to an official usually only called in to fold up what remains of a company, after the receivers have been and gone: the liquidator. Given the initiatives already taken by secured creditors like Exim, it seemed unlikely that much work would be involved. Still, some tricky legal issues might be in store and Mackey turned to one of the best City liquidators he knew: Christopher Morris. Would he care to take on the job, asked Mackey in the middle of Morris's dinner? It looked like 'a tidying-up job' for the most part, but it would need immediate attention.

Morris has had his share of famous liquidations over the years. His victims include Bernie Cornfeld's IOS and the London & Counties Bank. His base in Touche Ross's London headquarters, in Little New Street just behind Fleet Street, is a modest office at street-level opposite the Cartoonist, a public house where the walls are covered as the name suggests. Morris has taken to displaying one or two cartoons on his own walls; and on his desk sits an inkstand engraved as a souvenir of his central role in the dismantlement of Roberto Calvi's Banco Ambrosiano.

The first intimation that the Laker assignment might not prove entirely as billed by Mackey came like a piece of cloak-and-dagger business straight out of Italy's Ambrosiano drama. While Morris was visiting New York towards the end of February, he was telephoned by an anonymous caller. There were weighty legal actions pending over the Laker Airways affair, said the caller. Would Morris consider selling his rights in any future litigation? Morris never did discover the name of the mystery bidder. But he began to look into the legal background a bit more urgently – and it led him directly to Bob Beckman's office.

The two men could hardly be more different in appearance. Morris is short and dark where the red-haired Beckman stands over six feet tall. The Englishman, again quite unlike Beckman, is shy to the point of being self-effacing – an impression somehow reinforced by his coyly tentative handling of the occasional cigarette – but he has a twinkle in his eye much of the time which announces a quiet self-assurance. Above all, perhaps, Morris appears one of nature's traditional English city gents, whom it is hard to envisage dressed in anything but a meticulous business suit. His whole being exudes caution and steady judgement.

He was not, in other words, the man to jump for Beckman's plan on the spur of the moment. He needed time to test the US lawyer's mettle – and as it happened, there was a tailor-made opportunity for doing so.

Ever since the DC-10 crash at Chicago in 1979, Beckman had been at work on a claim for damages for Laker Airways against the US Federal Aviation Authority, McDonnell Douglas and American Airlines. By late February 1982, he had boiled the suit down to an action against AA but he was still certain of its merits, notwithstanding Laker's own collapse. This was the pretext for his first meeting with the Laker liquidator. Beckman said they should press for damages of more than £20m. Morris contacted AA, met personally with its chairman – who refused, however, to have anything to do with Bob Beckman – and walked away in March with a settlement of £3.9m.

It was not a bad start for the Beckman/Morris relationship. It developed quickly, as Beckman set out his case for exploring another, altogether grander suit. Morris, fortified now with the AA damages, agreed to pay Beckman a retainer to investigate the allegations of an anti-Laker conspiracy.

The opinion which Beckman served up in June – providing the basis for an antitrust suit – sparked off a furious debate inside Touche Ross over the merits of continuing. Conflicts of interest were rife. After all, the firm could count a number of major clients amongst those who might be hurt by a successful antitrust case. It even audited the accounts of the IATA itself in some parts of the world! But Touche did not belie its reputation: it would at least hear Beckman through to the end.

So Freddie's longest-standing champion was accorded a lavish reception on 10 November when he arrived at the London office to make his pitch. In the Touche Ross boardroom sat Douglas Baker, now chairman of Touche

Ross International, Peter Stilling, the firm's top auditor, Michael Blackburn, now the managing partner in London, and Rick Murray – a key figure in the background who ran the firm's legal department in New York and had already spent much of the autumn of 1982 acting as devil's advocate against the Beckman plan. Others in the audience included Touche's London solicitors, Durrant Piesse, Beckman's own wife and Freddie himself, whom no one doubted was going to be a star witness for any legal action that ensued.

It was the most important day of Beckman's career. And he handled it with aplomb.

He gave an impressive account of Laker Airways' short and troubled existence as the proud owner of Skytrain. He reviewed the attitudes and reactions of the airline world to Freddie's rise and fall – and he chronicled in detail what had happened, as he saw it, when attempts were made to rescue Freddie's business from oblivion at the end. There was much talk of US legal procedure, of the Sherman and Clayton Acts, of unlawful combinations and intentional torts. But what Beckman was proposing was starkly clear to everyone present.

He was proposing a civil action in the US courts on two grounds. First, that there had been a classic antitrust conspiracy organised by BA and a number of other IATA airlines to destroy Laker Airways: that they had arranged to fix 'predatory prices' which meant operating at below cost just long enough to finish off Laker and then raising prices all round immediately afterwards to recoup their own losses. And second, that the airlines had conspired together to wreck the rescue planned by McDonnell Douglas and the Midland Bank – which companies were to be seen, however, as willing accomplices.

The list of potential defendants was a lengthy one. The sums involved would be huge. The suit would seek full redress for the £350m. hole in Laker's accounts the previous February. They would request a trial by jury. And Section 9 of the 1890 Sherman Act (and Section 4 of the 1914 Clayton Act) would automatically require, in the event of a favourable verdict, that the defendants should hand over treble damages: not a cent less than $1.05bn.

For Touche Ross, the attractions were obvious. Indeed, in the financial sense, the firm had little to lose. The assets of Laker Airways had already been plundered remorselessly by the bankers. Exim, for example, had beavered away tirelessly through the summer to repossess the DC-10 fleet it had financed for Laker in 1980. McDonnell Douglas pilots and maintenance men had been hired to spirit the aircraft away at the earliest possible moment. (They had flown them from Gatwick to an airfield at Yuma, near Tucson, Arizona, where they were to sit until Exim could find someone to buy them.) The result of such prompt action by the banks was that Morris had precious little chance, in his liquidation, of producing more than a tiny fraction of the cash he would need to pay off all the creditors.

There were 14,000 ticketholders owed £4m., 2,500 trade creditors owed £13m. and 2,300 employees of Laker who were owed £5m. Then there was £7m. that the company owed to the Air Travel Reserve Fund. And that still left the banks and finance houses themselves, which had lent Laker £264m. and were unlikely to see half that amount recouped through mortgage seizures. Yet here was Beckman offering a different prospect altogether. Not only might there be enough to pay off the creditors, but there could even be a handsome sum left over for Freddie and his first wife as the injured shareholders!

But financial risk was not the only kind of exposure that Morris and his colleagues had to ponder that day. What if Beckman's case was simply based on a stream of arcane legal howlers? The bad publicity which could result for the firm was painful to contemplate, never mind the repercussions of a futile offensive against BA, the Midland Bank and the UK Government. And no one was in any doubt about the gravity of the undertaking.

When Beckman had finished putting his case, there

was a long interrogation. The Washington lawyer presented a dazzling array of papers. There was no doubting his intimate knowledge of the airline business, nor his profound conviction of the injustice done to Laker Airways. He made much of the 1974 episode, when the big three carriers (BA, Pan Am and TWA) and British Caledonian had climbed down so quickly in the face of an earlier complaint. And it was a critical precedent, insisted Beckman, precisely because he had now unearthed evidence of strikingly similar incidents.

Chief amongst these was a series of three discussions held under the auspices of IATA in Geneva during July and August 1977. The same hostile airlines had discussed a joint reaction to Skytrain's impending arrival. They had planned cheap, blatantly anti-Skytrain fares which would be offered in large enough numbers each day to match Freddie's prospective capacity. Beckman knew the details because he had obtained the transcripts by using the US Freedom of Information Act once again. He had not yet managed to obtain firm evidence of the wheeling and dealing behind later price discussions. But there were at least two further critical dates, said Beckman. One was 16 October 1981 when talks had been held at the offices of the CAA in London; the other related to an IATA conference at Hollywood, Florida, in January 1982. These were key episodes in the pricing war which brought down Laker. Beckman was asking the Touche Ross partners to believe that the exhaustive searches facilitated by US court procedure would soon turn up further incriminating evidence in connection with both.

They had to agree it certainly seemed likely. After all, the man on the Clapham omnibus surely wasted no time wondering whether Skytrain's rivals had acted in concert as a result of pure coincidence or of careful planning. The idea that it had been a coincidence was surely asking rather a lot. And the outside observer had arguably been encouraged to see a conspiracy at work by numerous public utterances from those involved. Had not William

Waltrip, Pan Am's chief executive, been quoted, for example, in a prominent industry newsletter as saying Laker would be squeezed out of its niche? Beckman had no shortage of documented quotes like that which carried, he said, the clear implication that prices would be lifted again once Freddie had departed.

Nor had the evidence stopped accumulating in February 1982. Months later, for instance, the managing director of TWA's UK sales agents had been quoted as saying that cut-price charter operators might be 'in for another dose of what the carriers gave Freddie Laker'.

In short, there was a glaring prima-facie case for inferring a conspiracy. Under US antitrust law, the inference might even prove strong enough, eventually, to make documentary proof superfluous. That, of course, led directly to some uncomfortable questions from the Touche partners: what exactly did US antitrust laws entail in this arena? Was it not the case that transatlantic aviation had traditionally been exempted from antitrust and handled by diplomats, not judges? The British and American governments had negotiated a complex agreement in June 1977, known as Bermuda II, to cover these matters. What hope had Beckman of sidestepping all the civil servants' painstaking efforts to prevent just this kind of suit?

Every hope, said Beckman. The fact was, the US authorities had been hopelessly embarrassed and irritated by the Bermuda II document almost from the moment it was signed. It was the swan song of a dying era, killed off by the deregulatory reforms of the Carter Administration between 1977 and 1980. The idea that IATA should provide immunity for price-fixing conspiracies was now anathema in Washington, said Beckman.

This ensured two consequences. First, any claims to immunity would be scrutinised very hard. And unfortunately for Laker's foes, argued Beckman, their discussions in July/August 1977 had never begun to fulfil the conditions laid down for the granting of immunity. Such price talks had to be approved by the Civil Aviation Bureau (CAB). In fact, they had been filed but never approved – and President Carter had gone out of his way to reject the CAB's conditional recommendations that had followed.

Second, the post-1977 mood in Washington – even allowing for a certain recidivism by the Reagan Administration – would remove any ambiguity from whatever evidence did surface from the 1977–82 years suggesting a plot by the US carriers. Indeed, Pan Am and TWA had themselves acknowledged the hypersensitivity of their position – under direct US Government pressure – by dropping out of IATA proceedings altogether. (They had joined in again, under supposedly rigid conditions, for the Hollywood, Florida talks.) All in all, said Beckman, the notion of immunity against antitrust would quickly be seen for the canard it really was. Why, the CAB itself was about to be broken up.

After all these subtleties, it must have been a relief for Beckman's audience to query the colourful evidence of a plot to sabotage the 1982 refinancing effort. Here, at least, tangible documents were already at hand. Beckman had copies of some of the outraged telexes sent to McDonnell Douglas and General Electric, protesting against their proposed equity support for Laker. There was one from British Caledonian's chairman, for example; if GE went ahead, it said, 'BCal has no further interest in McDonnell Douglas Aircraft'. That was clear enough. Threatening telexes of one kind or another had been received from several airline bosses. One, René Lapautre of the French carrier Union des Transports Aeriens (UTA), had even sent a copy of his telex to six other chief executives urging them to follow his example. The offending messages would later become known as the 'nastygrams'. Beckman was already confident of their impact on any US jury.

Finally it was all over and the time came for a decision. Should Touche Ross proceed with an action or not?

The partners retreated to a private meeting. Whether BA's privatisation entered into their calculations as a useful bargaining counter will never be known. But it can safely be assumed that they all understood the potential implications of a suit for the British carrier's prospects of flotation. 'It was not a push-over decision,' said one of the participants later. They emerged at the end of the afternoon with their minds made up. Two factors had won the day. Morris was anxious that he should be seen to be discharging his professional duty as the liquidator: to turn down the suit, he felt, might expose Touche itself to an action for damages by a determined creditor. Above all, though, the partners bought the presentation. Beckman had fired them with a conviction that he was right.

But the lawyer was not told immediately of his success. Rick Murray announced that the firm would be seeking a second opinion in Washington. Moves were made in this direction, indeed, though they petered out when Beckman reminded everyone that the firm which had been chosen for the second opinion was an adviser to one of the prospective defendants.

Finally, Morris rang Beckman in his office. The verdict, said the liquidator, was that they should go ahead provided that Beckman agreed to act on a contingency fee basis. Until now, he had worked for a retainer – though it was true he had hinted he might move on to a contingency fee if Morris ran out of money. The switch, as Touche knew, demanded a big commitment from Beckman himself. He was being offered a package which would yield him rather more than 20 per cent of any damages eventually secured in the courts. But if the case collapsed after years of work, there was no guarantee he would receive a cent.

Beckman took a few days to consider it. He needed to ensure that he could call on help from another Washington firm, which had already been helping him during the investigation. This was Metzger, Shadyac & Schwartz.

The firm had an international client list – Dick Shadyac is personal counsel to Colonel Gaddafi and the Libyan Government – and had worked with Beckman on many briefs over the years. In 1982 it took Carl Schwartz no time at all to decide to throw in his firm's lot with Beckman. It was agreed that Beckman, Farmer & Kirstein would concentrate on the refinancing allegations while the second firm worked on the price-fixing conspiracy. This was confirmed to Touche Ross. Morris gave the go-ahead for the suit to be filed.

'The Antitrust Defendants' Lawyers Relief Act', Beckman would jokingly call it later. But he knew, and everyone else knew, that it was going to startle the aviation world – and it did. The suit took the form of complaints and a demand for damages in the US District Court for the District of Columbia. It was lodged as *Laker Airways Ltd* v. *Pan American World Airways, Inc. (CA No. 82-3362)*. The defendants were cited as Pan Am, TWA, McDonnell Douglas and the McDonnell Douglas Finance Corporation, British Caledonian, Lufthansa, Swissair – and BA. It was agreed that parallel complaints against other names would be filed later.

And Beckman was playing hardball, as the US lawyers put it, from the start. Thanksgiving Day in 1982 was on Thursday 25 November and much of the legal establishment was heading off for a traditional long weekend. Beckman adhered to another tradition, long practised by US litigation firms. He filed on the afternoon of Wednesday 24 November. From that moment, the clock began ticking on the twenty days allowed for US defendants to file their replies. That spoiled a few weekends. The case had begun as it was long to continue.

7

Gentlemen Callers

THE DESTRUCTION OF LAKER AIRWAYS LIMITED
or
HOW THE MIDLAND BANK AND BRITISH AIRWAYS
COMBINED WITH FOREIGNERS TO FORCE A PROFITABLE
BRITISH COMPANY OUT OF BUSINESS

It was not the sort of thing City of London solicitors were used to at all. This was the grandiose, even slightly quaint ('combined with foreigners') heading to a seventeen-page document which Morris and a colleague personally delivered to the Midland Bank on 24 November 1982 – the very day that the US antitrust suit was filed in Washington against BA and its co-defendants. Risible or not, it caused apoplexy along the quiet corridors of the clearing bank. The Midland's reaction was immediate – and it landed the bank in open court a couple of months later, at a time when BA and the airlines were still struggling to come to terms with what had happened. The Midland's reception by the judiciary offered BA and British Caledonian some early encouragement and caught the flavour of much that was to follow.

Coward Chance, Midland's pukka City lawyers, could hardly believe their eyes. The document was known as Attachment 7 – it had been the seventh appendix to Bob Beckman's initial presentation to Touche Ross. When the solicitors checked its narrative content, they very quickly construed it as a missive from Cloud 9. Much of the content looked to them as fanciful as the title. (In fact, though they had not been told this, Beckman had deliberately written it in an inflammatory style. It had been composed not as a legal notice at all but as an indication of the kind of bad publicity the defendants could expect to get from sensational press coverage. Whether Beckman had ever intended that it should surface publicly is unclear.)

It was not just that it lacked any supporting evidence for its assertions. (This accorded with normal US practice, where allegations are set out uncorroborated at the outset, although Attachment 7 did seem to push the boat out rather far. 'Laker offered a simple and inexpensive service,' it read at the start. 'Laker was successful and profitable . . . In the spring of 1981, an economic misfortune befell Laker . . .') Far worse, to the Midland's solicitors, it teemed with tiny colourful details which were flatly denied by the bank executives involved.

Participants in some of the critical meetings on the eve of Freddie's 4 February confrontation with the Midland had been 'sworn to secrecy', said the document. Once Freddie and his solicitor had been shown safely inside the Midland conference room on that eventful day, the first bearer of bad news had 'entered and closed the door, putting his back against the door'. Later, he 'said that Sir Freddie could not make any telephone calls'. And so on and so on: the men from Coward Chance advised their client that Attachment 7 was preposterous – but a full and prompt riposte was needed.

Riding suitably high horses for the occasion, Geoffrey Taylor, the Midland chief executive, went straight round to the Touche Ross offices with the head of his legal department. He personally denounced the document as an outrage, reading from a prepared statement which he refused to leave behind at the end of the meeting. What followed came as no surprise.

Both Midland and its subsidiary, Clydesdale Bank, acted swiftly in the courts. They lodged their own versions of events in Washington. And in London, on 29 November, they issued a writ against Laker Airways claiming a permanent injunction to prevent themselves being joined as co-defendants in the main litigation. They were immediately given a temporary injunction privately, pending a further hearing in the Commercial Court of the Queen's Bench.

As for the clearer's relations with Touche Ross, they took a frosty turn. The bankers, aware of what was in the wind earlier in the autumn, had asked to be given forty-eight hours' notice of any legal action against them. Or else, they had threatened, Touche Ross would cease to exist as far as the Midland was concerned. Morris saw Attachment 7 as the warning they had requested: in fact, it gave them a few weeks' notice rather than forty-eight hours. By an unhappy chance, however, the document arrived at the Midland just as its senior men were preoccupied with the launch of a huge bond issue on the US financial markets. They thought the timing was deliberate. Relations between the two sides, it was quickly made clear, would not be returning to normal for some time . . .

In the following weeks, news of Freddie's personal experiences seemed to add insult to injury for many of those affronted by the Laker suit. Freddie was rebuffed by the Association of British Travel Agents; but the CAA awarded him a fresh air travel organiser's licence and he was telling anyone who would listen about his plans for Skytrain Holidays.

The Midland injunction came before Mr Justice Parker on the Queen's Bench early in February 1983. He renewed the November injunction until a full trial of the banks' stand could be arranged. And in open court, he echoed the view of many in the City about Attachment 7: it carried 'a title which savours of either fiction or journalism rather than legal exposition'. Its content, said the judge, was so inherently unlikely that he questioned the motives of those who served it. He contrasted it unfavourably with the 'cogent and direct' evidence which Midland had filed in Washington.

Mr Justice Parker then went further, with some remarks about the merits of the banks' position at a full trial. And he singled out an issue which was to weigh heavily on future events. All defendants in the Laker Airways suit faced the prospect of financial loss, whatever happened. For there was no provision under US antitrust law for successful defendants to have their legal costs re-imbursed. Touche Ross, in other words, would pay its lawyers nothing if they lost. BA and the others would pay handsomely even if they won.

Meanwhile, in the boardrooms of BA and the other non-US airlines, this striking truth was just beginning to mellow an initial disbelief that the suit had been filed at all. Telephone calls had been exchanged and lawyers consulted. To virtually all the European executives involved, the Morris initiative looked too ridiculous to be taken seriously. This was not the view taken in the US. No one seemed too clear about the reaction of McDonnell in St Louis, Missouri: the manufacturer kept its cards close to its chest, now as later. But in New York City, the American airline defendants, Pan Am and TWA, never had any illusions about the possible ramifications of the suit – though they regarded it as frivolous nonetheless.

Indeed, news of the filing was received at Pan Am's Park Avenue offices with some bemusement. Freddie himself had been there just the day before to see Ed Acker, the airline's chairman. Freddie had wanted to propose some new business between the airline and the nascent Skytrain Holidays. He and Acker, for all their bitter rivalry, had always got along well personally. Acker was still allowing his former adversary to use a free travel pass on Pan Am flights and Freddie was fond of saying how many friends he had at Pan Am. (Back in the summer of 1981, just before Acker was brought in as chairman from Air Florida, there had even been rumours – reported in *Fortune* magazine – that Freddie might get the top job at Pan Am himself.) The two men had had a very cordial meeting on 23 November. But according to Pan Am's in-house counsel, not a word had been whispered by Freddie about the approaching action.

As for Washington's legal establishment, no one there doubted the significance of Beckman's suit. But they had a monumental job persuading the Europeans of that.

Perhaps the least difficult task belonged to Len Bebchick, British Caledonian's US lawyer since 1961. Bebchick had originally been retained by chairman (now Sir) Adam Thomson some months ahead of BCal's inaugural flight. He had been intimately involved in the airline's licensing struggles from the start and, like Beckman at Laker Airways, was by now rather more than a strictly legal adviser. In fact, Bebchick and Beckman were old adversaries themselves, with a long-standing professional rivalry which had spilled over into personal animosity once BCal and Laker had begun to find themselves competing directly for new routes. (Bebchick had always presented BCal's opposition to the licensing of Skytrain, whether in London, Washington or Hong Kong.) When Bebchick flew over to Caledonian House at Crawley and explained the facts to the BCal board, they were ready to accept the potential gravity of the matter.

That left BA, Lufthansa and Swissair.

BA played a completely dead bat. 'We are aware of the development. We do not believe there is any justification in it,' said the airline publicly. And that was that.

Nor – in the initial weeks, at least – does there seem to have been much private concern at BA either. The British carrier lodged an application with the US District Court on 13 December, asking for an extension of the time allowed to respond. Otherwise, not much happened. It was true that some of the corporation's executives had been cited personally as co-conspirators; but with the revolving door on BA's executive suite spinning at its present speed, that did not appear to be an insuperable

72

problem. Gerry Draper, for instance, was one of the named men.

So when the chairman acknowledged just before Christmas 1982 that there would certainly be no BA privatisation before the next general election ('We have a long way to go'), he was thinking about balance sheets and profit margins, not protracted court battles.

The continental defendants scoffed indignantly at the news of the filing. Professor Alfred Rudolph, Lufthansa's in-house legal counsel, and his German-speaking counter-part at Swissair, Dr Andreas Hodel, do not give the obvious impression of men happy to take any corporate business altogether lightly. But the absurdity of Beckman's suit, as it appeared to them, left both momentarily perplexed about an appropriate response. Help was recruited, inevitably, from Connecticut Avenue.

Heinz Ruhnau, the new chairman of Lufthansa, had arrived at the airline six months before from Bonn, where he had been Under-Secretary for Transportation in the German Government. He had seen official briefs con-cerned with US antitrust matters dealt with in the past by a German US lawyer called Dieter Lange, at the London office of Wilmer, Cutler & Pickering, one of the leading US antitrust practices. Ruhnau arranged for the Morris suit to be handled for Lufthansa through the same channels. Additional assistance was later sought from Short, Klein & Karas, another Washington firm which also acted for Swissair. The two airlines were to move closely in tandem throughout the case. Their first step was a cheeky one and echoed the Midland chief execu-tive's personal visit to Touche Ross. If successful, it might well have pulled the rug from under the suit against the airlines as successfully as the Midland response appeared to be undermining an action against the bank.

Beckman's main partner, Don Farmer, had acted for Lufthansa in the past over some minor regulatory matters. In January, a senior delegation of US lawyers representing the counsel of Lufthansa, Swissair and their co-defendants marched into Beckman's offices to protest against his firm pursuing the Laker suit, since the action involved it in a conflict of interests. The implied breach of ethics was an outrage, said the lawyers. (There seemed to be a good deal of outrage about the place.) Beckman listened to the complaint, then reacted with a sharp burst of indignation that pressure was being brought to bear on his firm in this way. It was, in fact, outrageous. Nevertheless, a formal petition seeking his firm's disqualification from the case was lodged with the court the following month.

This did not endear the defendants to the judge appointed to the case; but it did give them an early glimpse of the reaction they could expect from the Honorable Harold H. Greene to anything smacking of an attempt to obstruct the proceedings of his court. Outside the US, Judge Greene is arguably the best-known American judge of the day; within his own country, he remains unidentified with any establishment and has a reputation for cleverness married to (for a judge) an unusually volatile temperament which leaves no one in his court uncertain of his authority.

He rose to prominence as an attorney working on civil rights in the US Department of Justice in the early sixties and was appointed as a judge to the Federal District court in 1967. But what really brought him to fame, between 1978 and 1982, was his handling of the US Government's antitrust case against American Telephone & Telegraph (AT&T). He was the third judge appointed to preside over the case. Fears were by then growing that it was actually unmanageable, rather as the antitrust case against IBM had become. But Judge Greene imposed himself on it, taking a tough line with both plaintiff and defendant, in a way which won him many laurels, a few mixed reviews and plenty of publicity. (He was profiled, for example, in both *The American Lawyer* and the *Washington Post*.)

He agreed to take on the Laker case even before the

74

AT&T imbroglio was straightened out. Indeed, there were to be several occasions when the pressure of the AT&T paperwork would bear down hard on the Laker litigation diary. But Judge Greene has an apparently insatiable appetite for the sensational commercial case – they are, as he says, 'better than dealing with car smashes'.

The motion for Beckman's disqualification he regarded as a flagrant abuse of his court's time. Counsel were abruptly told to continue the case, pending a formal opinion from the bench. In the event, the judge did not hand over his opinion for another sixteen months, by which time the issue had become academic. (Farmer had left Beckman's firm by then, after an acrimonious dispute leading to legal action between the lawyers themselves. Beckman had wasted no time cutting Farmer out of the case and surrounding him with impenetrable Chinese walls, just in case.)

This, though, was a mere portent of Judge Greene's determination to try the case. He was very soon confronted with a far bigger test which required him, in staking out the jurisdiction of his court, to acknowledge explicitly what was rapidly becoming clear to all: *Laker Airways* v. *Pan American* had the potential to be the most important event in aviation law for decades.

By January 1983, BA and its political masters in Whitehall had begun to think better of their initial reaction to the suit. In part, this merely reflected a finer appreciation of the unavoidable costs involved – a worry already aired by the Midland and shared by BCal. But there was another, far deeper issue involved. To put the matter bluntly, what right had an American court to start pronouncing on the UK-based relationship between one British company (BA) and another (Laker)?

To lawyers, the issue is a familiar one and passes under the jargon term 'extraterritoriality'. To Whitehall officials – and civil servants in other countries, too – the issue is a hardy perennial needing careful attention in the cultivation of good relations with Washington. And to companies with global business commitments, it is an issue neglected at their real peril. Extraterritoriality crops up whenever one government attempts to impose its legal fiat upon the citizens of another. In practice, the US has long been the arch-offender – and antitrust cases have given rise to all the most celebrated clashes in recent times.

Over Laker, the claim made by Judge Greene's court was simple. Domestic antitrust law was directly applicable because the plaintiff and all the defendants in the case had been involved (however directly or indirectly) in business together within the borders of the US. American consumers had been affected by the dealings before the court. They had every right to be protected by their own legal system. If other non-US companies did not like the implications of business on these terms, they had only to stay away from the US marketplace in future.

There were scores of subtle legal complications, naturally. How much business had the defendants really done together in the US? Was there not an overwhelming balance of convenience in favour of leaving any action to the national courts of the parties concerned? Were there good reasons for putting a blind eye to the telescope in aid of the cheerful coexistence of nations (what the lawyers call 'comity')? At bottom, however, the claim being made by Judge Greene's court dictated a stark choice. Either one accepted that it was inherently fair or one did not.

The British Government did not.

In Whitehall, the whole principle of imposing US domestic antitrust law upon companies intent on essentially international business was regarded – and still is – as frankly unacceptable. The concept went much further than anything in English law on the subject. It carried the risk of treble damages. It exposed UK companies to irretrievable legal expenses. Above all, it was incompatible as the British saw it with both the spirit and the practical application of international free trade. And the Americans could be relied upon to try their old tricks about once every ten years. In the sixties, it had been the international shipping industry which had resisted the antitrust menace; in the seventies, RTZ and the world's uranium mining industry had borne the brunt. Now it was the airlines' turn.

All this had been spelt out in a little book published only a few months before the filing of the Laker suit, *National Laws and International Commerce: The Problem of Extraterritoriality*. One of its authors, Douglas E. Rosenthal, a practising lawyer in Washington, was telephoned by counsel for BCal the very day of the filing and agreed to help prepare BCal's defence. His co-author, William Knighton, was the Deputy Secretary in charge of the Aviation Division at the DTI.

In short, BA – and BCal – had to fight the very notion of Touche Ross's Laker suit. Views about the substance of the suit, or lack of it, were superfluous in this respect. The extraterritoriality issue demanded a punchy response all of its own. So the airlines trod along the path signposted by the Midland: they asked the Commercial Court to rule that any Laker action against them should be confined to the English courts. Lufthansa and Swissair joined them in the motion. And on 2 March 1983, Mr Justice Parker handed them all a temporary injunction to that effect.

Opposition to their move came not just from Touche Ross, which served a countermotion, but from Washington as well. On 9 March, Judge Greene laid down orders in Washington that the other defendants should not turn to any foreign court for help to block the suit.

Despite a mounting jumble of legal paraphernalia, the outline of a headline-grabbing international row was becoming clear to everyone. The co-defendants – now including Sabena and KLM, the flag-carriers of Belgium and the Netherlands who had been added to the case in mid-February – were all appalled at the prospect. No one could be sure what defiance of the US judge's orders might lead to. Would aircraft be confiscated on the tarmac at Kennedy Airport?

The gathering seriousness of the situation was openly acknowledged by counsel for the British airlines on 24 March, when they came before Mr Justice Parker once again. They had decided to take up the gauntlet thrown down in Washington. They asked the English judge to renew his 2 March injunctions. The reasoning behind this bold move, it must be said, was bolstered by more than the official line towards extraterritoriality, important though this was. There was another, almost equally significant issue in the balance: namely, the sanctity of Bermuda II, the UK's bilateral aviation treaty with the US.

It was this double-barrelled aspect of the Laker antitrust suit which was really getting the Government and Whitehall excited by March 1983. It was managing to combine in one crisis two of the most troublesome aspects of the entire international legal agenda. Not only did it imply that British business should kowtow to US antitrust legislation. It also threatened, as the UK Government saw it, to drive a coach-and-horses through the delicate structure of Bermuda II – a treaty which had always been regarded, along with its immediate predecessor, as the model for bilateral air service agreements all over the world. And by March, rumours were rife in the airline world that BA had made rather more use of Bermuda II's supposed grant of antitrust immunity than had initially been realised.

There was no doubting this was a potential embarrassment. The suit was complaining that there had been inter-airline pricing discussions. The simplest defence would be to deny that any such discussions had ever taken place. But it was no secret in Washington legal circles that many top lawyers were sceptical this line could really be held. There was a widespread feeling that, once confidential documents began to surface, evidence of such discussions would be incontrovertible. (That was the suspicion, after all, which Beckman had persuaded Touche Ross was well-grounded.)

Unfortunately the second line of defence – were it to be appropriate – might have its drawbacks. It would consist of saying, 'Yes, we had those kind of discussions you complain of; but they were not against US domestic law because they were always held under the aegis of an agreement specifically written to exempt them from US jurisdiction.' But what if the discussions, once displayed to public view, revealed all kinds of chicanery and wheeler-dealing? What US lawyer could then predict how an American jury might react, regardless of Bermuda II's sophisticated provisions?

Behind closed doors in the opening months of 1983, this was exactly the dilemma facing civil servants in the Aviation Division. They were all too aware of the possibility: faced with the Skytrain innovation, why should BA and the other airlines not have reacted entirely in line with a long tradition of secret IATA bargains stitched up in smoke-filled rooms? If so it should prove, the Laker suit had all the ingredients to turn the regulators' lives into one long nightmare for years to come. How much better to scotch the US action now, by keeping BA and BCal barred from it by English law!

On the other side of the Atlantic, meanwhile, US Government officials in the Department of Justice were also thinking hard about the likelihood of finding some colourful evidence of a closed shop practice on the North Atlantic air routes. The lawyers in the Justice Department antitrust division, however, were poised to draw some very different conclusions from the men in Whitehall. Any lurid details that emerged of pricing discussions would be regarded in London as a tiresome obfuscation of the central point, that antitrust was irrelevant. In Washington, any such details would probably pull the trigger on a criminal prosecution.

News of this alarming possibility reached the UK Government early in 1983. Talks were held between the two sets of officials in February. There was distressingly little meeting of minds.

British efforts to dissuade the Americans from a formal inquiry grew steadily more desperate. But they were to no avail. The Justice Department was even loath to connect its interest in the North Atlantic directly to Laker's collapse. Finally, on 25 March, the Department announced the launch of a Grand Jury investigation into criminal antitrust activities by BA and the other North Atlantic carriers.

Four days later in the English High Court, Mr Justice Parker compounded Whitehall's dismay by rejecting the request of BA and BCal for a renewed temporary injunction – pending a full trial of the injunction motion – to keep them out of the dock. His lordship hoped they 'would do nothing which would exacerbate a situation which, in view of the differences of opinion between the governments of the two countries is, to say the least, somewhat delicate'.

It was going to get downright brittle before very long.

8

The Favourite

At precisely 12.52 p.m. on Sunday, 10 April 1983, television viewers all over Britain saw Brian Walden's ITV current affairs programme, *Weekend World*, fade out just a fraction earlier than usual. In the ad break that followed came a TV commercial which was really more of a miniature feature film: it lasted a full six minutes and included a sci-fi film of Manhattan, lit up like a cosmic gin palace, flying into Heathrow Airport at night over the suburban roofs of the metropolis and terrifying the honest citizens out of their beds in the process. It was not a peak advertising time, but there was generally a select audience for the spot, thanks to the influence wielded by Walden's programme. On 10 April, it was even more select than usual – all BA managers had been invited by their chairman to tune in for the occasion.

In the UK, the managers received their invitations by post. Overseas, every BA office received a copy of the commercial on videocassette; many country managers held drinks' parties for dignitaries in their local travel industry to watch it with BA's own staff. They were all treated to the sight of King and a newly appointed chief executive of the airline, Colin Marshall, reviewing BA's 1981–3 achievements. A massive new advertising campaign was then launched with the 90-second flight of the *Manhattan Landing* film.

It was King's way of announcing that the changes at BA were meant to alter more than its corporate structure and its accounting results. Also at stake was the self-respect of the workforce and the public image of the airline, which the board regarded as indistinguishable in practice. The new company was aimed at far more than just selling tickets. It was about corporate achievement and self-confidence.

The new man beside the chairman typified both. Always courteous and immaculately dressed, with a ready if slightly professional smile and a quiet passion for detail, Colin M. Marshall – the M stands rather curiously for Marsh – is the professional service industry manager through and through. He is also that rare animal, the British businessman who has made good in the US and returned to a career in Britain. (He speaks with just the trace of a midatlantic burr.) In 1983, at the age of forty-nine, he immediately struck BA's managers at all levels as the personification of everything lacking for years in the airline's boardroom.

Not that Marshall actually joined the board. Both he and Dunlop had to remain below it: their salaries were too high to be accommodated within the nationalised industry guidelines. And at around £85,000 a year – Dunlop was getting £66,000 and King himself £41,000 – Marshall was also earning rather over twice Roy Watt's current salary (Watts was staying on as deputy chairman). But then, as chairman of Avis, the US-based car-hire company which had been 'Trying Harder' for years, Marshall had already been making $345,000 a year by the end of the seventies.

Born and bred in London, he had left school in 1951 and gone straight into the ranks of the workers as a cadet purser with Orient Steamship. Seven years (and twenty-one voyages from England to Australia) later he joined Hertz, beginning in its Chicago headquarters and rising to be head of the US giant's UK and Benelux car-hire operations by 1963.

Another senior Hertz man, Donald Petrie, left Hertz just about this time to join Avis Rent A Car, alongside

Felix Rohatyn and a team assembled by Lazard's of New York which had bought Avis in 1962. The company was in bad shape and the bankers' team was busy turning it round. In 1964, they hired Marshall away from Hertz. He stayed with Avis for fifteen years – encompassing the period from 1965 to 1972 when it was actively managed as a subsidiary of Harold Geneen's legendary ITT – and he rose through astonishing energy and application to be its chief executive officer by 1976, one of the most powerful British-born men in US business. (Marshall still begins his daily engagements at 7.00 or 7.30 a.m. most mornings of the week.)

Marshall subsequently spent two years as executive vice-president of Norton Simon Inc., which acquired Avis in 1979. Then he returned to England in 1981 to take up a career in UK retailing.

Sears Holdings, the late Charles Clore's shoeshop empire and owner of Selfridges, had been a rival bidder against Norton Simon for Avis in 1979. Marshall had been told then that there would be an opening for him in the UK firm if he ever wanted it. He had been there less than eighteen months when he was approached on BA's behalf by Russell Reynolds. The challenge of taking over one of the biggest travel service corporations anywhere in the world must have been well-nigh irresistible to the old ('Car Marshall') Avis man. But King had to work hard to persuade Sears's chairman Leonard Sainer to let his new deputy go. ('National interest and all that,' said King later, recalling his plea to Sainer.)

It was only Marshall's fourth change of company in thirty-one years. But he was moving shrewdly, as before – and those who chose him knew exactly what to expect. King wanted a chief executive who understood how service businesses worked. He was not interested in finding another senior man with airline experience; he had enough of them already. Indeed, the very high calibre of BA's middle management was proving a revelation, now that the top layers of the airline hierarchy had been removed. (This in fact was the reason why King hired only two senior men in the end, rather than the three he had cleared with Mrs Thatcher early in 1982.) King was seeking an international marketing boss with all the other skills necessary to running a huge organisation.

Marshall did not disappoint him. On the day of his arrival, 1 February, Marshall formed a marketing committee of senior BA executives to look at the whole gamut of consumer services offered by the airline. And plans were laid for a central services staff under Jim Harris, formerly the head of UK passenger and cargo sales and now the airline's marketing director.

Harris and his services staff in London, reporting directly to Marshall, were soon to form the hub for all the airline's diverse marketing operations. It would be their job to coordinate the efforts of BA's local managers in sixty-two countries around the globe. Just as Dunlop had tightened up the accounting controls, so Marshall quickly imposed a far more rigorous approach to country managers' marketing budgets and policy. 'There will be no empire-building,' said Harris, announcing his four-man team. 'The new organisation will be very slim, since that is the way to get swift decisions. We now have a fundamentally different way of tackling how to sell our airline's services.'

There were going to be a lot of fundamental differences around BA before long. Marshall set to work immediately to review every detail of BA's management structure. Helping him was another newcomer, an American in his fifties called Michael Levin. A professional consultant who had worked with Marshall at Avis, Levin moved into an office next to Marshall's in Speedbird House on a full-time basis.

To the consternation of some BA executives, Levin remained outside the airline's formal management hierarchy; but there was no doubting his powerful influence on events from the outset. The results would be apparent a few months later.

It was not just structural weaknesses and reporting inadequacies that stood between BA and privatisation, however. Nor did those who knew Marshall expect him to busy himself exclusively with such matters. A deeper malaise afflicted BA – and it had been remedied not at all by the many disruptive changes since early 1981. Indeed, all the traumas of the last two years had greatly compounded this fundamental problem: the appallingly low morale of the workforce.

No company of 59,000 employees could possibly be shrunk to around 37,000 without a profound loss of confidence amongst all those remaining. When Marshall arrived, there were even rumours of another 2,000 forced redundancies amongst senior management staff. The man who had worn a red coat with his employees for so many years at Avis was not slow to appreciate the challenge. He would have to effect, he knew, a basic change in employee attitudes – towards the airline itself, its management and, above all, the customer.

Red coats and weekend motivation conferences on 'How to Love your Superiors' were not the only tools, though, which Avis had brought to the task of raising morale. In its 1966 advertising campaign, devised by the Doyle Dane Bernbach agency, Avis had had one of the most celebrated copylines in modern business: 'We're No. 2 – We Try Harder'. Marshall was keen to grapple with BA's corporate advertising plans as soon as he arrived . . . and he found the planning already well advanced for just the sort of campaign he had in mind.

The origins of the new campaign went back to the previous summer, that of 1982 – to the overthrow of Gerry Draper and to Dunlop's assault on BA's whole business strategy. During the expansionist Draper era, BA's advertising had naturally embodied his direct, price-oriented approach. (All commercials had had to carry fares information, for example – even though this dictated different commercials for, say, New York, Chicago and Boston because the three cities had different APEX fares to London.) When this was jettisoned in favour of the bigger margins/lower volume strategy, the advertising was turned upside down, too.

The change made up in speed for what it lacked in diplomacy. King was introduced early in the summer of 1982 to Charles and Maurice Saatchi – of Tory party advertising fame – through a shared friendship with a West End art dealer. He explained that he was looking for campaign ideas that would somehow convey the trauma of what had been going on at BA. He wanted BA's employees, too, to feel that it had all been worthwhile.

The Saatchis interested King with some of their immediate reactions. At the beginning of August, the BA chairman secretly invited the Saatchi & Saatchi agency to devise an alternative to the current campaigns run for BA all over the world by the international agency, Foote Cone & Belding. (FCB had been BOAC's agency since 1946. They had won the BA main account in 1973 and had been given exclusive, global responsibility for the airline in 1979.)

King liked what he saw from the Saatchis. On 13 September, he wrote a thirteen-line letter to Bill Barry, the chief executive of FCB in London: the agency's thirty-six years' service was over, as of that evening. The press was told next day of the Saatchi group's appointment. It was the biggest account switch in UK advertising history. FCB had 620 people employed worldwide on BA business and was earning millions in percentage fees on advertising and promotional work worth £42m. in 1982. King's letter knocked it sideways.

The agency could hardly pretend that the bolt came out of a totally blue sky. It had been asked to present its views about BA's strategy early in the summer. (There had been a bit of awkwardness when the FCB people first met King: it had taken several weeks to arrange the occasion. 'Why so long?' demanded King. 'I just want to have a look at you.' They were not accustomed, apologised the admen, to dealing with a chairman on such a spontaneous basis.) When FCB made a full presentation, its US head had flown over to participate in person; King told him he thought the presentation excellent. But the approach to Saatchis followed just the same – and was headlined in the advertising trade press in mid-August. The whole industry was seething with rumour by the beginning of September.

But the manner of the *coup de grâce* was vintage King. He offered no reasons and no personal explanation. When Bill Barry rang him back on the evening of 13 September, the BA chairman was unavailable. 'It seems a little odd, if not most mysterious,' wrote the FCB boss in reply, 'that a large public sector account, such as British Airways, was not put out for tender.' But it did him no good. The decision had been taken and that was that. Even the advertising world, used to the odd bit of knockabout stuff, was a little shaken. The influential *Campaign* magazine, which had first broken the story, summed up the general reaction: 'the least that common decency would have offered [FCB] now was the chance to compete openly for the business with other agencies, even if the dice were loaded against it.'

The bare truth was, though, that FCB and Draper had been too close. (It was Draper who had given FCB the global account in 1979.) King wanted to be rid of them both. And the 'We'll take good care of you' slogan had been in use at BOAC as long ago as 1948. On the advertising front as on all others, King wanted a striking departure in every sense.

There was a further reason why King wanted a dramatic new advertising campaign precisely at this time. He was anxious to show all BA's employees that he was no flash in the pan. Late in 1982 there were critics, he knew, who drew comfort from the fact that the nightmare of his chairmanship (as they saw it) could not last for ever. He had only been appointed for a three-year term, after all. King was determined to outflank any adversaries 'playing it long', as he put it. So he went to the Trade Secretary and had his appointment extended until after privatisation. A controversial change of advertising agency, King felt, was the best way to show that changes under his leadership were going to be permanent – and were going to be the biggest since 1946 in all sorts of directions . . .

Saatchis set up a special task force for its new account and hired one of the industry's best brains, Geoff Seymour, away from a rival agency. Seymour was responsible for such famous campaigns as those for Hamlet cigars and Heineken lager. The search began immediately for a slogan which would stress a brand image for BA in place of all the product emphasis – lower fares, wider seats, better frequencies and so on – which had distinguished the Draper years.

Two happy discoveries were made. Any number of world airlines were bigger than BA, including several in the US, according to all the industry's usual criteria of size. Even in the strictly international arena, Pan Am was bigger in terms of 'revenue tonne kilometres', the usual IATA measurement in such matters. But on the pure basis of passengers carried internationally, there was no doubt about it: BA was the world's No. 1. A new concept was born. The British flag-carrier could be 'The World's Favourite Airline'.

And when the Saatchi team came to look at the North Atlantic route in particular, they found to their delight that BA was carrying 1.4m. people over the ocean, compared to the 1.2m. population of Manhattan. So an idea was born, too.

By November 1982 the concept had been worked into a striking £12m. campaign built around ten separate 60-second commercials. When American footballers rioted in their changing-rooms or Humphrey Bogart's lover knocked his trilby off at Casablanca Airport or Thor, the God of Thunder, sent one of his handmaidens packing – as was to happen in three of the ten commercials – the idea in each case was to contrast their rages at being booked on some other airline with the cool confidence of Laurence Olivier or Joan Collins or Omar Sharif as they checked in with their BA tickets. And cool confidence was the concept.

The Manhattan idea developed into a plan for a 90-second film which was originally designed to be used for BA's privatisation campaign in 1983. King and his board gave the green light in November 1982 for filming to go ahead on *Manhattan Landing* and three of the smaller films.

This, more or less, was where things stood when Marshall arrived at Speedbird House. The Saatchi approach fitted perfectly with his own requirements. The old emphasis on products would have been no good: most passengers did not believe half the claims made, never mind BA's own employees. Marshall wanted a theme which could do something to help him rebuild the morale of the corporation. If he could persuade BA people to think of their airline as 'The Favourite' – just as Avis people had believed in 'Trying Harder' – then the advertising would be serving a valuable role internally as well as externally. (*BA News*, the company newspaper, was referring jauntily to 'The Favourite' within a couple of months.)

Staff reactions to the new campaign, in the weeks just before and after Marshall's arrival, were at best mixed. What bothered many of BA's local country managers was not only that the traditional approach had been abandoned, but that the series of ten films had been designed for use in thirty-three countries around the world. The campaign was, in fact, the biggest application yet of Saatchis' growing belief in 'global market' advertising. With different voice-overs, the campaign would impress the same image on BA's target markets throughout the world. But this implied a severe loss of financial autonomy for many career managers. The colossal £14m.

set aside for the global campaign left only £12m. out of the proposed 1983–4 budget of £26m. for the local, 'tactical' advertising over which they still exerted considerable control.

A few managers even had the temerity to suggest that 'The World's Favourite Airline' as a slogan had less than a global suitability. Cinema audiences in France would have cause to doubt it, since BA – like all of Air France's competitors – was banned from advertising on French television. And in Japan, the local manager simply refused to accept a copyline which so totally ignored JAL's 60 per cent share of the London–Tokyo market. As for the privately cynical reactions of all those on the staff who had become accustomed to the tired jokes about the Bloody Awful airline – they were the very people Marshall regarded as one of his biggest challenges.

By March, though, it was decided to rejig the budgets slightly. The global campaign – now including *Manhattan Landing*, since privatisation had been abandoned for 1983 – was assigned £12m. instead of £14m. and the tactical advertising budget for 1983–4 was lifted from £12m. to £19m., making a total of £31m. compared with £19m. the year before. This was an indication of the priority attached to changing BA's image. But it was also, perhaps, a sign of something else: the BA board by March was beginning to believe that the worst might really be behind it financially. The results for 1982–3 were looking far better than they could possibly have hoped early in the year.

As Peter Lazarus, the Transport Permanent Secretary, told the Commons Public Accounts Committee in 1984, 'They did rather better than we had expected or than those concerned had expected earlier in the year . . . It was only right towards the end of the year that the Department realised just how successful the turnaround had been.'

In fact, the Great Turnaround sought desperately since the spring of 1981 was evident for all to see. Labour productivity, for example, had jumped 15 per cent against a 6 per cent target, making a big contribution to a 9.3 per cent return on assets. As for cash-flow, BA had been required to meet an External Financing Limit (EFL) of negative £9m. – repaying £9m., that is, rather than adding to existing debt. In the event, capital spending had been reined back so far that, with the sale of the six TriStars to the MoD and the disposal of International Aeradio, BA had cut its external debt by £35m.

When the April launch date for the Saatchi blockbuster arrived, it was already clear that BA had made a very respectable profit for 1982–3 – in fact, it emerged a few weeks later that net profits had been made of £72m. (later revised to £77m.). Operating profits had risen from £6m. to £167m. Better still, trends in the airline industry suggested that the winter of 1982–3 might well have witnessed the trough in its economic cycle: Marshall had timed his arrival to perfection!

But if all this allowed a bit of leeway in the advertising budget, the new chief executive and his chairman were determined to win themselves a respite from the continuous speculation about imminent privatisation dates. In November 1982, the Trade Secretary had given BA a formal statement of his Department's objectives. They included the achievement of commercial profitability as soon as possible with a view to early privatisation. But at a press conference for the Sunday newspapers on 9 April, Marshall stressed again the same message preached by King since before Christmas: 'I believe that we need to have two good years of profit under our belt, on a rising trend in the airline industries, and then I think you have got a good scenario which might encourage the Government to go ahead with privatisation.'

In other words, no privatisation in 1983. He had ample grounds for his caution. Even 1982–3's net profits, as the auditors warned darkly, only meant BA was technically bankrupt to the tune of £185m. rather than £257m. as it had been a year earlier . . .

And there was something else, as well. Long before, in the summer of 1971, Marshall had seen the US Justice Department cast its long shadow over his career at Avis. (Divestiture of the car-hire firm had been imposed on ITT as part of a compromise settlement to Justice Department antitrust charges.) He was going to be positively the last person at BA to underestimate the importance of any Grand Jury involvement with the Laker affair.

He can hardly fail to have noted the Grand Jury summons for an Atlantic air transport investigation on 25 March. So, was Marshall already reserving just the tiniest of doubts about privatisation's timing on another score, too?

In the early summer of 1983, though, he and King had plenty of other, considerably more pressing concerns. Not least of these was that most basic question for any airline: what aeroplanes would it choose to fly in the future?

9

Substantial Refinement

Roy Watts's tenure of the chief executive seat at BA had had something in common with Dunlop's period at Commercial Union. The two men, both accountants, had had the unhappy experience of trying to steer a large company through a period of almost unparalleled disruption in its sector of the international economy – whilst being exposed to the most intense public scrutiny throughout their ordeal. It says a great deal for Watts's stamina and likeability, as well as his capacity to adapt, that he was still there at all when Marshall arrived in 1983.

A softly-spoken 59-year-old Doncastrian, Watts by then had been at the centre of events for just over ten years. Not unlike Colin Marshall, he had started off – as chief executive of BEA in December 1972 – with a lot of rousing talk about the importance of the customer and the supreme test of pleasing the passenger at all times. A decade and four chairmen later, Watts had had a career dominated by less subtle considerations. As its chief executive for most of the three years ending in March 1981, Watts saw BA notch up aggregate trading profits around £600m. less than had been anticipated in management budgets. And he had to preside over a contraction in the workforce from almost 60,000 in 1979 to 37,000 in 1983.

Clearly, he had far less influence over strategic matters after King's arrival. King believed Watts had been inside the industry for too long to see how deep the cuts would really need to be in 1981–3. But the new chairman valued Watts's huge knowledge of the business very highly and the early stages of BA's recovery owed much to Watts's own initiatives. Perhaps his role by 1983 had moved closer to that of chief operating officer, in US corporate parlance; formally, though, he remained chief executive and deputy chairman throughout. Most of the day-to-day direction of the airline's affairs remained under Watts's control, anyway, whilst King and his 'parallel management' team of Dibbs, Henderson and Dunlop went to work on BA's underlying policies. It was an exhausting role, whatever its aptest description, and Watts was a tired man when Marshall swept in.

In the ensuing reorganisation, Watts remained deputy chairman and was made director responsible for the airline's fleet requirements. It was not exactly going to prove a retirement job. One of his responsibilities was the presentation of BA's case at the public inquiry which began in January 1983 into the expansion of London's airport capacity. Should a Terminal 5 be built at Heathrow or should the contractors move in on Stansted with a vengeance?

Angry environmentalists advocated whichever solution distanced the affair furthest from their own back gardens. The British Airports Authority wanted the Stansted option. BA wanted Terminal 5. To have to relocate a significant proportion of its operations to Stansted, said Watts in his first written submission in January, would cost BA perhaps £200m. a year in additional overheads. (It was instructive, though, to see Watts warning in his evidence that it was 'idle to pretend that we can now predict precisely what the future trends will be' in passenger demand and air transport technology. The bold confidence of that 1978 plan belonged to a different era entirely.)

It was not airports but aeroplanes, however, that were to be Watts's chief preoccupation. The 'T5/Stansted' would rumble on; but fleet options were more pressing.

He had the gratification, first, of seeing his 1978 decision to order a fleet of Boeing 757s vindicated. There had been much public criticism in 1978 that BA was buying the 757 instead of a new aircraft from Airbus Industrie (AI), the European consortium based in Toulouse for which British Aerospace was then working as a sub-contractor. Watts justly argued that the 757 was the plane for BA's requirements – and it was the most logical choice from the point of view of the UK economy as well. For one of BA's main criteria was always to strive for a Rolls-Royce engine commonality throughout its fleet. The 757 could take Rolls-Royce engines. For the European consortium to fit them on its Airbuses, either BA or the British Government directly was going to have to shoulder the (not inconsiderable) certification costs. So BA went for the 757 on every count.

By 1983, Airbus A-310s were being delivered to several continental airlines – including, as it happened, almost all of BA's fellow defendants in the Laker action. But the 757 was also established by then as an infinitely more successful commercial aircraft. The first of seventeen deliveries was taken at Heathrow in February 1983 and BA was anticipating significant cost benefits for the financial year 1983–4.

Another expectation for 1983 was the long-awaited recovery in international passenger traffic. In the early months, BA itself was still looking at monthly returns lower than the same period for the preceding year. (Indeed, this unnerving vista persisted right through until December 1983.) All around BA, however, others were proclaiming the end of the long airline recession.

The prospect was far from certain: airline stocks on Wall Street did not really begin to move until the early summer, for example. But King and his fellow directors decided they had to be ready to meet new capacity demands. The existing fleet, in their view, would hardly fit the bill. It was still heavily dependent on outdated Trident 3 and BAC 1-11s – which were anyway due to be made redundant by new noise regulations by 1986. In short, Watts in 1983 was given the task of recommending a new aircraft to the board. BA would need it for short-haul routes, would anticipate buying perhaps a fleet of fifteen and would be budgeting for a capital investment of as much as £400m.

Whitehall took a different view. The outlay required for any new aircraft would make a big dent in the investment allocation currently set aside for BA by the Treasury in its public expenditure sums. As BA's sponsoring ministry, responsible in the usual way for second-guessing all the airline's key policies, the Transport Department took a hard look at whether the dent was really unavoidable . . . and concluded instead that it might be more appropriate for BA to give up some of its less profitable European and domestic UK routes – in which case, it argued, the need for the new fleet would conveniently disappear.

Alas, Whitehall still had a lot to learn about the hard men whom its political masters had chosen to set loose on BA. The civil servants were going to spend a great deal of the next two years enduring the same corrective lesson over and over again: King and his colleagues were not very good at giving things up.

The disagreement over the need for new aircraft was scarcely remarked at all in public. Behind closed doors, it led to a bitter row which presaged even worse to come in 1984. To the outside world, the only apparent drama was the purchase decision itself. Which aircraft would Watts and his team go for?

McDonnell Douglas had never managed to sell any of their planes to BA. The St Louis manufacturer tried desperately hard for this order. It was offering the 150-seater DC-9 Super 80, plus almost any financial terms BA would like to name.

Boeing was offering two versions of its 737, which BA already had in its fleet. The existing 737-200 was a 115-seater; the new 737-300 was a 150-seater. Both would have the big advantage of necessitating no pilot retraining or special ground equipment refitting for the British airline. And Boeing also had the implicit backing, though this was not public knowledge, of the Price Waterhouse report. It had strongly recommended that BA cut its costs by reducing the variety of aircraft types in its fleet. Sticking to Boeing would be the easiest way for BA to do that.

The other possibility was the third and as yet only embryonic member of the Airbus family, the A-320. This was a 150-seater with an innovative wide-bodied design offering attractive running costs and impressive mechanical efficiency. The only trouble was: it would still be a couple of years before one was built and first deliveries would not arrive before 1988.

It was never really certain later whether the BA board had been genuinely interested in the A-320 or not. But if they were only pretending to consider it that spring of 1983, in order to draw better terms out of the two US competitors, then they fooled a lot of people.

At King's instigation, Watts took a BA delegation down to Toulouse for talks in March. They held discussions with all the AI executives in their drably functional-looking office block just down the road from the public airport. And they were driven a few miles around the airport to the neighbouring suburb of St Martin-du-Touche: the headquarters of Aerospatiale, the French member of the consortium in whose back yard the Airbus parts are built into flying aeroplanes. There they saw the great construction hangars for the A-300s and the A-310s. They saw the old Concorde hangar where (as their hosts ardently hoped) the A-320 would one day be built. And – their hosts could hardly prevent it – they also saw row upon row of unsold aircraft, or 'white tails' as they are known in the industry, with their virgin paintwork glinting in the spring sunshine.

The BA men were in fact visiting Toulouse at the very worst point of a searing two-year recession in new aircraft orders. The airline industry's disarray was causing serious alarm in the boardrooms of all the major aircraft manufacturers around the world. That very month, there were reckoned to be some two hundred new wide-bodied white tails on the global market. Some twenty-four of them were lined up on the tarmac outside Aerospatiale's offices. The pressure was accordingly intense on BA to commit itself to the A-320 – Air France had ordered twenty-five – and so help ensure the launch of the construction programme.

British Aerospace, which since 1978 had taken a 20 per cent stake in the AI consortium and a rather higher share in the A-320 itself, was threatening thousands of redundancies at its factories in England if the A-320 were abandoned. The company was no longer in the state sector; but the Government was still holding 48 per cent of its shares, which the Treasury planned to sell soon. And another change since 1978 was the attitude of Rolls-Royce. Its engines were to be fitted to the A-320 from the start. So Rolls-Royce and British Aerospace were both involved directly in lobbying on behalf of the Airbus.

Perhaps BA initially believed that a purchase from AI might circumvent Whitehall objections to any fleet purchase at all. Was it not a reasonable hope, after all, that the additional expense might look rather more acceptable if it benefited not one but three (or, at least, two-and-a-half) public sector companies? But if that was indeed the plan, it badly misfired. For a start, burdening public expenditure to help British Aerospace or Rolls-Royce would hardly have appeared very logical to the Treasury: neither company came within the PSBR parish, since British Aerospace was now in the private sector and Rolls-Royce was always accounted as a private company anyway. Furthermore, the Treasury no more wanted to get involved in A-320 subsidies than it wanted to know the details of BA's fleet plans!

In fact, the airline stumbled into the middle of a classic Whitehall confrontation between the Treasury and one of the spending departments, in this case Trade and Industry. The DTI was campaigning on behalf of British Aerospace – which was still 48 per cent state-owned – to win government aid for the launch costs of the A-320: British Aerospace wanted a loan of £437m. to cover the costs of new jigging and tooling in the factories at Bristol and Chester where it was proposing to build the A-320's wings. (Rolls-Royce also wanted £113m. towards the cost of its involvement in a major engine development programme for the new Airbus.) If the aid were refused, said the DTI, it might seriously damage Britain's strategic interests in Europe.

This got short shrift from the Treasury. Loans had a nasty habit of not being repaid in the UK aircraft industry. True, there had been a tradition, provided for by the 1949 Civil Aviation Act, that half of any new aircraft's launch costs would be met by the Exchequer. But that tradition was going to be strictly historical. If the Treasury was to approve borrowing for grand aerospace ventures in the future, it needed persuading that the investment looked financially sound and that the cash would be repaid. As it happened, the Treasury had always looked askance at the Airbus venture. This attitude dated back to 1978 when Denis Healey and Joel Barnett had opposed the idea of British Aerospace going into the consortium. They had been overruled by the rest of the Callaghan Cabinet; but Treasury officials remembered the sound basis of the decision, as they saw it, and British Aerospace's membership of AI still rankled with officials in Great George Street.

Huge trouble was therefore taken over the finances of the A-320 project between October 1981 and the spring of 1983. But the best 'central case' that British Aerospace and the DTI civil servants were able to produce – relying, that is, on the most likely-looking assumptions – came up with returns of hardly 3 per cent stretching years into the future. No deal, said the Treasury.

Then along came the suggestion that BA borrow

another £400m. or so in order to place one of the very first orders for the A-320 . . .

Airbus's executives had to acknowledge their obvious credibility problem. Of the A-320's two predecessors, neither the A-300 nor the A-310 came anywhere near breaking even. They were a far cry from the Concorde debacle; but they were emphatically not the kind of projects that any private sector manufacturer would have been able to swallow with equanimity. On the other hand, it just happened that AI was now fired with enthusiasm for an aircraft which its executives – and many others in the international industry – passionately believed to be a world-beater. Pierre Pailleret is Airbus's youthful French marketing director. Built like a Toulouse rugby-club second row forward, with a scrum-half's shrewdness, Pailleret is a man to charm the birds out of the trees. But it was tough going with BA.

Intense talks went on through May and June. Details even emerged in the press of a remarkable offer made to the British carrier. Not only would AI offer each A-320 Airbus at a substantial discount on its $25m. 'list price'. (That much was the very least BA would have expected.) But AI would even arrange to lease a second-hand fleet of American planes for BA until 1988, passing them over with the lion's share of the leasing bill already paid.

Back went Watts and Dunlop to Whitehall. But the answer was the same. Any firm order for the A-320, whatever the timing, implied a firm balance-sheet liability. This had potentially unacceptable implications for public expenditure planning and a questionable impact on the prospects of privatising BA's already lurid balance sheet. It was left to King, as usual, to deliver the *coup de grâce* publicly. 'The A-320 remains a paper aeroplane,' announced the chairman in the middle of August. 'I am not in the business of launching a new plane. I have had enough trouble launching this airline . . . We have worked too hard to get this airline right to be able to afford to take a gamble on a new aircraft now.'

So that left just the US competitors: Boeing and McDonnell Douglas with its DC 9-80. But what the marketing men at McDonnell must have felt when they read King's remarks about a gamble can be readily imagined. The timing of the final purchase decision was set for the next monthly meeting of BA's board on Friday 2 September. There was little doubt that Boeing would win the day.

The Airbus adventure, though, had an important legacy: the idea of leasing the new fleet was snatched up eagerly by BA and looked the ready answer to its own balance-sheet worries. The aircraft would be purchased outright by a group of banks, who would then hand them over to BA in return for regular lease payments. That way, given some nimble accounting, the financial burden might be shouldered entirely by BA's income account: its balance sheet would not be involved.

But still Whitehall demurred. It was nervous of the many small-print items which inevitably accompany banks' leasing deals of this kind. While McDonnell and Boeing vied with each other to offer ever keener terms, the Transport Department continued to oppose any order whatever.

At the eleventh hour, the prospect was growing of another visit by the chairman to Mrs Thatcher. But with weeks to go, Derek Nicholls, BA's treasurer, tied up a deal with an international financial syndicate led by Chemical Bank to provide a leasing facility of up to $650m. (The syndicate included Britain's GEC and several other corporate lenders as well as the usual run of international banks.) The airline was now all set to take fourteen 737-200s on a short lease from Boeing, which would leave the maximum flexibility in future years for BA to replace the new aircraft with another (including, possibly, the A-320).

Confronted with a virtual *fait accompli*, the Transport Department finally backed down. Immediately after the board meeting on 2 September, Colin Marshall announced the Boeing order, worth around $300m. It was, he said 'the best deal all round'.

The press dwelt at length on the fierceness of the battle between the US manufacturers. For those directly involved in BA's progress towards the private sector however, there was no doubt which battle had really been the more significant. King and his colleagues had scored a first major victory over their supposed masters in the Transport Department.

Another aspect of the announcement was noteworthy too: it came from Colin Marshall, not Roy Watts. In fact Watts had just resigned. His departure from the airline had been the subject of gossip and speculation almost since the time of King's installation. Much of it had been premature because it had underestimated how vital were Watts's experience and knowledge as stabilising factors during all the turmoil. But once Marshall was aboard as a chief executive who clearly knew his own mind, Watts accepted that the time had come for him to bid a dignified departure.

There were rumours early in the summer that King was manoeuvring to have his deputy chairman appointed head of the British Airports Authority in place of its existing chairman, Norman Payne, who was proving a doughty adversary in the T5/Stansted squabbles. But it was not to be. Watts left in August for another public sector job far removed from the anguish of massive redundancies and management upheavals he had had to endure at BA.

A mischievous story went the rounds that the Prime Minister had summoned Watts to Downing Street to tell him his new job. 'Ah, Mr Watts,' said Mrs Thatcher, as he entered the room, 'I do hope you will agree to be the new chairman of TWA.' A short and ghastly moment of misunderstanding had reportedly ensued, to the delight of the mandarins. Whether Watts's new subordinates at the Thames Water Authority thought it was quite such a good joke was unclear; but the story was probably apocryphal anyway. (Watts had not been there very long before he emerged as an enthusiastic proponent of privatising water. Did it cross his mind late in 1983 that the Thames Water Authority might just make it to the private sector ahead of his old employer?)

While Watts was still preparing to leave, the anguish at BA reached a new pitch. For by the beginning of July, Colin Marshall and Michael Levin were ready to unveil the management structure which they had been designing since their arrival. The episode was also going to reveal the hardness which had helped take Marshall to the top of a leading US corporation. It led to emotional scenes reminiscent of the first big shock administered by King and Watts in September 1981. Only this time, tears were not the monopoly of the check-in girls at Heathrow.

Back in January, rumours outside BA had spoken of thousands of lay-offs in the senior management ranks. The numbers had been absurd, since the airline only had about four hundred staff earning over £15,000 a year. But the gist of the rumours had correctly foreshadowed Marshall's thinking on the matter. He wanted a much smaller, more compact management team at the centre of BA's operations.

On Monday, 11 July 1983, King and Marshall gave a press conference to announce the consequences. They demolished the new structure of International, European and Gatwick-based services established less than a year earlier. In their place, Marshall was setting up eight profit centres for passenger operations, defined by geographical area. Cargo, charter and package-tour operations were three additional centres. All eleven would report to Jim Harris. All would be, with more commercial than grammatical sense, 'more customer responsive and more profit responsible', said the chief executive.

Most shocking of all, though, the centres would answer to a headquarters team of just a hundred managers, reporting directly to Colin Marshall. The names of the chosen would be made clear in the following weeks. Those not chosen would be leaving for good – and that would mean about seventy senior managers taking premature retirement. Out came the tumbrils once again.

A period of acute anxiety followed for all those unsure of their position in the new scheme of things. But a handful of top men were at least spared the waiting: their departures were announced there and then, on 11 July. They represented the last of the pre-King senior management. Most conspicuous were the three heads of the disbanded 1982 divisions: Ossie Cochrane, 62, who had succeeded Gerry Draper the previous summer, Peter Hermon, 55, and Stephen Hanscombe, 50. At the same time, Charles Stewart, 55, chose to announce his resignation as head of industry affairs 'for personal reasons'. Not one of these four individuals was mentioned by name anywhere in BA's subsequent report and accounts for the 1983–4 year (though Watts, a board member, was offered 'sincere thanks for his long and distinguished service to the airline and to British aviation . . .').

Heading the new structure would be a six-man task force: Colin Marshall, 49 (chief executive); Gordon Dunlop, 55 (chief financial officer); Jim Harris, 54 (marketing director); Howard Phelps, 56 (director of operations); John Garton, 54 (engineering director); Peter Bateson, 38 (director of marketplace performance [sic]).

The moves stunned the airline world which had hardly heard of Colin Marshall six months before. There were predictable protests from inside and outside BA that the airline was being pulled apart by a man with insufficient experience to know what was needed. The speed with which Marshall was moving – and Levin at his side – could hardly fail to excite some nervousness about the haste, even amongst favourably inclined observers. But no one listening to Marshall debate the points for and against the various aircraft options that summer doubted the new chief executive's ability to master a complex brief in double-quick time. As for experience – that had proved an expensive commodity for BA in the past. Marshall had no qualms, anyway, about being a new broom.

Consistency, finally, was no more a sticking-point for the chairman than it had been before. 'We are taking a second bite,' as he put it in *BA News*. 'Our moves in May last year were made to put in a structure at relatively short notice which gave us a view of what we needed to look at. This is now being very substantially refined.'

Rather, he might have added, as Samson substantially refined the temple.

10

Bermuda Blues

Taking BA's executive management by the scruff of the neck was one thing. Relying on an assertive approach to shake BA free of its legal problems was quite another. By the summer of 1983, the airline was at the centre of what was fast becoming a celebrated episode for the international lawyers.

Professor John Oakley of the University of California put the situation as succinctly as anyone – if a touch morbidly for those involved – in an article written for the *Sunday Times* that July: 'The Americans think Sir Freddie was mugged in Central Park. Perhaps not. He collapsed in Britain, and it may have been from natural causes. But the [UK] Government's efforts to keep the body buried are only likely to make the Americans dig deeper, with everyone wondering what secrets lie in the grave.'

By then, the Government was openly lending its weight to moves to halt both the Justice Department investigation and the Laker civil suit. At the outset, though, it was the imminent prospect of Grand Jury proceedings which really concentrated officials' minds. Arguably private litigation would have to be seen (grudgingly) as falling beyond Bermuda II's reach. But if a department of the US Government itself could not be bound by the treaty, then who knew where the affair would end?

There had been acute disappointment in Whitehall back in March that the Justice Department's offensive had not been headed off before it really got going. But after the announcement of the investigation – into 'possible anti-competitive practices in transatlantic air service' – a furious campaign was mounted to extricate the British airlines from its field of fire before the actual appointment of the Grand Jury and the start of its hearings. This was scheduled for 27 June. In the meantime, the Department had the power to subpoena documents and commit individuals for cross-examination before the jury, whose job it would be eventually to determine the grounds, if any, for a Federal criminal prosecution. After that date, there might be little or no hope of salvaging BA.

So there were just three months to pull off the rescue. It did not fail for lack of endeavour.

In the middle of April and again towards the end of the month, officials from the Department of Trade and Industry and the Foreign Office flew to Washington to press their case. British Embassy personnel there offered encouraging news that US State Department officials appeared slightly embarrassed by the affair. But in Washington, as usual, it was lawyers not diplomats who were calling the tune – and the Justice Department insisted its inquiry was well grounded.

Justice officials were not impervious to appeals from airlines involved in the Laker suit; indeed, the apparent success of some of BA's co-defendants at putting their case for exclusion was rather galling for the UK officials. Andreas Hodel, Swissair's in-house counsel, paid a visit to the Justice Department with one of his embassy's diplomats in April, for example. Elliott Seiden, the senior official in charge of the investigation, confirmed the same day, according to Hodel's own account, that there would be no further interest taken by the Department in Swissair's activities.

No such luck for the British airlines. A delegation representing four departments of the US Government made a reciprocal trip to London the next month for more talks at the DTI's own offices. By now the Grand Jury's inauguration was just a month away. The discussions were becoming less and less friendly – and they were given even more urgency by a side row which blew up over a UK licence for a new US Atlantic carrier, People Express.

There was not much doubt why the CAA was taking its time over the licence. To outsiders, it looked just the kind of bureaucratic nonsense Freddie Laker had had to endure in Washington back in 1973–4 over his Skytrain clearance. Now the boot was on the other foot. People Express planned to land its first 747 jumbo to Gatwick at the crack of dawn on 27 May, ready for take-off on a return trip a few hours later. The deadlocked discussions at the DTI on 23–24 May threatened to mean no licence for the flight and endless ugly consequences . . . The antitrust negotiations stretched late into 25 May. But it was all to no avail. The US delegation left its hosts empty-handed, People Express collected its licence – and the Grand Jury loomed ever closer.

What no amount of discussion could get round was the gathering conviction within the Justice Department that it was going to find something worth all the bother of a Grand Jury – that Professor Oakley's body in the grave, so to speak, was going to reveal some nasty signs of foul play. Evidence belonging to the Grand Jury was for the most part held strictly confidential. But some of the documents before the jury were being used in the civil suit and a few were even finding their way on to the public record at the US Federal Court House opposite the National Gallery of Art in Washington. Some fruity quotes began to circulate in the press.

The fulminations of the European airline chiefs over McDonnell's intended rescue package were providing predictably colourful material. There was even, rather absurdly in the circumstances, a high-school essay about Freddie Laker written by the teenage daughter of the McDonnell Finance Corporation president, Jim McMillan.

International interest in this revered document was attributed to an apparent cooperation between father and daughter which lent ominous significance to its version of events. 'The Midland group's intransigence', ran one much-quoted sentence, 'made any effective rescheduling effort impossible to achieve' (though why the Midland, like any other bank in the world, should not have had the right to behave intransigently over a bad debt if it wanted to – that was less widely aired).

It was emphatically not the specific substance of the Justice Department case, however, which was consuming so many hours of government time in London and Washington. Rather, it was the conflict of views about Bermuda II which really divided the two sides. And this looked a matter of principle which it was hard to fudge. The two governments were taking a diametrically opposed view of their 1977 treaty.

The British said it provided lock, stock and barrel of the regulatory framework for the North Atlantic air routes: capacity, prices and every other aspect of competition was covered by the treaty. More than that, Bermuda II even provided elaborate guidelines for what was to happen in the event of any disagreement. Articles 16 (Consultations) and 17 (Settlement of Disputes) saw to that. If all else failed, resort was allowed to an independent arbitrator. But by no stretch of the imagination did a US judge fit that description: the US courts were simply trespassing.

On the contrary, said the Americans. The treaty specifically provided in its Article 12 for exemptions to be made in the general application of the air service agreement where it threatened to impinge on US domestic law. Nowhere were these exemptions of more importance than in the area of antitrust law, which every international company knew perfectly well had to be respected as the ark, as it were, of the US economic covenant. Nor would independent arbitration necessarily change the position: Article 17 included the proviso that each side need give effect to an arbitrator's judgement only so far as was 'consistent with its national law'. Hence BA's predicament.

To Whitehall's considerable chagrin, it was the American version which by mid-June was attracting the sympathy of the civil courts – not just in the US, which had been expected, but in England as well. With just days to go before the first hearing of the Grand Jury, in fact, there was every reason for the Justice Department to expect that the civil antitrust suit might eventually run along in parallel with its own investigations.

Mr Justice Parker had refused to renew the temporary injunction for BA and British Caledonian on 29 March, supposedly exposing the airlines to Judge Greene's court. But the Court of Appeal had promptly replaced the injunction, pending a full hearing of the arguments for and against a permanent injunction in April. Mr Justice Parker presided over the April case, too. Before passing judgement, he chose to hear what Judge Greene himself had to say about the attempt being made by the defendants in his US court to divert their case to England.

The US judge pronounced on 4 May. Not for the last time, he had some grand historical parallels to draw – and the strength of his feelings was very evident: 'What is in jeopardy is the enforcement of the Sherman Act with respect to a market – travel between the United States and Europe – in which this nation has the highest interest. The Sherman Act, as has often been observed, is our charter of economic liberty, comparable to the importance of the Bill of Rights with respect to personal freedom, and there is thus the highest kind of public interest in preventing the Act from being emasculated in this important area.'

It was all very well, concluded Judge Greene, surrendering jurisdiction over some other kinds of private litigation from time to time. 'But the antitrust laws of the US embody a specific congressional purpose to encourage the bringing of private claims in the American courts, in order that the national policy against monopoly may be vindicated.' In other words, far from it being unjustly hard on the British airlines, in that no comparable suit could be brought against them in England, this was precisely the reason for holding them down to his court in Washington. They wanted to take advantage of more lenient laws in England. He was not going to allow it.

Three days later, the English judge listened to counsel for the UK Attorney General presenting his Government's contrary view of the position. It had no obvious effect on his judgement, finally delivered on 20 May.

Mr Justice Parker ruled against BA and BCal: they would have to take what was coming in Washington. He acknowledged that the case touched on questions of government policy; but at issue were matters of rights and obligations. These depended on law, not government policy. No English laws had been put before the court to justify blocking the liquidator. (It was a first hint of the ultimately fatal flaw in BA's case: Bermuda II had no statutory backing.) As for US law, the relationship between antitrust legislation and the treaty, said Mr Justice Parker, offered no basis for an injunction. Above all – and echoing the view from the other side of the Atlantic – the plaintiff really had nowhere else to go. English law would provide no remedy for his complaint. 'What is unjust in allowing the UK airlines, if the facts are established, from answering . . . for breach of the laws of the country by permission of whose government they were operating?' asked Mr Justice Parker. If there really had been malpractice and Laker Airways were now to be barred from righting the wrong, it would be 'a manifest injustice'.

And so matters stood, through into June, past the Tories' re-election and through the weeks leading up to the inevitable Appeal Court hearing.

As the civil servants readjusted to Aviation's move from the DTI to Transport, their new Ministers arrived to tackle their first briefs. For both Cecil Parkinson at the

DTI and Tom King at Transport, there was one manifest injustice which had to be rectified without delay – and with the full backing, somehow, of the courts. It looked a tall order; but the Government's lawyers had been preparing the appropriate measures for some time. Out came the 1980 Protection of Trading Interests Act.

The PTIA, as it is known, had been put on the statute books in response to an earlier bit of extraterritoriality trouble from the US. It empowered the Government to prohibit a party in the UK from cooperating with a foreign court where the result seemed likely to compromise British trading interests. Cooperation in this context included turning up at the foreign court in person or producing documents to help it. (There was also a specific dig at antitrust actions: any UK company having to pay triple damages could use the PTIA to reclaim the punitive element of the damages. This aspect was going to add its contribution to the Laker case, too, though not quite yet.) The PTIA had been used on only one or two occasions to date. In June 1983 it seemed to do the trick very nicely.

Orders invoking the PTIA were passed on 24 June. They forbade BA and BCal from complying with instructions handed down by Judge Greene's court. This extraordinary step – hardly the stuff of a relationship between two closely allied nations – was not surprisingly accompanied by all kinds of mollifying statements for Washington's consumption. Of course no escalation was intended, insisted Government spokesmen, and of course the bilateral talks over Bermuda II were continuing. In reality, they continued – in London on 27–28 June – only so that US officials could express their dismay at the UK action and warn that the Grand Jury's deliberations could not be so easily spiked.

But in the English courts, the PTIA dealt its anticipated blow against the civil action. After an eleven-day hearing between 4 and 18 July, Sir John Donaldson, the Master of the Rolls, sitting with Lord Justices Oliver and Watkins, ruled on 26 July that it would in the new circumstances be quite unreasonable to allow the Laker liquidator to pursue his case against BA and BCal in Washington. Exposing the airlines to such an ordeal, said the Appeal Court, would be 'a total denial of justice'. The PTIA had made the cases against them 'wholly untriable'. They were awarded injunctions halting the Laker liquidator in his tracks.

The Master of the Rolls went out of his way to say that the rag now being waved at the American judiciary was any colour but red. 'We, and all other English judges, would deeply regret any misunderstanding on the part of our brethren in the US of what exactly we are doing and why we are doing it,' said Sir John; '. . . neither the English courts nor the English judges entertain any feelings of hostility towards the American antitrust law or would ever wish to denigrate that or any other American law.' Nevertheless, it was conspicuous that the Appeal Court, whilst critically influenced by the 24 June order, had not rested its judgement exclusively on the PTIA.

Some account had to be taken, said the court, of the fact that BA and BCal had been relying on an interpretation of Bermuda II handed down to them by the UK authorities. As for the question of the relevance of government policy, Sir John remarked that it would be odd indeed for the courts and the executive of the nation to be speaking with different voices about an aspect of the UK's relations with a foreign power. Taking these points into consideration, as well as the PTIA's impact, the court had no choice but to disregard the fact that the Laker liquidator had nowhere but the US to pursue his complaint.

Touche Ross and its lawyers went to work on the judgement the next day. There was never much doubt that they would try to appeal to the House of Lords.

In Washington, lawyers began to speculate that Judge Greene would sidestep the Appeal Court by having a trustee of some kind appointed within the US to pursue the antitrust action against BA and BCal on Christopher Morris's behalf. The judge himself described the injunction order as 'premature and improper'. But the liquidator was determined to play the hand himself if at all possible. And by the early autumn, the Laker camp was confident of the chance to appeal. The lawyers pinned down arguably erroneous interpretations of statute in the July judgement: the fact that the suit could not be launched in England had been wrongly disregarded, for example. They asked for permission to challenge both the injunction and the PTIA order in the House of Lords.

The Law Lords' Appeal Committee announced its decision on 10 November. It was the anniversary of Beckman's triumph at the Touche Ross offices in Little New Street – and the date proved a happy augury for the Laker camp. The Law Lords granted Morris the right to appeal. As it happened, all sorts of momentous decisions were by then lining up for BA in 1984. Their Lordships merely added another to the list.

11

Goodbye, Mr Morrison

Just the week before the Law Lords' Appeal Committee decision, on 1 November 1983, a junior Minister at the Treasury made one of the most important political speeches about the UK economy for many a long year. The speech, by John Moore, was a product of months of reappraisal by the Tories, before and after the June 1983 general election, of their whole privatisation policy. Moore announced little that was new in detail. But his speech proclaimed a profound advance in the Government's commitment to privatisation – and it helped spark off an explosive debate over the future of the British airline industry which guaranteed another climactic struggle for BA in 1984.

In the years before 1983, privatisation had been a successful part of the Thatcher record but hardly a key tenet. Indeed, BA's repeated setbacks had been partly responsible for limiting its impact. One of the original motives for announcing BA's sale as the first target in July 1979 had been the airline's status as a major state monopoly. When the sale had had to be postponed, the Government had opted to aim a little lower. The 1979–83 Parliament had therefore witnessed a string of sales limited to companies which happened to be owned by the Government, for one reason or another, but which in almost every other respect were no less commercial than their private sector rivals. Britoil, Amersham International and Cable & Wireless, for example, all fitted into this category.

Nor had privatisation been much trumpeted in the wider political context. It had been only sparingly referred to in the 1979 election manifesto and was regarded as a peripheral area of Conservative policy by large sections of the Parliamentary party in the years that followed. This is not to deny that much had been done since Mrs Thatcher's arrival in Downing Street. All or part of some ten corporations had been sold, including large stakes in BP and British Aerospace, raising almost £2bn. for the Exchequer. But privatisation was only one of the strands in radical Tory thinking. Others, like the promotion of home ownership, were just as important or more so: council house sales had even raised more for the Exchequer (£3.5bn.) into the bargain.

Events in 1982–3, not least the Tories' landslide re-election, changed all that.

Imperceptibly at first but with a surprising suddenness in due course, privatisation sprang forth as Thatcherism's response to the nationalisation programme of the postwar Labour Government, with an equally central role. This evolution in the Tory Government's thinking was not a neat and tidy one. In fact, it was not even entirely deliberate. Samuel Brittan, the influential writer on economic affairs for the *Financial Times*, described privatisation as emerging 'almost by default as the main theme of Conservative supply-side or structural policy . . .'* For as Brittan explained, other themes were explored first – most pertinently, the idea of unlinking the nationalised industries from the arithmetic of the PSBR by allowing them access to private funding channels in the Eurobond market or wherever. But advocates of 'unlinking' in this way found it heavy-going.

Treasury officials allowed no fudging of the issue. State entities which tried to borrow without a government guarantee would be charged higher interest rates and even then the market would probably demand some sign

---

* Samuel Brittan, 'The politics and economics of privatisation' (1984).

of tacit government backing. In such circumstances, said the Treasury, an explicit guarantee was invariably the best policy. (It was all laid down in what were known as the Ryrie Guidelines, after the Second Permanent Secretary who devised them following the 1979 election.) But it was not a policy calculated to foster a successful 'hands-off' attitude towards the nationalised industries (though a 'Buzby bond' to raise money for British Telecom in the private sector had in fact been welcomed by Chancellor Geoffrey Howe as a promising innovation).

In short, advocates of 'unlinking' gradually came round to thinking that the best solution was to go the whole hog: if private capital financing was so desirable, why not push the putative borrowers back into the private sector altogether? Come the spring of 1983, the radical implications of this conclusion were beginning to look attractive for all sorts of reasons. Privatisation, in fact, was a most promising concept. It had everything to offer: a supply-side tonic, a powerful antidote to macro-economic woes and a banner for the philosophers of the Party.

The direction of the political current was increasingly evident. Legislation was passed in February 1983 to liberalise entry into the telecommunications industry. The Tories' June election manifesto was not exactly a clarion call for the new policy, but its aims were stated clearly enough: 'Reform of the nationalised industries is central to economic recovery . . . The old illusions have melted away . . . We shall continue our programme to expose state-owned firms to real competition.' BA was on the list of sale candidates.

The intellectual current was moving fast, too. In July 1983, the *Lloyds Bank Review* carried a widely noted analysis of the prospects for privatisation by two distinguished academics. 'The scope for privatization,' they concluded, 'is substantially greater than is commonly believed. Consumers would benefit, directly or indirectly, from appropriately designed privatization schemes in

117

industries covering over four-fifths of the presently nationalized sector.'* Again, BA was a prominent name.

Changes in the Cabinet, meanwhile, were matching the trend perfectly. The new Chancellor after the election was Nigel Lawson – undoubtedly one of the cleverest members of the Tory Front Bench and a strong champion of privatisation. His support went far beyond intellectual advocacy, though. As Secretary of State for Energy, Lawson had overseen the sale of Britoil, a pioneering effort in its scale and complexity. He had experience of implementing the policy: he was determined to push it further from his new, infinitely more powerful position.

Whitehall's most significant response to all this lay, naturally enough, within the corridors of the Treasury itself. In the past, privatisation had been piecemeal and very largely left to the initiative of whichever Government department was responsible for the company involved. Now it was to be the target of a much more coherent programme. And the Treasury's own Public Enterprises Group would take an active interest in promoting the success of that programme. (Plenty of scope here, the cynics noted, for more battles between traditional adversaries at the Treasury and the spending departments of Whitehall . . .)

One immediate consequence was a bonanza for the professionals of the City of London. Every big privatisation meant enormous fees for the chosen advisers, even leaving aside the delicate matter of profits taken on early trading in some of the new stocks. The Public Enterprises Group officials, notably Gerry Grimstone, were responsible for overseeing the day-to-day implementation of the programme. They took great pains to ensure that the Treasury always paid percentage commissions significantly lower than the City was used to – but nothing could detract from the absolute scale of the business. Here were a few civil servants, flexing the kind of power previously

* Michael Beesley and Stephen Littlechild, 'Privatization: Principles, Problems and Priorities'.

only wielded in the Square Mile by a handful of potentates from the private sector. But this, of course, was a spin-off effect. Others were of far greater importance.

The programme's five chief motives were spelt out clearly by Ministers and their officials to all interested parties (who were soon to include many government delegations from overseas – even one from China early in 1985). These were: the promotion of efficiency; the reduction of the public sector relative to the rest of the economy; the financial benefits to the Exchequer; the encouragement of employee participation in business; and wider ownership of shares throughout British society.

The priority at this stage still rested with the reduction of the public sector and the promotion of efficiency. But wider share ownership was the dark horse which many senior politicians discreetly fancied from the start. Indeed, in the City, the Wider Share Ownership Council and the Stock Exchange had been trying to arrest declining public interest in equities for years. In the autumn of 1983, preparations for the flotation of British Telecom raised the first serious possibility that a different set of priorities might be appropriate for the privatisation policy in general.

Ministers were nervous of the political risks of any Hard Sell for share ownership. And there were practical problems: the Independent Broadcasting Authority, for example, effectively rules out any commercial which includes both a corporate puff and information about a forthcoming sale in the same company's shares. But the DTI that September called in Dewe Rogerson, a leading City public relations and advertising agency, to formulate a professional selling effort for British Telecom. Early indications from them of an astonishing degree of popular interest in the topic – and signs, too, of a massive impact by the Power Behind the Button corporate image campaign devised for British Telecom by the Dorlands agency – were straws in the wind.

Not until British Telecom had finally confounded the

pessimists in December 1984, though, did the Government espouse the wider share ownership motive whole-heartedly. For the present, it was enough that privatisation itself was to be accorded pride of place. This was the message of John Moore's speech in November 1983.

Moore had been one of Lawson's junior Ministers at the Energy Department. After Cecil Parkinson's abrupt departure in October, the ensuing Cabinet reshuffle saw Moore succeed Nicholas Ridley as Financial Secretary to the Treasury – that is, he resumed his role as a junior Minister to Lawson – and he was given responsibility for the privatisation policy. Everything in Moore's back-ground – he had worked in US investment banking and broking with Dean Witter Reynolds before entering politics – ensured that, handed a ball of this importance, he would run hard for the line. (An appropriate meta-phor in his case, since he is also something of a fitness fanatic.)

On 1 November, Moore was invited to the City's Plaisterers' Hall to address a conference held annually under the auspices of stockbrokers Fielding Newson Smith. His speech had been painstakingly prepared in the Treasury and was entitled 'Why Privatise?' It set out unashamedly – and at some length – to provide a tract for the times and Moore delivered it with gusto. It was Thatcherism's sharpest and most substantial answer yet to the nationalisation theories of Herbert Morrison and the prewar architects of Socialist Britain. And the answer was quite explicit: 'Good-bye, Mr Morrison.'

Moore attacked the performance of UK nationalised industries on every front: prices, productivity, job creation, capital investment, customer satisfaction. They were contrasted with the private sector generally – and with the companies newly privatised since 1979, in particular. And the conclusion drawn was simple: the fault lay not with wicked employees nor even with damaging government interference over the years. The fault lay with the original concept itself. The key passage left no doubt about the Government's chosen solution.

> The primary objective of the Government's privatisation programme is to reduce the power of the monopolist and to encourage competition. As the programme moves into the heartlands of the public sector, maximising competition will become of dominant importance. No state monopoly is sacrosanct. We intend through competition and privatisation to open up the State sector to the stimulus of competition and reverse the creeping bureaucratisation of the last 35 years. The long term success of the privatisation programme will stand or fall by the extent to which it maximises competition. If competition cannot be achieved, an historic opportunity will have been lost . . . Less government is good government. This is nowhere truer than in the state industrial sector. Privatisation hands back, to the people of this country, industries that have no place in the public sector. Long may the process continue.

No longer was privatisation to be just one of several radical policies. It was to be the very touchstone of Thatcherism, the ultimate test of the Government's historical significance. Underlying this was a tacit acknowledgement also of another truth. Such fundamental upheavals could not be brought about without the application of colossal political willpower. Moore was not saying so in as many words; but he knew that every big privatisation was bound to encounter enormously powerful vested interests at all levels of political and corporate life. These interests would do their utmost to sap the momentum of the sale process. Added to this, there were the inevitable unforeseen complications which lawyers, bankers and accountants would herd along in droves.
Hence the importance of speeches like Moore's.

Nicholas Ridley, a leading torchbearer for Thatcherism in the traditional Tory shires and now Transport Secretary, made a speech along similar lines at the Chartered Institute of Transport on the same day. And hence, too, the vital need for a Prime Minister like Mrs Thatcher with such an evident resolve to get her own way.

None of this, though, was to deny that many candidates for privatisation raised serious complications which could not properly be brushed aside as so much sophistry. Nor were these complications necessarily restricted to the cases of 'natural monopolies' – telecommunications, gas, water and the like – where post-sale supervisory guidelines obviously had to be established with some care.

There were, too, some 'natural competitors' whose privatisation would not preclude the need for continued regulation. What made this especially complicated was not hard to see. Many of the natural competitors prior to privatisation enjoyed some of the trappings of a monopoly, at the state's behest. The rules of their post-sale regulation would have to reflect a decision by the state about how much of the artificial monopoly it wanted to see surviving for one reason or another. Otherwise, public sector monopolies would simply become private sector monopolies – and what would happen then to all that talk of promoting competition?

BA fitted roundly into this latter category. It was not a natural monopoly. But it had a quasi-monopolistic hold over UK aviation which the Government would have to approve or remedy via the appropriate regulatory agency. And as if this were not complicated enough – given the nature of the aviation industry and its resilience to change – the British Government in the particular case of BA had added yet one more twist. It had proclaimed a firm commitment to BA's sale before so much as starting to think about the regulatory aspect. All those keen to see as fast and big a privatisation as possible, including the Treasury, therefore had a vested interest in the status quo. Privatisation, dangled as a carrot, might have been used to speed up whatever regulatory changes (if any) were thought desirable. Instead, the Government by its timing had turned privatisation into a formidable obstacle to regulatory change.

Britain's independent airline bosses did not need to be academic economists to get the message in all this. If they were going to tame BA, the sooner they started the better.

For Nicholas Ridley, arriving in the Cabinet after twenty-four busy years in the Commons, the consequences were momentous. For in the months following the general election, the Civil Aviation Policy Division under William Knighton had been transferred with all its civil servants from the DTI to the Transport Department. In other words, Ridley's journey from the Treasury to the Department of Transport set him down, one of the acknowledged high priests of privatisation, right at the centre of the 'artificial monopoly' debate – just where he would be most torn between conflicting views of what was required on the regulatory front in order to make privatisation a successful vehicle of competition.

On the one side was King's heavily entrenched BA board; on the other was the independent airline lobby under British Caledonian and its chairman, Sir Adam Thomson. The argument between them was fraught with political danger, as Ridley very quickly discovered.

At BCal, a three-man team – Peter Smith, the planning director, Mike Carter, the general manager for corporate planning, and David Beety, the airline's solicitor from the City firm of Knapp-Fishers – had spent much of their summer preparing a document which was christened the Blue Book. A copy had been handed to Ridley's predecessor, Tom King, in September and another copy was presented to the new Transport Secretary just ahead of Moore's speech.

In essence, the Blue Book took all the economists' caveats about privatising public monopolies and applied them directly to the case of BA. It provided an impressive

123

array of statistical evidence. Sir Adam Thomson summarised the conclusions in a statement for the press:

> The problem is that British Airways controls around 83 per cent of the UK scheduled air service output. Endowed with profitable routes and public funds, rescued from bankruptcy by a benevolent Government and operating from a virtually impregnable position at Heathrow, the world's busiest international gateway, British Airways in private hands would be in a position to stifle us.

The 169 pages of the Blue Book had a better idea. The book was called *A Strategy for British Civil Air Transport in Private Ownership* and its proposals were suitably grand. BA's share of scheduled services should be reduced to around two-thirds by the sale of a selection of its routes to BCal. Naturally, Thomson and his managing director, Alistair Pugh, had their own selection: they wanted the routes to Spain, Portugal and a number of other European cities, the Gulf and the Caribbean. For these flights – and the planes providing them – BCal would pay £200m. cash. At the same time, just for good measure, BA should also be required to hand over its domestic routes to UK regional operators. Alternatively, said the Blue Book, if this was for any reason deemed impractical, then BCal should be allowed to move all its operations lock, stock and tartanwear, from their present base at Gatwick to Heathrow.

The result of all these recommendations, said Thomson, would be a completion of the job begun by the Edwards Report of 1969. (This had been the last comprehensive review of UK civil aviation: it was prepared by a parliamentary committee under Professor Sir Ronald Edwards and its recommendations for a 'second-force independent airline' had led directly to the creation of BCal itself.) BCal's market share stood to be increased from 17 to 29 per cent – offering the prospect (in BCal's view) of a truly competitive UK airline industry.

In his speech of 1 November, John Moore acknow-ledged many of the problems addressed by the Blue Book. 'We are not so naive,' said Moore, 'as to think that an unrestrained monopoly in the private sector would be less inclined to exploit its position than the monopolies in the public sector. The key here is to ensure that . . . where competition is not practical or is slow to develop, regulation or franchising can ensure that the harmful effects are minimised . . .'

Next day, BCal's chairman went to see Nicholas Ridley to explore what the Financial Secretary's words might mean in practice. It was the culmination of an auspicious month or so for Thomson. His airline had knocked BA off the top of a popularity poll run each year by *Executive Traveller*, a UK travel magazine. The flag-carrier had been defeated in the courts over an attempt to block new competition on the Belfast–Heathrow route from another fast-growing independent operator, British Midland Airways. Most important of all, Thomson's Westminster lobbying campaign to recruit MPs to BCal's cause – orchestrated by Tory MP Bob McCrindle, a consultant to the airline – had moved into a high gear.

Ridley and Thomson had a long talk. The word in Whitehall was that Ridley had been impressed by many of Thomson's arguments – and the word reached St James's.

The repercussion was immediate. King reacted to Thomson's suggestion as though he were a sly fox that had just run under his lordship's mount after a long and particularly arduous ride. He seemed in two minds for a moment whether to admire Thomson's cheek or set the dogs on him. But not for long: the dogs it was going to be. 'We intend to get into any market where we think we can make a profit,' said King on 4 November. 'We will compete wherever and whenever we can. The independents have built their businesses on the lack of competition from British Airways. They are always preaching competition. Now they are going to get it.'

No less than Thomson, King had plenty of background factors that he thought were moving in his direction, too. For a start, there were BA's interim results, which he was announcing on 4 November. The airline had lifted its net profits after interest and tax from £80m. in the first half of 1982–3 to £162m. in 1983–4. Thomson and his friends had mistimed their 'smash-and-grab raid', said the BA chairman. They would have had a better chance of succeeding when BA was on its financial uppers.

Again, King and Marshall took the occasion of the interim results to announce a generous profit-sharing scheme for BA employees. It was straight out of American business practice and nothing remotely like it had ever been seen in the UK public sector before. It was also straight out of the Treasury's own model privatisation schedule: Stage Two – 'Introduce private sector attitudes and methods'.

'There are no catches,' said Colin Marshall, announcing the scheme. 'There is no ceiling. The more we bring in, and the more we save, the more we'll get. I hope the bonus at the end of the year is going to be a large one. It's one bill that British Airways will find it a pleasure to pay.' And a bill, he might have added but did not, that any Tory Government was going to find it extremely embarrassing to curtail, as Thomson's plan would inevitably require.

Finally, King opted to take the offensive in public over the timing of BA's sale.

Within a fortnight of the general election, it had been decided at Cabinet level to try selling off 100 per cent of BA as soon as possible. Over at Speedbird House, the flattering attentions of Wall Street's research analysts had helped dispel the more cautious attitude struck by King and Marshall only a few months earlier. Encouraged by the Government's enthusiasm, BA's board was already taking a bolder stance before the BCal assault began. In the face of Thomson's manoeuvrings, it became openly aggressive.

The City had only just begun to take a serious interest in the idea of a private BA by November 1983. But it seemed at least a possibility that BA's sale could be arranged by the following autumn. King and his colleagues on the board made sure this was duly noted in the press. If necessary, the message read, BA would be ready to step in and take British Telecom's place in the privatisation queue.

Gordon Dunlop went even further than this, to the private dismay of one or two civil servants. BA as understudy to British Telecom was one thing; but Dunlop had grander ambitions. 'The October [1984] slot for floating British Telecom is dead,' said the finance director. And he was bursting with ideas for the recapitalisation of BA's balance sheet – including, rather improbably, a giant bid for the company by its own management!

(If nothing else, this rather cavalier style was very revealing about the BA board's attitude to the civil servants of the Aviation Division. It was none too respectful. William Knighton, the Deputy Secretary in charge of the Division, had just turned down a request from BA for two new aircraft for its Highlands operation, which did not help matters. As far as BA was concerned, there were market realities and political realities. Civil servants did not fit easily into this scheme of things.) For more than four weeks, the two sides harangued each other, with Ridley forced to equivocate in the middle.

Not least of the Transport Secretary's problems was a genuine confusion over how best to effect BCal's suggestions, even assuming they were thought desirable. The only obvious approach lay with enabling legislation, which would risk interminable delays for BA's privatisation schedule. BCal insisted that Ridley had no choice but to hand the whole subject over to the CAA for them to produce a considered list of recommendations. But Ridley seemed reluctant to do this. Perhaps it went against his political instinct to put his trust in such an unknown quantity. It would still be unclear at the end of the day, anyway, how to implement any decisions which emerged. And would it really be wise to pretend that sweeping regulatory changes were still an option when the Government had already been committed to BA's sale for well over four years?

A reference to the CAA, however, undeniably had the great attraction for Ridley of relieving the immediate pressure for a solution. He was certainly in need of some relief. As well as the question of BA's future shape, he was faced with the choice between a fifth terminal for Heathrow and a major expansion of Stansted Airport – and with a growing debate, too, about the general licensing policy of the CAA. Nor was the background entirely conducive to calm reflection about all these matters. In the House of Commons, MPs on both sides were being lobbied furiously by BCal and the independent airlines and – in a rather hastily assembled defensive move – by BA itself. (King appeared in front of both the Tory Aviation Committee and the all-party Aviation Committee early in December.) In Whitehall, meanwhile, a period of adjustment was inevitably causing some dislocation as the Aviation Division settled into its new home at the Transport Department.

In the end, Ridley took his civil servants' advice and ran for sanctuary. On 12 December 1983, he told the House of Commons that the sale of BA would go ahead as soon as possible, which in the real world meant early 1985. (Reports of British Telecom's death, evidently, had been premature.) In the meantime, he was asking the chairman of the CAA to review the implications of BA's privatisation for the future of competition in the UK airline industry – and to report back with recommendations for the industry's sound development.

It was apparent within weeks that Ridley had raised the stakes in more ways than one.

12

The Travelling Circus

The British defendants before his court were giving
Judge Greene all kinds of problems. The legion law firms
involved had always guaranteed that the Laker proceedings, like the mills of God, would grind slowly and
exceeding small. But in the year from the filing of the suit
to the authorisation of the House of Lords appeal, they
had almost ground to a complete standstill.

One week after the appeal decision on 10 November
1983, the US judge brought in yet another influential
lawyer to the case. He instructed Stephen J. Pollack of
Shea & Gardner to act as an independent go-between for
the court – an amicus curiae, in legal parlance – to explore
the positions of the US and UK governments and report
back on what might be its most appropriate course 'in
light of the decisions of the English authorities and the
resulting incapacity of the plaintiff'.

Some action was clearly needed. It was not just that the
liquidator's situation vis-à-vis BA and British Caledonian
had been riddled with complications. The British stonewalling had affected virtually all the other parties to the
action, too.

West Germany's Department of Transport, for example,
seemed determined that Lufthansa should hand over no
documents to the court before BA did so. Like Swissair,
Lufthansa had protested vigorously to the Justice Department about the Grand Jury investigation and thought it
had made its point successfully. (In fact, Justice officials

flew over to Germany early in December for lengthy interviews with the airline's personnel and it was not dropped from the Grand Jury's deliberations until May 1984.) Encouraged by this, Lufthansa was not inclined to be very helpful in the civil case either. As for TWA and Pan Am, they seemed to have been regarding themselves for much of 1983 as innocent spectators at a legal ringside: Uncle Sam and John Bull were slogging it out in a contest which looked bound to go fifteen rounds at the minimum.

Now, with the amicus curiae settling down to his task, Judge Greene determined to quicken the pace of the proceedings. The number of co-defendants had just risen to a dozen: a third suit had been filed on 22 September joining UTA, the privately-owned French overseas airline, and SAS, the Scandinavian airline, to the action. With many of the twelve defendants hiring specialist antitrust lawyers in Washington as well as retaining their general purpose US counsel, matters were threatening to get out of hand unless some visible progress were made soon.

The most obvious place to start was with the US carriers. Ever since May, they had produced only a trickle of documents for Beckman. Under a laborious procedure known as 'creeping compliance', they had made papers available only under sufferance. Beckman was more than once notified that documents were ready for his inspection at either TWA's or Pan Am's offices in New York City . . . only to discover, when he arrived there, a room full of flight schedules and brochures that he could almost have collected on a diligent trip round the travel agents' shops.

It was largely Beckman's fault, however. Under normal circumstances, the counsel in a US civil suit of this kind abide by a Protective Order of the court. This obliges all the parties to restrict access to discovered documents strictly to the litigation lawyers involved on the case. Only on this basis, after all, will companies surrender confidential commercial information of possible value to their competitors. But Beckman refused to accept the normal protocol. He maintained that he was now fighting a second front in the European courts and needed to be able to use the documents there. The US carriers refused to play along with this – hence, very few documents changed hands.

In November, counsel for TWA, Pan Am and the Laker camp were prevailed upon to accept an informal protective order amongst themselves. It let loose a torrent of papers. Over the next nine months, TWA alone produced about 60,000 pages for the plaintiff. It handed over more than 100,000 separate documents eventually – and Pan Am did the same. Then came the contributions of all the other defendants. Affidavits, interrogatories, answers and objections, motions and depositions: they all came flooding over the court in a Niagara of legal bumph.

American law affords a plaintiff powers of investigation which are undreamed of – and largely unenvied – in European courts. His counsel has three main lines of attack. He can request access to all properly relevant documents in the possession of a defendant. (The defendant can put up any number of obstacles and often does; but the judge has the last word and discovery orders from the court, as they are called, leave defendants with no choice but to comply.) Again, so-called interrogatories allow plaintiff's counsel to put written questions to corporate bodies and obtain written answers which can be used as evidence in court. Finally, and most demanding of the court's time and everyone's patience generally, individuals associated with the case can be obliged to submit to cross-examination on the record by plaintiff's counsel. (This ordeal is known as a deposition, with the individual deponents being deposed with all due ceremony.) Taken together, these powers guaranteed a sea of paperwork for all the lawyers involved (and a handsome source of revenues for their firms, with a good Washington partner worth up to $300 an hour for his services).

From late in 1983, Civil Docket No. 82-3362 in the first-floor records department of Washington's Federal Court House began to fill up rapidly – and it went on filling ever faster through the whole of the following year. By the end of 1984, there were twenty-nine volumes containing nearly nine hundred individual documents – and these were just the pleadings of the various parties to the action, with associated evidence!

The bulk of the case material naturally accumulated at Beckman's offices. His firm moved to new and larger premises in October 1983 just to accommodate the weight of papers. They were for the litigation lawyers' eyes only: crates and crates of them, for example, from the European airline defendants ('Please release all documents in your possession between x and y dates,' ran the typical discovery request, 'in which the name of Laker is to be found . . .') By 1985, over one million papers had been gathered by Beckman. Perhaps 10 per cent came from Laker Airways, about 30 per cent from the US carriers and the rest from the Europeans – including BA and BCal.

BA had used the Protection of Trading Interests Act (PTIA) to avoid handing over documents held in the UK; but there was nothing to stop Beckman obtaining access to BA papers located in the US, many of which he claimed were highly relevant to his allegations. As for BCal, the second British carrier had despatched a choice selection of its most sensitive papers to Washington at the outset of the Grand Jury case, leaving the consignment with its Washington lawyers for them to work on BCal's defence. Beckman demanded discovery of the lot.

All the continental airlines, with the single – and curious – exception of UTA, resorted to blocking tactics against discovery, each one choosing a slightly different course depending on its national law. But Beckman's persistence wore them all down in the end. But what, one might ask, was the purpose of all his industry? Could anyone possibly have supposed that the jury in the eventual trial would ever be able to come to terms with a fraction of the information at the Laker camp's disposal?

Of course not. But that was not the point. The jury would actually be required to see only what counsel to the two sides put before them. The purpose of the rest was to enable the lawyers to strip out the critical issues of fact which they wanted the jury to see in order to weigh the arguments put before them. It was a process of distillation.

Or at least, that was the neat theory of what was happening to the Laker civil suit in 1983–4. Sometimes theory and practice moved closely in tandem. Sometimes they did not . . . and then the whole, dizzy process began to look like something only too familiar to outsiders watching the US system at work: legal trench warfare. And in these trenches, the business of the occasional night raid was known as the taking of depositions.

Depositions began in earnest early in 1984. They normally begin in major US suits only when all documents have been collected and the trenches are fully dug; but Beckman launched his partly in response to the difficulties he was encountering over the discovery process. For this reason, too, he reversed the usual approach of starting at the bottom of the hierarchy of responsibilities: Beckman went straight for the board-rooms, starting with General Electric and moving on to the various airline chiefs.

Each deposition was preceded by the same elaborate rigmarole. Video cameras and microphones had to be trekked from one occasion to the next and set up anew at the start of the proceedings. And at the side of the room, for easy reference, Beckman and his associates would display three huge white boards headed 'Laker Airways History'. Covering them was a typewritten chronicle of the airline's tortured past, stretching from its first application to the old Air Transport Licensing Board on 15 June 1971 all the way through the next eleven years.

133

Some questions were common to all the cross-examinations. Had the chief executive, for example, ever been to a weekend gathering on the Wyoming ranch run by the Conquistadores del Cielo? (This is a highly secretive, men-only club whose members are exclusively drawn from the top executives of the US aviation industry. It is widely regarded as a potent meeting-place for the men at the top of all the worlds' airlines – with obvious implications to anyone suspicious of conspiracy in high places.) Other questions concentrated on specific details of the deponent's personal involvement with the Laker Airways History.

The answers rarely if ever lived up to the drama of the setting. Typical was the deposition of Ed Acker in the boardroom of the Pan Am building in Manhattan at the beginning of May 1984. About twenty lawyers turned up to hear Bill Barrett of Metzger, Shadyac & Schwarz conducting the interview. The lights hummed and the videos whirred – but the Pan Am chief sang not at all. If the Laker camp was looking for dramatic revelations, they were sadly disappointed. The whole affair was blandness itself.

This was most emphatically not the case a week later in Paris, where Bob Beckman arrived in person – he disliked depositions and did as few as possible – to handle the cross-examination of Rene Lapautre, UTA's diminutive but highly combative chairman. It proved, in fact, one of the highlights of the year – though not necessarily as Beckman might have hoped.

Lapautre is a former Inspector in the French Ministry of Finance who became head of UTA in 1981, at the age of fifty-one, after seven years in the airline business. UTA, the product of a successful merger between France's two biggest independent airlines in the early 1960s, had enjoyed a period of steady growth through the seventies. By the date of Lapautre's arrival, it had expanded from its main operating base, developing a network of African routes built around France's former colonies with a high priority on cargo.

UTA was not, as this suggests, a conspicuous competitor of Laker Airways – but Lapautre, whilst busy like everyone else in the industry with the effects of recession, had watched the progress of the Laker suit through 1983 with more interest than most outsiders. On the one hand, he had played an unabashed role in the nastygrams episode between McDonnell Douglas and its European customers. On the other, he had a passionately held view about the appropriate response of any non-US defendant to the antitrust suit – and it was uncompromising.

Lapautre believed the European governments ought to have got together at the outset and told the White House in so many words that the action was unacceptable. By the time UTA was joined to the suit on 22 September 1983, however, it was already a little late for this. When Beckman's request for documents arrived at the UTA tower in Puteaux, the modernistic new business zone just across the Pont du Neuf in Paris, Lapautre authorised the immediate dispatch of hundreds of documents to Washington. No blocking tactics for him: he had nothing to hide and wanted everyone to know it. In fact, he was bursting to express his indignation about the whole affair.

When the next request arrived – seeking his attendance, which French law did not oblige, at a deposition in the US embassy in Paris – Lapautre grabbed his chance. The session opened in the US Consul-General's office overlooking the Place de la Concorde, at 2.00 p.m. on May 1984. A phalanx of American lawyers sat around the room to hear Beckman conduct his cross-examination. Lapautre, with a red French Legion of Honour stripe in his lapel, sat ready for the questions.

But when Beckman began, the Frenchman demanded an interpreter. Beckman remonstrated. Was it not the case that the UTA chairman had an American wife and spoke perfectly good English? Well yes, said Lapautre. But General de Gaulle had once said no Frenchman should speak anything other than French at an official

135

engagement in France – and Lapautre agreed. It was hi
right to have an interpreter and that's what he was goin
to have. (He was also going to have two hours for hi
lunch the next day, because that was how long
Frenchman needed for his lunch.)

So there was a break in the record until the service
were obtained of an elderly lady interpreter. While th
lawyers sat waiting with scarcely concealed mirth at hi
discomfort, an exasperated Beckman turned to Sand
Miller, UTA's US lawyer who spoke no French either
'If I was having a drink with Monsieur Lapautre,' sai
Beckman to his compatriot, 'I'm sure he would spea
English with me.' Lapautre insisted on having th
remark translated for him. Then he requested Sand
Miller, in English, to please inform Mr Beckman that he
Rene Lapautre, would never accept a drink from M
Beckman – in any language.

At length the lady interpreter was in place and th
business of the meeting began. It had not run very fa
when the UTA chairman, by now evidently enjoyin
himself hugely, stopped the interpreter to correct he
translation. This brought the house down. But Lapautr
stuck to his guns: he was perfectly at liberty to spea
English if he wanted to – but it made no difference to hi
inalienable right to deal with Beckman's questions solel
in French.

He might as well have answered them in double Dutc
for all the apparent use they seemed to be, though
Lapautre. Beckman asked him, for example, to explair
the significance of digits on the top of telex forms. It wa
almost as though the Laker lawyer were suggesting th
presence of sinister coded messages. On another occa
sion, Beckman wanted to know the exact telephon
number and zip code of UTA's office in New York
Lapautre said he did not know them – and what was th
point of asking, anyway? More than once, Sandy Mille
had to remind his client that he was under an obligatio
to answer the points which were put to him. And behin

all the tomfoolery, as everyone knew, there lay some weighty matters. Beckman was intent on establishing that Skytrain's expansion round the world had been a threat to UTA's global pretensions. And he tried hard to elaborate on the idea of a cartel at work behind the nastygrams to McDonnell.

Lapautre used the occasion as he had planned to, even ignoring the advice of his US lawyer in some respects. Broadly, he had three ripostes. First, UTA did not consider Skytrain a competitor anywhere in the world. Second, as its chairman he had if anything been favourably disposed towards Freddie's low fares initiative: low fares from Heathrow to Paris could open up a potential feeder route for UTA's network to Africa and the Pacific. Third, the nastygrams were the legitimate action of a group of consumers banding together to protect their interests against a producer. Yes, he had sent copies of his telex to McDonnell to the chief executives of six European carriers, urging them to make the same protest. And he had had every right to do so. Then Lapautre made a sally of his own. The complaint filed by Beckman against UTA, said its chairman, had made a number of defamatory allegations. Beckman should be on notice that Lapautre was considering the possibility of suing him!

Whereupon the proceedings came to a close. Lapautre returned to his office in the UTA Tower in Puteaux, and there – figuratively speaking – he stayed for the rest of the action. Beckman left other European depositions to his colleagues.

In a sense, the mixture of farce and tedious detail which had dominated the Paris session was the essence not just of the depositions but of the whole pre-trial proceedings, as they meandered along – far from the public eye – into the summer months of 1984. As the various parties' lawyers came to know each other better, though, their periodic excursions for the depositions acquired the jollity at times of a travelling circus. There was always the risk of a high-wire act going wrong or a bear breaking loose, just to keep an element of suspense in the air. But most of the fun was just being there, amidst the noise and the lights. And for some of the less widely travelled US lawyers, it was a marvellous way of seeing Europe for the first time – on first-class expenses. The first week of June found them all in Zurich. Then it was off to Stockholm at the end of the month for SAS's depositions. (The return flight on that trip was diverted from Kennedy Airport to Montreal and they all ended up driving back to New York in an overnight limousine together – all except Beckman's partner David Kirstein, that is: he slept the night in Montreal's airport terminal.)

But they never went to London. The PTIA and the Appeal Court's permanent injunction barring the plaintiff from pressing his action against BA and BCal had put the British airlines beyond the reach of the deposition circuit. Worse, from the Laker Airways point of view, it had put the UK offices of BA and BCal beyond the reach of Beckman's various discovery procedures. And as the months of 1984 slipped by, the conviction grew amongst outsiders in Washington that incriminating evidence – if it existed anywhere – was most likely to be found in the office files of the British carriers.

It did not appear to have been found anywhere else: this was the most glaring reality by June 1984. It was impossible to be sure, given the protective order on the discovered documents. But really sensational disclosures had a way of reaching the streets in the US: and there were none. Hundreds of cupboards had been opened all over the place, expelling not one real skeleton amongst the lot of them. Or that, anyway, was the public impression – nurtured, naturally, by the airlines themselves. It was a source of much privately expressed surprise amongst independent observers. As for Beckman and his associates, they were putting a brave front on it; but there certainly appeared to be little for them to celebrate so far.

Nor were the empty cupboards their only source for concern. The amicus curiae's report, commissioned the previous November and submitted to Judge Greene at the end of February, had produced no visible change at all in the attitude of the court. The report's eighty-eight pages amounted to an encyclopaedic review of the legal precedents and choices facing the judge, including the possibility of counter-injunctions against the English Appeal Court. But it had come to no very compelling conclusion, for all its professional refinement. ('Under the circumstances, resolution of the conflicting considerations is a matter within the Court's discretion, which will be further informed by briefing from the parties in response to this report.')

Most discouraging of all, perhaps, the Justice Department had announced in Washington on 11 May that it was heavily curtailing the scope of its own investigations. It had unearthed no evidence, said the Department, which could provide the basis for either criminal or civil antitrust proceedings against parties involved in the unsuccessful attempt to refinance Laker Airways in 1980–1981.

After all, it appeared, the Justice Department had come round to the view taken by the British Government and succinctly expressed in the amicus curiae report: 'Her Majesty's Government is satisfied that the offer by McDonnell Douglas to participate in the financial restructuring of Laker remained open. The judgement that that offer, and other financial offers of support, were inadequate to keep Laker alive was made by the Civil Aviation Authority.' The Justice Department had also informed BCal, Lufthansa and Swissair that it was closing its files on their affairs altogether.

There were no public reactions from Touche Ross, Beckman or anyone else in the Laker camp. But the wind was hardly blowing in a favourable direction. Still, there were two immediate grounds for consolation. The Justice Department, after fifteen months of inquiry, had chosen to push ahead with more work on the predatory price-fixing conspiracy. And, as at least a few commentators noted, the strictly domestic writ of the Grand Jury had undoubtedly been a significant restraint on the evidence brought before it.

Christopher Morris and his lawyers could hope to do rather better than that – but only, it was becoming increasingly clear, if the House of Lords would free their hands in England. Then they could get to grips with the one defendant they now prized above all the others: BA.

It all depended on the House of Lords. The appeal against both the PTIA and the June 1983 injunction began before the five Law Lords on 5 June 1984.

13

The Immaculate Prospectus (1)

Martyrdom has been a Ridley family tradition for three hundred years. Nicholas Ridley was himself named after the unhappy Bishop of London, his forebear, who was burnt at the stake as a heretic by Bloody Queen Mary. As the arguments over the future of British civil aviation became steadily more heated through 1984, the Transport Secretary found himself in danger of producing history's second Ridley conflagration.

His cause was an honourable one – the promotion of greater competition and a more open market economy – and Ridley had espoused it throughout his political career, not infrequently to his own disadvantage. He had become a junior Minister in 1970 with a reputation as a Powellite in economic matters, only to be left behind by the Great U-Turn of the Heath years. He had spoken out strongly against the 1972–4 sequel and, in opposition through the later seventies, had cut rather a dash in the Commons as an effective critic of the Callaghan Government's industrial policies. He had made many speeches and written long and thoughtful newspaper articles attacking the 'bloated and expanding' UK public sector – and the Whitehall establishment, too, which in his view helped make the curtailment of the public sector so difficult. But when it came to applying some of his competitive principles, Ridley was to confront a choice between political necessity and theological rectitude which might have been familiar to a Marian Bishop of London.

As a junior Minister at the Foreign and Common-wealth Office from 1979 to 1981 – a bizarre appointment from the start – he contained a crisis over policy in Central America and avoided provoking an Argentinian invasion of the Falklands with an adroitness which won him respect. As Financial Secretary at the Treasury until 1983, he toiled patiently to elucidate doctrinal matters close to his own heart. Neither job, however, left him quite prepared as the new Secretary of State for Transport for the decision required late in 1983 over the future regulation of a privatised BA.

Setting up the CAA review at least allowed, as was intended, a cooling of passions for a while on both sides of the debate. The CAA sent out letters on 19 December 1983, inviting submissions from over a hundred different parties in the aviation industry. It was obvious immediately that its review was going to be painstaking – so the media's interest switched elsewhere while the CAA got on with its task.

There was never any doubt that British Caledonian and all the other independent companies in British aviation would do their very utmost to see BA's wings clipped in some way before privatisation. But just in case they needed it, the flag-carrier had obligingly provided a reminder in 1983 of the dangers posed by a private BA, red in tooth and claw.

In 1982–3, BA made operating profits of £6m. on its no-bookings shuttle services from Heathrow to Glasgow, Edinburgh and Belfast. In October 1982, however, British Midland Airways had begun a bookable shuttle from Heathrow to Glasgow. It added an Edinburgh shuttle in March 1983. The BMA flights, puncturing BA's virtual monopoly, offered an alternative kind of service: booking facilities, hot meals and a bar included (plus a cheaper return price). By May 1983, BMA had snatched about 30 per cent of the market. This brought a straightforward response from Colin Marshall: on 1 July 1983, BA announced that it would be introducing a Super-Shuttle with hot meals and a free bar at the end of August. But a few weeks later, BMA won CAA approval to launch a shuttle on the Belfast route. This provoked a less commercial response.

BA appealed to the High Court against the CAA decision, bypassing a furious Transport Department which would have been the normal arbiter of such an appeal. It was a questionable legal tactic – the judges rejected BA's case, though they did acknowledge an apparent departure in CAA policy – but BA seemed determined to snub the CAA and to draw attention with a series of colourful public statements to the damage threatened to its own interests by increased domestic competition.

All this – not to mention the introduction of Concorde on occasional Super-Shuttle flights – struck BA's opponents as a menacing portent of things to come. By February 1984, Marshall's new marketing men had restored much of BA's lost competitiveness simply by improving the Shuttle product on offer. But this, of course, was proof in a sense of the competition pudding favoured by the independents. They, meanwhile, did not forget the bullying tactics glimpsed the previous autumn.

Leading the independents, inevitably, was BCal under its chairman, Sir Adam Thomson. BCal's 1983 Blue Book was condensed and repackaged in gold covers with a subtly amended title: *A Competitive Strategy for British Air Transport in Private Ownership*. This was submitted to the CAA on 31 January 1984. It included a list of BA routes – about a fifth of the flag-carrier's total network, including long-haul routes to the Caribbean, the Far East and the Gulf and short-haul routes to the Eastern Mediterranean, Vienna and Helsinki – which the CAA was urged to recommend should be switched from BA to BCal, as a basis for future competition in the industry. The list itself, however, was omitted from a bowdlerised Gold Book which was released for public circulation. All BCal would reveal was that its proposals, if accepted, would just about double the size of its own operations.

Some observers castigated all BCal's talk of competition as rather bogus. International airlines were not to be compared, ran this argument, with the simple rivalry of butchers and bakers in the High Street. The whole industry – outside the deregulated US, at least – was one enormous cartel operation. Most routes were subject to bilateral treaties which divided them between carriers of the two connected countries. And many of these were subject to pooling arrangements, which meant the carriers split the revenues on the route according to a pre-agreed formula which took no account whatever of passengers' preferences for one carrier or the other. 'Competition' was so much baloney.

But the BCal case was slightly more sophisticated than this seemed to acknowledge. The Gold Book admitted the shortcomings of 'head-on competition'. Where the CAA licensed a second British carrier to operate directly in competition with BA – extending the usual bilateral arrangements to allow for 'dual designation' of BA and one other – the UK companies would have to share the revenues left in the pool pot by the non-British carrier. This practice did not have a glorious history. (BCal referred in a footnote to the demise of British Eagle in 1968 as well as Laker in 1982.) Fortunately, BCal discerned other ways to improve competition. Most importantly, these included awarding BA's rivals sole licences to cities adjacent to existing BA destinations.

In the middle of February, the CAA showed exactly how this might work. It gave BCal permission to fly from Gatwick to Riyadh, the capital of Saudi Arabia. BA, which already operated flights to Jeddah and Dhahran, the other two major Saudi commercial centres, was incensed. And the significance of the move was plain to see. Once the principle of 'indirect competition' in this way was accepted, said BCal, logic demanded that it be given a chance to compete more evenly with the help of

144

some reallocation of BA routes. As late as April, Thomson was still making public offers of £250m. in exchange for the routes BCal had in mind.

By this time, BCal felt not unjustly that it was making all the running. Its executives – especially Alistair Pugh and Peter Smith – had attended endless meetings with middle-ranking officials at the CAA, sitting for hours in the authority's London offices, at Space House in Kingsway, to present every detail of the Gold Book's recommendations.

Some of them were less contentious than the routes reallocation proposal. The establishment of a route networks hub at Gatwick, for example, and the separation of BA from its holiday charter operation, British Airtours, were warmly espoused by the leading tour operators, Horizon, Intasun and Thomson Holidays. These three companies banded together to form the Airport Users' Study Group and worked hard to add their weight to the anti-BA lobby. What they and the other charter independents most feared was the prospect of a predatory BA willing to dump surplus capacity on to the charter market as passenger traffic cycles allowed. But this would only be the most conspicuous symptom of a widespread cross-subsidisation of its operations by BA which all the independents feared.

By the middle of March, the CAA had received 135 written submissions. Five weeks later, on 18 April, it produced an Interim Report. More time was needed to study the options, said the CAA. But it was clear which way the wind was blowing. While cautioning against any strategy that might lead it 'to dismember an airline', the authority saw a prima-facie case for revising BA's route network and for liberalising domestic aviation, including its charter sector.

Twelve days later, on 30 April, Thomson was attending a demonstration of the A-310 Airbus at Geneva Airport. He took the occasion to welcome the Interim Report. It indicated, he said, 'a desirable change in the shape and structure of our industry and we welcome it'. Then, no doubt well aware of the fact that BA was presenting its 1983–4 results the next day in London, the BCal chairman boldly suggested that BA's privatisation should be postponed to allow time for the CAA's ideas to be implemented. 'The fundamental changes which the authority points towards cannot happen overnight. They must be prepared meticulously . . .'

This was little more than a statement of the obvious – provided one accepted the premise that those changes were indeed going to happen. John King did not astonish the world when he expressed BA's reaction the following morning. 'Claptrap,' he said – that was what Thomson was talking. 'It will not happen. We will not allow it.' The BA chairman then made clear just how inflammatory was the material which Ridley had asked the CAA to present to his Department. 'The Government will not have the blessing of me or my board to take away anything from British Airways,' said King. 'I would regard it as a resignation issue.'

When someone had the temerity to ask him whether this meant he would in fact resign, King's reply was as blunt as it was truthful: 'I accept resignations. I don't submit them.' In other words, if the Government told him to institute sweeping CAA changes, he would simply refuse. Since he would not resign, the Government would have to submit or sack him. That would produce a few political fireworks and no mistake. (Some senior civil servants spent an idle moment or two musing what, if any, legal steps would be available to sack him.) Ridley must have detected a burning smell there and then.

The Interim Report, however, brought home to BA, too, just how serious was the growing confrontation. Part of the airline's difficulty to date had been the sheer demands made by the CAA on its executives' time. Marshall, Dunlop and their colleagues simply had too many pressures on them in the first half of 1984 to orchestrate an effective response.

For these were critical months in a variety of ways. At the most basic level, the new management was busy inculcating into BA's entire workforce the changes of attitude towards the customer which Marshall believed would be the key to the airline's success – in the private sector or the public. In this, as in a few other important respects, BA was unashamedly following in the path of one of its closest IATA allies, the Scandinavian airline, SAS.

SAS had brought in a dynamic new chief, Jan Carlzon, nine months before King's appointment. He had managed to turn round SAS's financial position quite dramatically. He had introduced a Euroclass business fare which looked modelled on the club class introduced by BA in the spring of 1980. Since then, though, he had been setting the pace. He had hired Landor Associates, a Californian design consultancy, to refashion SAS's presentation of itself. Late in 1983, King had given a similar mandate to Landor (much to the disgust of some leading figures in the British design world, who were enraged that BA did not even invite them to bid for the job). Above all, Carlzon had adopted a flip motto – in SAS's case 'Let's Get In There And Fight' (sic) – and had hired a Danish staff training consultancy to get the SAS girls smiling sweetly, come what may.

In December 1983, Marshall had brought in the same Danish consultancy, Time Management International, to evangelise BA in a similar way – this time to the gospel of 'Putting People First'. For seven months, until the end of June 1984, some 15,000 BA employees went on two-day courses in groups of 150 at a time to attend classes on personal relations and the successful management of the passenger. (The programme continued after the summer: by June 1985 all 37,000 of BA's employees had attended a two-day course.)

It was easy to debunk the gung-ho aspects of all this from outside – and a 24-hour strike by cabin crews in February suggested there were still plenty of employees whose priorities were not much different from what they had been in the past. But Marshall never doubted the efficacy of the TMI courses. With his 'I Fly the World's Favourite Airline' lapel button proudly to the fore, the chief executive spent a huge amount of time flying around the world in order to address as many of them as possible in person. It was quickly evident inside the airline that those who ridiculed the courses were generally those who had not yet been on one. By the middle of 1984, the results – with BA captains strolling down the aisles before departure, for example, to chat with passengers – were evident even to the least observant.

There were other changes in store for the cabin crews, too. As one spokesman from their trade union put it: 'The job has a history of being manned by ex-debs and men off the boats, but all that has changed.' For hostesses of an uncertain age, the changes were regrettably terminal. BA introduced five-year contracts and an age-limit of twenty-six on new hostesses. All those commercials for British Caledonian's Girls might have been toe-curlingly embarrassing for some; but they had evidently found their mark with others and BA apparently felt its girls were suffering by comparison. Elderly BA matrons were to be a thing of the past.

Throughout the airline, in fact, past practices and assumptions were being re-examined. A more sophisticated segmentation of BA's various markets by Jim Harris and his staff was throwing up all sorts of fresh marketing ideas where the Super-Shuttle had led the way. (Renewed efforts to attract the budget traveller, for example, produced the 'Poundstretcher' fare packages.)

Finally, the CAA had to play second fiddle until June to all the intense preparations now being launched for privatisation itself. King visited the Prime Minister in Downing Street on 22 February 1984. Their discussions were not publicly disclosed. But from this date onwards, the official position in Whitehall seemed to be that the first tranche of British Telecom would be sold late in 1984 and BA could be expected to follow it into the market early in 1985.

So there was a lot to be done in the spring and early summer of 1984 to prepare the mechanics of privatisation.

In March, BA appointed both bankers and stockbrokers to protect its own interests. Merchant bankers Lazard's were brought in first. They and the BA board then recruited two prominent brokers: Phillips & Drew, a firm which could boast one of the City's leading research departments, and Rowe & Pitman, the Queen's stockbroker and probably second only to rival broker Cazenove in its ability to place stock with the investing community.

In May, the Government and Hill Samuel appointed as their two brokers Wood, Mackenzie, the Edinburgh-based firm with a strong research team, and Cazenove itself. (The latter's services, uniquely, had been sought after by the Government for all but one of the privatisations to date.)

On 19 April, the day after the publication of the CAA's Interim Report, all four of the stockbrokers attended a conference together at BA's Speedbird House Headquarters. It was chaired by Keith Wilkins, the airline's planning director. The broad campaign for privatisation was sketched out that day. In particular, work was set in train for the writing of a sales prospectus; but plans were also laid for a comprehensive brokerage research report on BA, which it was hoped might fulfil the same vital marketing role which two such reports had already played for British Telecom's gathering sales effort. Bill Seward of Phillips & Drew and David Morrison of Wood, Mackenzie were the analysts given responsibility for this daunting task.

Through May and June, the City professionals worked to a tight timetable. As well as the bankers and brokers, BA's auditors, Ernst & Whinney, were set to work (again) on a Long Form report to be filed with the Stock Exchange in readiness for the sale. The Long Report

149

work helped the brokers in their struggle to present the investing community with a fair but readily comprehensible survey of the elaborate workings of a huge modern airline. And as the survey's parts were completed, they had to be cleared, laboriously and paragraph by paragraph, with a regiment of lawyers. The target publication date for the report was early autumn. That would set the scene neatly for an early 1985 sale – or even, if the BA board found its secret wishes fulfilled by a sudden snag over British Telecom, for a sale before the end of 1984.

BA for its part seemed now to be avoiding at least financial snags with a novel aplomb. Certainly the airline's results were at last springing only helpful surprises. On 1 May – with British Airways just one month old as a plc – King was able to announce net profits for 1983–4 of £214m. against the £77m. recorded for 1982–3. There were admittedly one or two accounting oddities in there; but the operating profit of £293m. was a striking achievement and transcended general expectations. (It was also by a more comfortable margin than BA had made on its operations over the whole 1970–82 period in toto!)

Meanwhile, the protracted resolution of the pension fund problem appeared to be reaching a happy if long overdue conclusion. Dunlop had eventually talked Whitehall round to the solution put together by Duncan Fraser & Partners the previous spring: employees were invited to switch from the old scheme to a new one before a deadline of 30 June. It was soon clear that a respectable percentage would choose to move – in the event, 53 per cent did so, leaving the residual index-linked scheme a manageable problem for the prospectus writers.

Most wondrous of all, BA had recorded a positive cash flow, strong enough in 1983–4 to repay a net £164m. of borrowings. With a little help from a timely £122m. revaluation of its fleet, the airline was actually in the black! Debt to equity stood at a sobering 89:11 ratio.

But as King reminded his audience when he announced the financial results on 1 May, he was now the chairman of 'a solvent business with a positive net worth of £124m.'.

And it was at this point – with all these figures and issues behind them – that King and his colleagues began to concentrate on the threat posed by the CAA. From BA's point of view, it was not a moment too soon.

Since the start of the inquiry in December, the flag-carrier had been conspicuously on the defensive. BA had given its written views to the CAA in the first week of February; but they were far less forcefully presented than the arguments paraded in the Gold Book. Nor did BA executives have the time to spare for the CAA which BCal and the other independents made available. No one, though, doubted BA's opposition to any attempt whatever to reduce the size of its operations.

Hostile observers discerned an array of unspoken motives behind this unsurprising response. Some were commonplace, like a desire to wield as much commercial power as possible in the private sector. Other alleged motives were more subtle. It was argued, for example, that BA could not face any significant cut-backs in its route network because this would entail a confrontation with BALPA, the trade union representing the airline's pilots. (All the other unions at BA had been reconciled to lay-offs – if not exactly to the end of all their elaborate manning agreements – by a combination of hard talking and ready cash. But it was conspicuous that BALPA had emerged virtually unscathed from all the redundancy programmes. Critics attributed this to BALPA's enormously strong position inside the company. 'Touch our pilots and we will ground the airline,' was the union's message for King from the start, said insiders.)

Whatever its real fears, BA's public case against the independents in these early months was essentially a rearguard action. It had four main thrusts.

First, BA's planning director – one of the most knowledgeable and respected men in the company – set out the consequences which he anticipated would arise from any order that BA should lose a fifth of its routes. Wilkins's key figures were 9,600 more redundancies and lost operating profits of £103m. That, said BA, was the cost of the Gold Book plus the various other independents' proposals. (The figures were shown to Ernst & Whinney for authentication.)

Second, the idea of BA needing more competition was ridiculed on the grounds that its business was substantially international and involved constant competitive pressures from overseas carriers.

Third, statistics were presented which seemed to question the image of an all-powerful BA. As King wrote in December 1983 in the first of a stream of letters to the *Financial Times*: 'if we include the important charter market, the total [BA share of operations by UK-owned airlines] is less than 64 per cent. This can hardly be viewed as a monopolistic situation.' (The share of UK airlines' scheduled operations was 83 per cent – and 100 per cent of all those from Heathrow.)

And fourth, the motives of BCal and the other independents were challenged. They might be talking about the intellectual merits of reorganising the aviation sector, came the response, but actually it was all just a try-on to grab whatever was going. 'Some people seem to think we are about to become easy prey,' as Marshall put it in March at the end of the period for submissions to the CAA. 'They are acting like vultures waiting to swoop.'

But it was relatively weak stuff. The BA board's forte was argument by assertion, not scholastic disputation. What it needed was a positive case, to project with vigour. In June 1984, King at long last took up the cudgels.

Britain needed the strongest possible flag-carrier, to make sure UK civil aviation went to the top of the world league and stayed there. That was to be the message.

King ordered a £2m. advertising campaign to put it across. Then he launched himself into the fray with an interview given to the *Financial Times*:

> We have let them [the independents] get away with it for too long. We are going to hit back . . . We are being asked to fight with one hand tied behind our back [since BCal would not disclose its route aspirations]. What is Sir Adam frightened of? Why does he not come out into the open and tell everyone just what he wants to grab from us? Furthermore, would Sir Adam really be capable of taking over the routes he wants, without any interruption in the continuity or quality of service? . . . Who has produced that magical figure of £250m. Sir Adam says is the value of the routes and aircraft he wants to acquire? . . . All these things should be publicly spelt out by Sir Adam and his other independent airline friends . . . Then BA itself can give its own blow by blow answer to this attempted predatory raid on its assets. . . . They are frightened of our power after privatisation. We are going to show them before privatisation just what competition is.

A few days later, King addressed a group of Wall Street brokerage analysts, flown over to London in Concorde for an investment briefing by the company. In case Ridley had still not appreciated the change of climate, King was more emphatic than ever. The Government, he warned, had no power to transfer routes as the law stood. Even if fresh legislation were introduced, he would stand his ground. 'I would not resign – they would have to sack me – and the board.'

It must have looked to Ridley as though every worry he had expressed the previous December about a CAA reference was now being vindicated. All he could reasonably hope for was a Final Report from the authority mild enough to allow an honourable fudge. Instead, the opposite happened. When an advance copy of the CAA Report reached Whitehall in the first week of July, it was even more prescriptive than Ridley had feared. A wholesale restructuring of the aviation industry was being recommended! Those busily at work on BA's sale documents wanted what was being called an 'immaculate prospectus', with no last-minute reorganisations which could only impair the prospects for a favourable market reception. The report appeared wholly incompatible with their demands.

'Be of good cheer, Master Ridley,' Archbishop Cranmer had told the Minister's ancestor as they faced the flames together. There followed the famous quote about lighting a candle that would never be put out. Well, here was the CAA urging Ridley to light a candle on behalf of Free Market Competition. But how could he possibly do that, without endangering BA's privatisation timetable and upsetting Treasury calculations of the sale proceeds? Yet the only alternative appeared to be a recantation of the arguments advanced for appointing the CAA in the first place. That would jar with everything Ridley had always believed in and could prove politically disastrous as well.

Doctrinal purity or the immaculate prospectus: it was not a happy choice.

14

The Immaculate Prospectus (2)

Of all the remote corners of the British Isles least likely to produce a temperament suited to a successful career in public relations, none can be more remote than the twenty-five or so square miles of North Antrim in Ulster. Facing Scotland's Mull of Kintyre twenty miles across the sea, it is a rugged and self-contained farming community. Even the people of Belfast, just to the south-west, consider the natives of North Antrim to be for the most part provincial and narrow-minded.

This, however, was not at all the impression made on King and Marshall by one David Burnside at the beginning of June 1984. The 33-year-old Antrim man approached them with an introduction from a City editor in Fleet Street. Within three days, they had hired him as exactly the kind of public relations man they had been looking for, to help mastermind the counteroffensive against the CAA which lay ahead. But then, David Burnside had come a long way from the hills of Antrim by 1984 – via a most unusual route even by the eclectic standards of BA's senior management.

Ten years earlier, a fervent young Unionist just down from Queen's University, Belfast, Burnside had thrown himself into the very thick of Ulster sectarian politics. Ulster politics still consume a great deal of his time: Burnside, for example, was one of the key organisers behind a rare briefing for Fleet Street editors given by Unionists in London to attempt to rally support against

Anglo-Irish talks in October 1985.) His chief role in the mid-seventies was as press officer for William Craig's Vanguard Party – one of the many extremist groups flourishing in Ulster in the first half of the 1970s – and it was Craig who later sponsored Burnside to go off to the Council of Europe for a year in 1978.

From Strasbourg, Burnside made the leap to London by becoming public relations officer at the Institute of Directors. He was not universally liked at the IoD, but he was extremely effective. He is the least ingratiating of men and his Antrim dourness can mean lunches punctuated by long silences and only the most wintry of smiles. He is not a humourless man, but is more given to caustic asides than casual joking. (When he arrived for his interview at the IoD, he saw portraits of Cromwell and William III hanging above him. 'With those on the walls you can't fail to give me the job,' said Burnside.) For nearly five years, he promoted the IoD's views tirelessly in Westminster and the media – for a while turning Walter Goldsmith, the IoD's director-general, into a minor celebrity in the process.

It was exactly this resourcefulness which the BA board needed in the summer of 1984. Burnside had failed to win the North Antrim constituency in the 1982 Ulster Assembly elections – he had been away from the locality too long, opponents said – and was on the brink of joining the staff at Central Office. But he took the job at BA – he was not formally appointed until 1 September, but that was a nicety – and it was made clear that he would have complete charge of all the group's public affairs in due course, assuming all went well.

It did.

Between the second week of June and the end of September, BA's board crushed the protagonists of the CAA and the independent airlines in one of the most ruthless and highly charged lobbying campaigns ever witnessed in British politics. It was also undoubtedly the most serious crisis in the history of UK civil aviation

The outcome – a virtually unchanged BA – ensured the survival of the immaculate prospectus and therefore of the plan for BA's privatisation in 1985. More than that, though, it helped to set the framework for the future of British aviation for decades to come.

King was absolutely determined that that future should hinge on BA's ascendency to become the world's No. 1 international airline. In this vision of things, the CAA's was a hopelessly parochial study. Nor was the threat to fragment UK aviation its only besetting sin. It was also demanding a betrayal, as King felt profoundly, of all the people left at BA after the bloodletting of recent years. The tone of the BA campaign was set precisely from the outset by a full-page newspaper advertisement which ran on 12 July:

BRITISH AIRWAYS WELCOMES COMPETITION

In fact, every day British Airways competes with hundreds of foreign airlines from all over the world. Faced with that competition, it is only by providing a better service to passengers that British Airways has achieved a pre-eminent position for Britain as the world's favourite airline.

Now, certain of our local competitors wish to see some of British Airways' routes taken from us and handed to them on a plate. To those airlines we say this.

If they do believe in true competition let them say so and act accordingly. Let the customers decide which airline they prefer on the basis of the service offered to passengers. And may the best one win.

King

Since BA already controlled all overseas flights from Heathrow, the above invitation contained disingenuous elements to say the least. But this was not going to be an intellectual sparring match. It was a bruising political confrontation. Burnside needed no time to appreciate this. In his assessment, anyway, BA's delay in countering British Caledonian's campaign since December (and earlier) meant that it had already lost the chance to win over the editors and leader writers of Fleet Street, the men who would weigh the principles of the matter and talk about competition doctrine – 'the philosophers', as Burnside would scathingly describe them.

As if to confirm this prejudice, the CAA's Final Report, when it appeared on 16 July, made no bones about its intellectual detachment from the immediate practicalities facing the politicians and businessmen. '[The CAA] cannot judge an airline,' it opined, 'solely by the style and quality of its management and by its operational performance in the immediate present . . .' There followed a lengthy quotation (complete with footnote) from Gibbon's memoirs. 'Gibbon was of course writing of the universities of Oxford and Cambridge but, allowing for the vigour of his expression, the underlying thought is valid for all monopolies.'

Neither King nor Marshall nor Dunlop had been to Oxbridge, nor any other university for that matter. What concerned them was not highfallutin notions of monopoly but the fact that the CAA was recommending a significant contraction in BA's operations. Colin Marshall was genuinely taken aback at the breadth of the recommended action. He telephoned Gordon Dunlop, who was in Inverness at the time. Dunlop had been reassured that he should not worry unduly about the report and he had taken a week's fishing holiday on the River Ness. Dunlop, too, was 'devastated' (a very Dunlop word, spoken with a ringing Perthshire cadence).

The chief financial officer hastened back and the two men sat down to plot the next steps. Keith Wilkins was assigned to calculate the cost of the CAA's proposals. There were fourteen of them and all but five were seen as openly hostile by the BA board. It was suggested that BA should lose to BCal its long-haul routes to Harare, capital of Zimbabwe, and to Jeddah and Dhahran in Saudi Arabia. BA should further be deprived of all its scheduled services from Gatwick, plus all European flights from other provincial airports, in favour of BCal and the other independents. These reallocations – which were at the heart of the ensuing battle – were to be enacted by the Secretary of State via enabling legislation. This would inevitably entail delaying the BA sale – and would reduce the prospective sale price for the Exchequer, too. This, said the CAA, should be regarded 'as a modest contribution to the sounder development of the industry'.

Wilkins concluded that, from BA's point of view at least, it was not so modest. The CAA claimed it was proposing a putative cut of 7 per cent in BA's revenues. Wilkins argued that the correct figure was nearer 10 per cent and possibly rather more over the longer term. The airline, he said, would face 3,600 redundancies with a loss of revenues of £293m. and an operating profits shortfall of £76m.

Marshall and Dunlop turned themselves into shop stewards overnight. In groups of two hundred or so at a time, the workforce at Heathrow was invited into a series of meetings in the main engineering base adjoining Speedbird House. Jim Harris did the same with staff in BA's offices around the country. The seriousness of the challenge to BA's integrity was stressed over and over again for several days until no one in the airline was in any doubt what they had to do. And off went many of them to do it. (Not quite all, though. One, a self-professed 'mole' who surfaced from time to time throughout the summer, wrote to the chairman of British Midland Airways ridiculing BA's talk of international competition. 'The airlines make Swiss bankers look like the Brownies,' he said.)

Local MPs were bombarded with protests. Petitions were signed and Cabinet Ministers besieged with complaining letters. (Douglas Hurd exclaimed to King a few weeks later that he had received 130 letters: what was going on? Most of his colleagues, though, had had a good many more.) Meanwhile, the board devised its own plan of action. Cabinet Ministers would be left to the chairman's tender mercies. Fleet Street's City editors and Westminster's special political advisers would be approached by Burnside. All Members of Parliament – and that meant all – would be lobbied in person, if at all possible, in the first few weeks. Help was sought in this from Ian Greer Associates, a prominent public relations consultancy in the field, hired in July.

King and Marshall spent hours trekking around the corridors of the Palace of Westminster calling on MPs in their rooms. Many members were wined and dined at local restaurants like Lockett's, where BA's directors argued their way through endless lunches and dinners. The extent of the lobbying, one senior backbencher told the press, was 'unbelievable'. MPs who demurred when asked for their support were not let off lightly. Nicholas Soames, MP for BCal's home constituency of Crawley, pointed out that he had a lot of BCal employees amongst his voters. 'You've got more who work for BA,' retorted King, 'and a few who work for Babcock & Wilcox besides!'

If all this was a predictable reaction, its vigour startled BA's opponents. Sir John Dent, the CAA's chairman, knighted in the 1986 New Year's Honours, gave a press conference on 25 July to announce profits of £2.3m. for the CAA itself – and took the opportunity to express his view of BA's stance. 'We need British Airways to play a leading role,' said Dent, 'to behave responsibly and considerately to the rest of the industry . . .'

King would deal with him later. For the moment, though, the BA campaign had only one object: to prevent Ridley from committing himself to the CAA's proposals, however vaguely, at the Cabinet meeting on 26 July.

In this it succeeded triumphantly. By the time the Cabinet assembled that Thursday, it was only too obvious that Ridley had a terrible dilemma on his hands. There was a lively discussion there and then, too. As if Ridley were not facing enough angry BA employees outside, there was even an ex-BOAC pilot in the Cabinet – Norman Tebbit – and both he and Nigel Lawson were strongly opposed to disrupting the immaculate prospectus in any way. Ridley was supported by George Younger, the Scottish Secretary, and one or two other colleagues; but it was clear that more debate was needed before he could reach any decision. And on 30 July, Ridley told the House of Commons so.

But if the BA board thought this was the beginning of the end, they were quickly disappointed. The following Thursday – after a week which had seen BCal employees parading through the streets of Crawley and the eight leading independent airlines writing directly to Mrs Thatcher for her support – Ridley was really no nearer presenting a solution to the Cabinet. The Prime Minister decreed that a Cabinet sub-committee should be set up to iron out a compromise. (Members included John Wakeham, the Chief Whip, and Lord Cockfield, the Trade Secretary, as well as Lawson, Tebbit and Ridley himself.)

A compromise was not what King and his colleagues were after. Next day, the BA chairman decided it was time to say something about John Dent and the CAA. Their proposals, said King on Radio 4's *World at One* programme, amounted to 'a vicious, violent and very unattractive attack'. He himself doubted, in fact, whether the CAA was actually qualified to decide the size of an airline at all – qualified commercially, financially or in any other way.

The day after that, Adam Thomson bluntly pointed out that King was 'relatively new to the industry' and that his attack on one of the world's most respected civil airline authorities was nothing less than shocking.

Then the two sides broke off and everyone left for their August holidays. Ridley went fishing in Scotland. He must have had trouble concentrating on his line. There was no doubting the crisis that the CAA Report had landed in his lap: his political career could easily be ruined by it. His position was roughly analogous to that of a barrister who had broken that cardinal rule of advocacy: never ask an expert witness a question to which you do not already know the answer. He had asked the CAA for its recommendations and they had delivered them. Unhappily for him, they were hardly compatible with the brief Ridley was advocating. Now at least half the jury was laughing and jeering at his discomfort.

There were changes in the Transport Department. Unkind observers joked that William Knighton, the Deputy Secretary at the head of the Aviation Division, had been reassigned to the Vehicle Licensing Department in Swansea. He was indeed switched from Aviation to vehicle licensing and taxation (though he in fact remained responsible for the intricate dealings over the Laker imbroglio, as well as maritime affairs). The new Deputy Secretary at Aviation, a shortish man with thinning hair and sharp, angular features, was David Holmes, an old hand at privatisations. The change of style was abrupt. Knighton is a jolly man with a perpetual smile but he is inclined to dwell on his syllables and is more loquacious than the general run of Whitehall mandarins. It is easy to suppose he would be no match for the new man around a poker table: Holmes, who arrived at Aviation at the beginning of September, is more given to a quizzical slant of the eyebrows than long discourses on legal philosophy.

This probably suited Ridley rather well. The Minister had had his fill of philosophy by now – in his case, the philosophy of competition as so warmly espoused by John Moore in his November 1983 speech. Those third parties who were howling down the CAA Report seemed to be showing precious little understanding of the agonising conflict between doctrine and practicalities. Asserting any firm policy was going to require all the decisiveness and personal authority he could muster, in a situation where expert opinions were proliferating by the day. As Ridley himself put it, in an article for the Bow Group's *Crossbow* quarterly published a few months later: "Being Secretary of State for Transport is not as easy a job as it might sometimes look . . ." But at least he could see one issue all too clearly: did he really want to go to the stake over an official report which had been authorised against his better judgement in the first place?

King was fishing in Scotland, too, but the BA chairman was spending a great deal of his time on the telephone. There were radio interviews to be given, public figures to be lobbied and fresh recruits to be garnered for the lobbying campaign: Sir Gordon Reece, the Prime Minister's own public relations adviser at election-time – and another beneficiary, like Dent, of the 1986 New Year's Honours List – was hired away from Armand Hammer in California on a three-month contract from 1 September. (Contrary to popular belief, however, King deliberately decided against trying to recruit the help of Cecil Parkinson, who was on his board at Babcock & Wilcox.) Above all, though, King wanted to clarify with his BA colleagues exactly how they would pursue the airline's interests as the search began in Whitehall for a compromise solution.

The mood at Speedbird House by now was a lot more confident than it had been on 16 July. There was a growing feeling that BCal and its allies had shot their bolt: they had no fresh arguments to press, yet opinion in Westminster had rallied quite conspicuously round the flag-carrier.

BA opted to push three points forward more aggressively at the next critical Cabinet meeting which would be in September. With the new arguments, BA would do its utmost to block a fudged solution which might concede important parts of the CAA menu.

First, it would argue that BCal's 'competition' in fact amounted to 'substitution'. If the Government wished to replace one airline with the other, that was its political prerogative; but competition had nothing to do with it. (The CAA surely saw substitution as a preparation for future competition; but the BA rejoinder had its rhetorical value undeniably.)

Second, BA would invite more direct competition on scheduled routes while giving assurances of good will towards competitors in the charter market. It would challenge BCal to fly alongside it to far more destinations than in the past (presupposing more so-called 'dual designation' routes could be negotiated with other countries).

And third, the flag-carrier would remind Ridley at every possible juncture that all his predecessors since 1979 had given their word that BA would not be broken up ahead of privatisation. King suspected that Ridley had not been made aware of this aspect of the sale's history until it was too late: he was determined to embarrass the Minister if he persisted in ignoring it.

Once again, BA won hands down. The opposition did not give up and it ran some effective advertising. (The three largest charter airlines, for example, warned of BA's real intentions: 'The truth is that behind the kindly grandmother muttering platitudes of goodwill . . . lurks a monopolist wolf. And the Little Red Riding Hoods of the charter airlines are in danger of being gobbled up.') But BA's pressure was relentless.

On 5 September, Marshall unveiled BA's 'dual designation compromise' at a reception at the Savoy. By accepting direct competition on sixteen specified routes, BA was offering a cut in its revenues of £24m. and lost operating profits of £16m. Not altogether surprisingly, this did not go down well with BCal. Its chairman remarked that BA was 'arrogantly using a dominant position in an attempt to regulate the air transport industry. This apparent attempt to usurp the function of the CAA should be treated with the disdain it deserves.'

In the following days, a piped band delivered a BA petition to Downing Street with 27,000 signatures – and King returned openly to the fray. In a BBC radio interview, he reiterated the board's total intransigence: 'We will have to refuse to implement that part of the CAA Report which relates to the transfer of routes.' And in a stinging and effective feature article in *The Times* of 10 September, King wrote, 'Integrity of one's word is a vital necessity in all forms of human relationship in all walks of life', having reminded his readers that three Ministers before Ridley had guaranteed no arbitrary transfer of routes.

When the Cabinet meeting of 13 September arrived, the issue was postponed. All options, announced Ridley, were still open. Nothing could have made plainer that they were closing very fast. In fact, the discussion of principles was dead. All that remained was the horse-trading. None of King's friends had much doubt how that would end. Lord Hanson, chairman of Hanson Trust, sent King a sheet of notepaper inscribed with a few apt words: 'The victory is not always to the swift, nor the battle to the strong. But that's the way to bet.'

For three weeks, the British civil aviation industry seemed to be in a state of open civil war. BA suspended all its preparations for privatisation, supposedly still going ahead in less than six months' time. There was no point working for a sale, said King, if they were going to lose 30 per cent of their assets in the meantime!

There was more than one uncomfortable personal encounter between Ridley and King. Meeting at a cocktail party on one occasion, for example, Ridley startled onlookers by accusing King of orchestrating a move to force his resignation. Both men liked fishing and they were both engineers. Beyond that, the contrast could hardly have been deeper between the patrician politician, educated at Eton and Balliol, and the ebullient, self-made industrialist. It was well reflected in the striking physical disparity between them: the one tall and thin with a heavily lined face much given to anguished expressions between frequent cigarettes, the other stocky and apparently burdened with not a care in the world.

But King had a care all right, and was passionate in its

165

cause. On 21 September, he went to see Mrs Thatcher. Days later, the Prime Minister made clear that the fighting had to stop: Ridley had to have a solution ready for the Cabinet's approval before the start of the Tory party conference at Brighton on 9 October.

The Minister's position was almost hopeless. Unless those concerned were prepared to bow voluntarily to the CAA, implementing its ideas was always going to be difficult, whatever the circumstances. Ridley needed both a carrot and a stick to encourage a spirit of army-style voluntary cooperation. (The only alternative – enabling legislation – could scarcely be contemplated in the present mood of the Commons.) But the Government's prior commitment to privatising BA robbed him of the one carrot which might have been really effective: no sale before a reorganisation. And the BA campaign had shown the futility of trying to use a stick. In short, as Ridley and his advisers themselves concluded, all that remained for the Minister was to try to extract some concession from BA which might give the final agreement at least a measure of compromise for appearance's sake.

In the last week or so of September, King and Marshall were spending most of their time on a tour of provincial cities to win support from opinion-formers all over the country. (They visited Edinburgh, Glasgow, Belfast, Birmingham and Manchester.) From Whitehall came a series of increasingly urgent telephone calls exploring BA's reaction to a limited exchange of routes with BCal.

Throughout the month, BA had played a wily game by insisting at every turn that it could accept no route swaps which did not leave it with either the Atlanta or the Houston/Dallas routes to the US, both of which belonged to BCal. In the last days of the month, the Atlanta route emerged, for no very obvious reason in retrospect, as the last real bone of contention. So it was that the whole negotiation was concluded – perhaps a touch absurdly, given the issues – with BA making the grandly magnanimous gesture that it would surrender its demand for the

Atlanta route. It would give up, in other words, what it had never had in the first place.

Thomson watched the last days of the battle with a growing sense of bitterness. 'What we are seeing now,' he told the press on Monday, 1 October, 'is how the entrenched monopolistic interests are calling on short-term political expediency to wreck the last real attempt to create a strong airline industry for Britain which would be soundly based for future competition.'

On the Wednesday, Ridley told both sides that he had at last reached a decision. His long-awaited White Paper, entitled *Airline Competition Policy*, would be published that Friday, 5 October.

On the Thursday, King left St James's to take a flight to West Berlin for the monthly BA board meeting. (It is generally held in a different country each month.) He was waiting in the departure lounge at Heathrow when Marshall and Dunlop rushed in unexpectedly with some urgent news. Ridley's office had just communicated the terms of the compromise that the Minister was intending to announce twenty-four hours later. In essence, most of the CAA Report would be ignored. But BA would have to hand over its Jeddah and Dhahran routes to BCal in exchange for BCal's South American routes (which had been loss-making since the Falklands war in 1982). And there were any number of loose ends still to be tied up. The three executives conferred hurriedly about what to do. Finally, King went on to West Berlin – and a grand official reception – while Marshall and Dunlop raced back to Marsham Street to see Ridley and David Holmes.

Ridley's position offered several options for BA, for example over the possibility of a new route to the Falkland Islands. The BA directors argued as late as they dared for the best deal they thought they could get – then they caught the last plane, via Frankfurt, for West Berlin. As they waited in Frankfurt, Marshall spent half an hour on the telephone with Holmes . . .

Arriving at their hotel in West Berlin at 11.00 p.m., the

two men went straight up to King's suite. There, the rest of the directors were assembled waiting for them. What followed was one of the more curious board meetings in the history of the airline. The directors finally went off to their rooms at 1.00 a.m., resolved to accept the Ridley package. After another brief meeting of the board over breakfast on the 5th, Marshall and Dunlop returned to London. They were just in time for a press conference on the White Paper that afternoon.

The first sentence of the White Paper said it all: 'Uncertainties affecting the privatisation of BA must be resolved . . .'

The Saudi/South American route swaps were not the only significant changes. There was to be some reorganisation of BA's network as between Heathrow and Gatwick. BA was given an MoD contract to fly twice a week to the Falklands. CAA plans for deregulating UK domestic fares were approved. Above all, the Government committed itself to helping BCal win 'dual designation' on many of BA's routes and to working harder for a greater liberalisation of European skies generally. But there were no route transfers to BCal's fellow independents, no restrictions on BA operations at or beyond Heathrow and no plans to kick BA out of the charter market. In virtually every respect, the flag-carrier could fly on to the private sector with its dominance of the UK industry undiminished.

The CAA was 'disappointed'. Thomson bemoaned the loss of 'an historic occasion'. Ridley – saved at last from the flames – acknowledged that the July report had been viewed 'in the light of practical politics'.

For BA, Colin Marshall welcomed the White Paper, as well he might. The immaculate prospectus had survived. Privatisation could go ahead with its timetable unimpeded. Marshall must have felt that the rushing to and fro of the previous twenty-four hours had proved worthwhile. What he could not know was just how many last-minute flights and telephone dramas still lay ahead.

15

The Smoking Gun

The tug-of-war over the CAA Report had attracted most of the public attention given to BA through the summer and early autumn of 1984. Behind the scenes, though, the airline's struggle with the law had moved dangerously closer to more than one climax of its own.

Three days after the release of the CAA Report on 16 July, Christopher Morris and Bob Beckman were sitting together in the Touche Ross boardroom in Little New Street. They had plenty to talk about.

The House of Lords appeal, begun on 5 June, had lasted until 19 June. The last day had been quite an occasion. The barristers had brought their wives along; Morris and Beckman had retrieved posted notices of the hearing to adorn their office walls. But a month later, they were still awaiting the judgement. And if it went against the liquidator, it was not obvious what should be the next step.

Late in the morning of July 19th, the telephone rang with a call for Morris. It was a journalist from the *Daily Express* offices around the corner. 'You've won the Laker case, Mr Morris,' he said. 'I thought you'd like to know.' Morris gave no reaction and went off to check the situation. It was true. He hurried back to the boardroom and announced the news to Beckman. The American gave a great whoop of joy. It was the kind of thing that usually only happened to him on 10 November each year.

The two men jumped into a taxi and went straight down to the House of Lords. Several people from BA and

British Caledonian had beaten them to it. The disconsolate executives were sitting around in the main hall of the Palace of Westminster: they could barely conceal their gloom. Morris and his lawyer grabbed copies of the full judgement and stood reading it in the corridor. It was almost too good to be true: a unanimous verdict – 5–0!

But true it was – or very shortly became so, once all the parties had filed into the chamber of the House and heard Lord Diplock present it as a motion for their Lordships to approve. There were very few there, as usual on such occasions. But the ceremony was no less impressive for all the parties to the action. They were witnessing, they knew, an historic judgement. It reduced the July 1983 injunction to rubble. The Court of Appeal's judgement was swept aside and the ruling of Mr Justice Parker, adorned with lavish praise from their Lordships, was restored to its original place. BA and BCal found themselves turned out of the English courts, with the door slammed behind them – and nowhere left to shelter from Judge Greene's angry summons. Lord Diplock, Lord Fraser of Tullybelton, Lord Scarman, Lord Roskill and Lord Brightman had produced a judgement which caused some surprise, not to say widespread disappointment, and considerable legal controversy.

Morris had challenged the Government's right to invoke the 1980 Protection of Trading Interests Act, which had apparently barred the British defendants from participating in the Washington court. The Appeal Court had seen the PTIA as the principal justification for its permanent injunction against him. The five Law Lords upheld the Government's action – but concluded that the Appeal Court had been wrong to see the PTIA in quite such black-and-white terms.

The 1980 Act was not necessarily a bar to the British airlines' participation in the case, said the Lords. If triple damages were to be awarded in a US judgement against the airlines, for instance, the PTIA would be no protection. More pertinently, perhaps, the PTIA's general

170

block on disclosure of documents did allow for exceptions to be made by the Secretary of State in response to specific requests. If anything, said the Lords, this made the PTIA a powerful ally for the British airlines' counsel. Where they wanted to keep a document under wraps, they would have the Government's June 1983 order as a pretext for withholding it. Where a document struck them as useful to their case, they could seek consent to reveal it – which the Government would presumably grant, in keeping with the spirit of the original Act!

Having pulled away the foundations of the Appeal Court argument, the Lords picked off the rest, brick by brick. They stressed the importance of the fact that the US was the only legal forum for Morris to press his claim. They acknowledged that Laker had effectively joined the scheduled airlines' club; but they rejected the view that this precluded him from complaining about the club's rules. One could elect to tramp into the jungle, in other words, and still cry foul if the beasts turned nasty. A protest in such circumstances, to use the legal terminology, was not to be held 'unconscionable'.

As for the illegality of the beasts' behaviour, that was a question for those who would interpret the Bermuda II treaty. The Lords said they would not and could not. (Their only reservation about Mr Justice Parker's ruling was that he had strayed in that direction.) The critical point was that the treaty had no standing in English law. But it was recognised under US law: so the US courts would have to deal with it. They would have to judge the implications of the fact that, as it appeared from the evidence, price-fixing sessions had been held by the airlines without the formalities needed to obtain antitrust immunity.

The Lords only addressed themselves to the underlying question of international law with respect to the longer term. If the absence of antitrust immunity meant breaches had been made in Bermuda II, with domestic legal consequences in the US, then it was clear that UK public interests were involved. The most appropriate remedy would be action at a diplomatic level by the two governments concerned. In the meantime, though, it would be 'a total denial of justice' to prevent Morris from pursuing Laker, unobstructed by the English courts.

Or so the House of Lords decreed on 19 July 1984.

There were many who doubted the wisdom of their Lordships on this occasion. Admittedly, too many incompatible expectations had existed. 'They were all disappointed,' wrote A. H. Hermann, legal correspondent of the *Financial Times* and author of a noted work on the issues involved.*

The critics had at least three good points. The judgement left the workings of the PTIA shrouded in confusion. It also disclaimed any interpretation of Bermuda II – yet that was exactly what the judgement amounted to, insofar as it accepted that actions in the area covered by the treaty were susceptible to domestic US law. Had not that been the bone of contention between the two governments all along? Above all, the judgement acknowledged that British public policy was involved – and promptly ignored it. The unedifying spectacle of the judiciary and the executive moving in opposite directions was just the anomaly the Master of the Rolls had warned about, the year before, and it left many Washington observers grateful but perplexed. There was much loose talk in the British press about John Hampden, Charles I's ship money and the glory of the English constitution. It ignored the awkward fact that this was not some domestic feud, but a clash between government and judges over a vital matter of relations with a foreign state.

The Government reacted with understandable consternation. For Whitehall's lawyers were only too aware that trial by jury in the civil action posed an inevitable risk for BA and its privatisation plan. Worse than that, by the summer Whitehall was becoming genuinely anxious

* A. H. Hermann, 'Conflicts of National Laws with International Business Activity: Issues of Extraterritoriality' (1982).

about the progress of the Grand Jury investigation. Its proceedings were strictly confidential. Still, there was a strong suspicion that BA was going to be on the receiving end of some pronouncement fairly soon. This could be a double blow now, spurring on the efforts of Morris, Beckman and all their colleagues as well as landing BA in the US criminal court.

There was only one course open to the Government: heavy action through diplomatic channels. So while Beckman busied himself making up for lost time against BA and BCal – notice was served of depositions against twenty BA personnel in August alone – the Department of Transport, the DTI, the Attorney General Sir Michael Havers (who was taking an intense personal interest in the issue, with hostile intent), the Foreign Office and its Washington embassy . . . all went to work behind the scenes to bring off a daunting piece of sabotage. Their target: the Grand Jury investigation.

In US constitutional terms, a President who aborts the work of a Grand Jury is pushing hard against the limits even of the White House's powers. Between 1945 and 1984, it had happened only twice. President Truman, at the very end of his second term in 1952, had squashed an investigation into the international oil industry which had threatened to embarrass US interests in the Middle East; an investigation into the domestic US copper industry was snapped shut at the beginning of the sixties. Neither precedent much worried the Justice Department in 1984. The evidence put before the Grand Jury was beginning to shape up into a real case. The DoJ was determined to pursue it.

What very few outsiders appeared to suspect, however, was that the DoJ's case was emphatically not an echo of the civil suit. Astonishingly enough, in some key respects it was exactly the opposite. Morris saw Laker Airways as the victim of a conspiracy to cut Atlantic fares, albeit temporarily until Laker had been bankrupted. The Grand Jury saw Laker as one of the principals in a conspiracy to fix Atlantic fares, occasionally leaving them – irony of ironies – higher than they might otherwise have been.

It had not always looked like this. Back in 1983, Freddie himself had appeared before the Grand Jury and emerged something of a hero. He gave evidence behind closed doors for two days, while the ever-faithful Beckman waited in the corridor outside. Occasional bursts of laughter from the courtroom suggested that Freddie was exerting his usual magic. When his testimony was over, the Grand Jury broke into applause and Freddie emerged to greet Beckman, with people offering their congratulations from every side. Over the following months, however, the picture of a martyred Freddie Laker began to pick up some interference. The vertical hold slipped for good in the middle of November 1983.

What the DoJ placed before the Grand Jury were documents suggesting that Skytrain, from its earliest days in 1977, had relied heavily on a succession of secret understandings with British Airways – and possibly others – over North Atlantic fare schedules. Especially notable was the following internal memorandum:

From: JOHN JONES	To: SIR FREDDIE LAKER
	c.c. R. ROBINSON
Subject/Ref:	Date: 9th NOVEMBER 1978

In accordance with our discussions the following proposal was made to British Airways:

In consideration for British Airways standing aside from any objection to the currently proposed amendment to our Skytrain Licence, Laker Airways would revise the Skytrain fare structure with effect from 1 April 1979 as follows:

| BASIC | £65 Westbound | $149 Eastbound |
| PEAK | £75 Westbound | $169 Eastbound |

(Peak Season Westbound – 24 July to 31 August
Peak Season Eastbound – 04 July to 15 August)

On condition that:

a) British Airways maintain a differential of at least £7 Westbound or $15 Eastbound over the above Skytrain rates.
b) That British Airways took Pan Am and TWA with them on the above agreement.

If any of the above conditions fail to be satisfied then the proposal made by Laker would no longer be valid.

British Airways further indicated that if Laker were to apply to the Civil Aviation Authority to vary the Skytrain Licence to remove the tariff provisions from the body of the Licence and make these subject to normal filing requirements, subject to the 75 day prior filing requirements of the Bermuda Air Agreement, they would not object.

(Signed)

John Jones

Here, in Washington's court vernacular, was Laker nabbed holding the smoking gun: a memorandum to the chief executive from one of his own senior employees confirming price-fixing arrangements. No document could possibly have crystallised the DoJ's suspicions more sharply – or the grounds for its opposition to the British approach. Meetings of this kind were positively encouraged by the CAA in London. Its officials expected scheduled carriers to discuss their tariff structures together before presenting them for the CAA's approval. This was what Mr Jones had evidently been doing with BA – at one of a series of meetings, concluding with an agreed price differential between BA tariffs and those of Skytrain . . .

But wait a minute, said the DoJ officials. Laker was not even a member of IATA. Even if it had been, this kind of meeting and discussion could only possibly be considered immune to antitrust prosecution if held formally under the aegis of Bermuda II, then filed and accepted by the Civil Aviation Bureau (CAB) in Washington. And as Jones had obligingly noted in the last paragraph of his memorandum, the Skytrain tariffs at that time were not yet the subject of normal filing requirements!

If any member of the Grand Jury still wondered where the investigation was leading, he must have known by the end of a two-day session on 15–16 November, 1983. John Jones appeared in person before the jury and delivered himself of a candid and comprehensive 'debriefing'. What he revealed was an astounding rebuttal of the idea that Laker Airways' Skytrain had ever been an innocent party fallen amongst predators. Instead, he presented a chronicle of Skytrain's affairs which would have sounded familiar to any student of competitive practices between international airlines for years past – what Anthony Sampson has summarised as being 'chiefly a question of air-routes and frequencies which have been thrashed out in hundreds of tough secret deals . . .'*

Jones described many deals and many meetings: at BA's Victoria Air Terminal in London . . . at the Intercontinental Hotel opposite Hyde Park . . . in bedrooms at the Waldorf. His evidence, in fact, presented a fair picture of the close and not unfriendly relations which had existed between Laker and BA between 1977 and 1981. The dramatis personae of his briefing included men like Hugh Welburn, the BA executive generally credited with the invention of the Apex cheap fare and a long-standing admirer of Sir Freddie. BA itself had a worthy history of trying to push through radical pricing initiatives against IATA opposition. The two British airlines, Laker and BA, emerged on more than one occasion from Jones's testimony as quasi-allies in the rough-and-tumble of the global industry.

* Anthony Sampson, *Empires of the Sky: The Politics, Contests and Cartels of World Airlines* (1984).

176

Unfortunately for BA, that was not the only message which came across to the Grand Jury. As Jones's testimony recorded it:

> They [counsel for the DoJ] asked whether I thought Monks [a BA negotiator] was aware that discussions were a breach of anti-trust violations and I explained that I thought it very likely as during the period of the five years that we'd been speaking to British Airways phrases like 'the illegal telephone' had been used. I was aware on one occasion that a British Airways official flew to New York to have discussions face to face rather than use the telephone at all and during all of the discussions with Monk and others it was made clear that these were very sensitive matters and, therefore, it was very likely that he was aware that there was some risk attached.

It was exactly the kind of colourful evidence that UK officials had feared might surface when they pressed the DoJ not to launch an investigation in February 1983. Whitehall lawyers could read out Bermuda II clauses until the cows came home; but was that going to expunge the impression left on any jury by talk of illegal telephones and the like?

There were even more graphic passages in Jones's evidence. Take, for example, this description of a notably bizarre meeting with a group of BA executives:

> On the 16th of July [1981], Sir Freddie Laker and I went to Victoria Air Terminal and because there was building work going on [in] the tower block where the meeting was scheduled, we had to take a somewhat devious route getting lost on the roof-tops [sic] and being redirected by Charles Stuart [of BA] who happened to be having lunch with travel agents to the Board Room where we were

meeting with Ossie Cochrane, Bernard Monk,
John Elliot, perhaps John Meredith, perhaps Hugh
Welburn. At the meeting on the 16th of July, the
fares sheet that I had prepared with comparative
analysis of our fares and British Airways fares . . .
was examined and I explained the writing in the
differential column which was Sir Freddie's and my
own figures . . .

When the time came in October and November 1984 for
the defendants' lawyers to cross-examine the Laker boss
himself, Freddie was led painstakingly through every
available detail of meetings like this one.

There was one other aspect of the Jones testimony
which must have excited the particular interest of his
American audience. The alleged purpose of the 16 July
meeting was to agree the discount which Laker's
competitors would be prepared to see it offering on the
tickets for Skytrain's Regency service. This was to be
Laker's first foray into the first-class travellers' market.
It was to be announced in the autumn and Freddie
knew the other carriers would be extremely nervous
about it.

The Laker employee referred many times to his own
firm impression that, on 16 July and on subsequent
occasions, BA had been acting on the basis of a clear
understanding between itself and the other leading
carriers, TWA and Pan Am:

[Laker] subsequently filed on the 31st of July a
package which consisted of a differential of £15 and
£10 respectively on the peak shoulder and low
season Apex fares . . . this was advised as being
larger than British Airways could accept subsequent to that filing in a telephone call with Bernard
Monk [of BA]. He telephoned to say that other
carriers were concerned and I took this to mean
TWA and Pan Am . . .

Jones was quite explicit on the point. Indeed, he even recalled a time when someone had handed him a paper that 'had to be a Pan Am document because the underlining was not of the type that anyone at Laker Airways had ever used . . .' And Freddie, during his own deposition in 1984, was going to emphasise the same point many times.

Freddie's allegations in this respect were at the heart of his often repeated insistence that 'the truth should be told'. He himself had more than one chance to tell it. Here, for example, is Freddie replying to a question from Beckman during his 9 October 1984 deposition about the basis of Freddie's stated understanding that BA was acting throughout in cahoots with TWA and Pan Am:

> British Airways knew full well and knows full well and so do I, and so does Pan American and TWA, that it isn't possible to make an agreement like this without all the parties going along. It just isn't possible and it's inherent in the whole structure of the IATA type of airline business. It's inherent. There's no way that any agreement that would give advantages or otherwise to a competitor could possibly, it just couldn't, happen without the IATA airlines agreeing to the total agreement.

So, as the investigation went into 1984, DoJ officials started to push hard for any evidence which could be used to tie the US carriers into the prosecution case which was slowly emerging. They used every means at their disposal under domestic law. They followed up all the leads provided by the various Laker Airways' documents and testimonies. They went through the US carriers' papers. They brought a string of US airline executives before the Grand Jury. And the result of all their efforts was: nothing.

TWA and Pan Am publicly protested their innocence at every opportunity. There was no documentary evidence to contradict them. They flatly denied that they

179

had ever been a party – directly or indirectly – to the sort of pricing talks so vividly described by Freddie and his staff. As for his homilies about IATA, that was exactly why they had left IATA in the late seventies, said the two big US carriers. Both airlines, whom so many Washington lawyers had rather suspected at the outset might be tripped up by the Laker saga sooner or later, were emerging unscathed.

By midsummer, British Government officials were becoming aware of the US airlines' position. It caused considerable puzzlement. And indeed, to many outsiders, the subtleties of US antitrust law were beginning to look unfathomable. After all, there was no dispute that Pan Am and TWA had charged exactly the same fares over the Atlantic during that crucial period from October 1981 to February 1982 when the alleged conspiracy against Laker had supposedly reached its climax. The US carriers had matched Laker and BA fares, dollar for dollar and pound for pound. What could be plainer than that?

Alas, it was not so simple. In US antitrust law, plots amongst competitors to rig a market in some way – so-called 'horizontal conspiracies' – do not require one party to write to another, 'Dear Bill, I have this market-rigging idea . . .' The law is sharper than that: it acknowledges that any self-respecting conspiracy is far more likely to consist of nods and winks in high places. The existence of a conspiracy, in other words, has often to be inferred from circumstantial evidence of changes in the relevant marketplace.

But are two competitors to be accused of conspiracy whenever, say, they charge identical prices for their goods? No, say the US lawyers. It is possible, indeed quite likely, that competitors in some industries will have a perfectly innocent marketing pretext for matching each other's prices exactly. (There are in fact numerous industries where this happens every day.) So the law recognises this kind of action, calls it 'conscious parallelism' and takes care to sever any automatic link between its presence and the inference of a conspiracy.

All of which, not surprisingly, has carved out a new face deep inside the mountains of US corporate law, bearing a seam rich in ambiguity and matters of degree. Where two companies act together in the marketplace, are they just indulging in conscious parallelism? Or are they betraying conclusive circumstantial evidence of those nods and winks?

The cases of Pan Am and TWA had DoJ officials scrutinising their case law with the utmost care. It was not encouraging. There was even one civil case with more than a passing similarity to the Atlantic fares battle. A gentleman called Jack Weit had launched a suit in 1980 against five big banks, alleging a conspiracy by them over credit card interest rates. The courts had established a motive for the conspiracy, opportunities to arrange it and even examples of identical behaviour in the marketplace. But in 1981, after a succession of appeals, it had all been put down to conscious parallelism by the banks (which included Continental Illinois in Chicago) and Mr Weit lost his case.

The DoJ feared the same view might be taken of the behaviour of the US airlines if it charged them with conspiracy – either against Laker, as alleged in the civil suit, or in league with Laker, as the DoJ thought applied to BA. In the words of a treatise recently published by the Antitrust Law Section of the American Bar Association: 'By itself, mere conscious parallelism will not compel a finding of concerted action . . . Conversely, where each defendant has legitimate business reasons that would rationally lead it independently to engage in the challenged conduct, the inference of conspiracy is weakened.'

In short, the case against Pan Am and TWA looked highly contentious – unless, of course, some trace of another smoking gun could be found for the Grand Jury with US fingerprints, as it were, clearly on the trigger.

And the search for this, ironically, led the DoJ men directly to the door of those officials in London who were still anxious to undermine the whole investigation.

For in some ways the most promising line of attack for the DoJ against the US carriers promised to be a full frontal assault on their participation in formal IATA-type discussions. There were the July/August 1977 talks at the CAB – the starting point, in Beckman's complaint, of the predatory pricing scheme against Laker – and there were the IATA talks at Hollywood, Florida in January 1982, where Pan Am and TWA had at least been present. To challenge the legitimacy of these talks, however, was to go straight to the heart of the intergovernment row over Bermuda II. And the British sabotage campaign was now becoming desperate. In mid-September, Sir Michael Havers, the UK Attorney General, flew to a meeting in Washington with Fred Fielding, President Reagan's White House counsel. There were long talks, involving officials from the DoJ directly. As a sop to British interests, it was finally agreed that the 1977 meeting and the Hollywood meeting should be dropped entirely from the DoJ's agenda.

So what was left? Quite simply, the evidence of senior BA personnel like Hugh Welburn, Gerry Draper and the others named in that incriminating John Jones testimony. Their revelations might indeed have been intriguing. (There was that meeting at the CAA on 16 October 1981, for example, to review Pan Am's new cut-price fares. BA had sided with Laker and opposed them in the morning. After lunch, it had apologised for misstating its true position and had changed sides, leaving Laker alone against all the big carriers. The conspiracy theory alleged that BA and Pan Am had consorted in the interval. The innocent explanation was that in the early afternoon [London time], BA officials had arrived at work in the US and discovered to their dismay that Laker had clearance from the US authorities to launch its new Regency service, threatening the big carriers' first-class traffic head-on for the first time ever. Which was the true version of events?) But the UK Government refused point blank to allow the BA men to appear before the jury.

At a senior government level, the Americans pointed out to the British that their refusal was obstructing the possibility of an indictment against TWA and Pan Am. It made no difference.

By October 1984, indeed, nothing that the US Government could say in mitigation of the Grand Jury's work was going to make any difference. The British Prime Minister had become involved. Mrs Thatcher was absolutely adamant that the British airlines should have no truck with the investigation – and the DoJ, what is more, had to be forced into abandoning it. She would be Chief Saboteur herself, if that was what was needed. The extraordinary judgement in the House of Lords, as the UK Government saw it, had been irksome enough. To have a department of the US Government spurring the civil suit along with all this talk of a criminal indictment as well – it was simply intolerable, said the Prime Minister. BA in every other respect had made the most remarkable progress: the airline was at last ready for privatisation. It was time to grasp a few nettles and sort out all this legal nonsense over Laker.

And this was the moment at which the Americans delivered their bombshell. A senior US Government delegation arrived in London to give Mrs Thatcher and her colleagues a friendly private warning. The Grand Jury's investigation was nearing its close. The DoJ was about to launch a criminal prosecution over air transport between the UK and the US. The charges would allege price-fixing and market allocation conspiracies. One of the defendants – perhaps even the only one! – would be BA.

16

The Numbers Game

Relations between BA and the Transport Department were edgy from the start, that October of 1984. The personalities involved had been so often out of sympathy that this was probably inevitable, even had there never been the bruising confrontation over the CAA Report. Each side, too, sometimes struck the other as the embodiment of its worst fears about any involvement beyond the great divide separating the public and the private sectors.

The civil servants saw themselves as the victims of endless indiscretions, impatience over details, blustering attitudes in negotiation and tunnel-vision blindness to all the complex issues raised by the sale in Whitehall. The businessmen in their turn thought they were having to put up with incessant dithering, mysterious delays, constant resort to minutes and memoranda to discuss all points great and small, and long, tedious meetings to surmount even the most obvious of obstacles.

Whatever the difficulties, though, the sale preparations were back in full swing by the second week of October. Work on the prospectus, so rudely interrupted by the CAA row in July and shelved since then, was resumed at drafting meetings between the airline and the civil servants – each with their patient City retainers – on Tuesday or Wednesday of each week through the next two months.

The first critical issue to be decided was obviously the timetable for the sale. King and his board were not too interested in detailed analysis of dates: they wanted to go at the earliest possible moment and made no bones about it. The professional advisers on both sides – that is, for the airlines and for the Government – had to judge that moment with a weather eye for all sorts of complications, however. It was manifest that a huge amount had still to be done.

It was not just policy decisions that still needed to be settled, though work on BA's totally unsaleable balance sheet had hardly yet begun. Arguably even more pressing were the practical steps which had to be set in motion as part of the basic mechanics of the sale. Which overseas markets, if any, were to be offered shares in the primary flotation? Which perks, if any, should be dangled in front of small investors? Which advertising agency should the Government appoint? (BA insisted adamantly that its own agency, Saatchi & Saatchi, could be left to get on with it – especially since Dorlands, which was handling British Telecom so successfully, was its sister company. But Whitehall had matching advisers of its own on every other front and did not want to make an exception over advertising.) And how much time would have to elapse between British Telecom's sale and the launch of the BA campaign?

The Treasury as usual kept its real views about timing closely under wraps. But the message which went out to the Transport Department stressed urgency at every turn. (As the old joke has it, this started out as 'Send us reinforcements, we're going to advance . . .') Transport Department officials then laid it on good and thick for the City: the Chancellor, it was told, wanted the proceeds of selling BA to be paid over within the financial year ending in April 1985. ('. . . Send us three-and-fourpence, we're going to a dance', as the message had become by the time it reached the end of the line.) As the weeks passed, the advisers were put under more and more pressure to stick to an outline timetable which had been agreed as early as August.

February 14 1985 was its target date. No one pushed

it harder than King and his board; but it had its own credibility amongst the civil servants. St Valentine's Day, it was thought, came long enough after the beginning of December to avoid the risk of a market overlap with British Telecom which was proceeding nicely towards the private sector that autumn. And it came far enough ahead of mid-March to avoid any intrusion on the pre-budget purdah observed everywhere in Whitehall. So 14 February it was to be.

Accepting this, Hill Samuel began to ponder the marketing for a sale date of 14 February. It would have to begin with an all-singing, all-dancing roadshow for the investing institutions starting as early as possible in the New Year. Invitations, to be sure of missing the Christmas post chaos, would therefore be despatched in the first week of December. Once the invitations had gone out, there could be no looking back – or else the privatisation of BA, after so many delays since 1979, might have to be postponed for good. So Hill Samuel fixed on the planned posting day, 3 December, as the point-of-no-return in the sale timetable.

There was just one other little matter which had been tabled back in August, along with the 14 February date. This was a concern raised by Hill Samuel amongst others over the Laker litigation. The merchant bank knew there were plenty of civil servants who were by now haunted with anxiety over Bermuda II, the Grand Jury investigation and all the associated problems. The bankers were anxious not to be seen as teaching granny to suck eggs. But when October arrived, they were still taking pains to stress that the sale prospectus would need to provide convincing comfort for the investor, over the Laker civil suit as well as the Grand Jury business . . .

Bermuda II was therefore one of the running discussion points through October, even in the City. The Government was already looking at the possibility of thoroughly renegotiating it – perhaps even looking for a Bermuda III treaty to replace it – and care would have to be taken over any references in the prospectus to the US/UK air services agreement, to ensure they were not upstaged by events.

There was also a move by BA's board to initiate discussions of a government indemnity for the airline against US legal problems, though this did not get very far. The general presumption in Whitehall was that, somehow and at some stage, the lawyers would either settle matters out of court or else provide adequate reassurance to satisfy potential investors. Both solutions were indeed being explored throughout the autumn by lawyers on either side of the Atlantic – though the quip about two peoples separated by a common language had never, for some observers, seemed more apposite.

But it was the financial shape of BA which was at last moving to centre stage in the privatisation preparations. The airline moved into its new West End headquarters at about this time: Enserch House, a newly refurbished address in St James's adjacent to the Libyan Embassy and only a stone's throw from King's personal office at Babcock & Wilcox's Cleveland House. As the board members settled down into their new premises, there was one problem above all others which struck them as central to the pre-sale talks: BA's capital structure. The 14 February target date lent the search for a solution more than a note of urgency.

BA needed government cash, and a lot of it, if there was to be the faintest chance of attracting investors in the near future. The question was: how much would the Government be prepared to hand over?

At one level, the figures were relatively straightforward. The critical equation was the proportion of BA's total net debt to its shareholders' equity, the so-called gearing ratio. In the US, airlines were just emerging from years of dire recession with balance sheets which typically paraded as much debt as equity – a high proportion, which was widely reckoned in the City to be less than ideal for BA at its debut. Price Waterhouse's

1982 Report had recommended a 25:75 ratio for debt/ equity. Certainly the British carrier was going to need an exceptionally good sale story if it arrived in the marketplace with debt/equity ranking worse than 50:50 in its balance sheet. Yet at the end of March 1984, the BA balance sheet boasted shareholders' equity of exactly £126m. Piled up on this meagre base was no less than £901m. of gross debts. Even reducing this amount marginally to take account of BA's cash, the gearing emerged wildly over the top, with about seven times as much debt as equity.

The much improved operating performance of the airline since March at least offered a grain or two of comfort. The research report which Phillips & Drew and Wood, Mackenzie had been labouring over so hard for much of the summer was finally published during October. With the kind of precision considered normal in the City in such matters, the stockbrokers forecast net earnings of £183m. for the year 1984–5. Adding this £183m. to the March 1984 equity and deducting the same sum from the March net debt figure produced a putative debt/equity gearing of roughly 7:3 – which, as it happened, translated as £700m. of debt and £300m. of equity. With the help of such conveniently round numbers, the City quickly came up with a consensus view that BA, to be sellable in the stock market, would probably need those figures to be reversed. At the very least, though, it woud still need to see debt no heavier than equity. In other words, it would need a cash injection by the Government of between £200m. and £400m. – and BA, naturally, wanted £400m.

So much for the basic figures.

Gordon Dunlop, presiding over BA's privatisation team, was not expecting Her Majesty's Treasury to hand over £400m. with a smile. The prevailing wisdom was that the total proceeds of the sale would amount to about £1,000m. (Assuming BA paid a dividend of £70m., this would imply a yield of 7 per cent, which would compare nicely with the yield offered on British Telecom's forth-coming issue.) The BA board was privately expecting the Treasury to question the very idea of hidden subsidies to the airline – which is what any cash injection would amount to – but a request for £400m. might be a useful opening gambit in the balance-sheet negotiations.

(The airline's expectations were to be amply fulfilled, though the basis of the Treasury's opposition to a subsidy was not always clearly appreciated. Some com-mentators thought that 'returning' a large portion of the sale proceeds in order to salvage BA's balance sheet would have a damaging impact on the PSBR. But there were several ways to skin the balance-sheet cat: the Treasury had the accounting means to adopt as much BA debt as it wanted, without affecting public expenditure or the PSBR in the slightest. Something else concerned the gentlemen of Great George Street rather more, however – particularly after the summer's events. This was the danger of upsetting Sir Adam Thomson at BCal, as well as the rest of the civil aviation industry, by being seen to bolster BA's cash resources just as it entered the private sector.)

Dunlop and his advisers had at least three arguments for seeking public money. These were pushed hard as October wore on and the days were ticked off towards 3 December – and they got a wide airing in the media, too. (King made sure the press knew about the 14 February target. If this annoyed the civil servants – and it did – it put even more pressure on both sides, as intended, to come up with a figure very soon.)

The first of BA's arguments was really an exercise in market sophistry. The more the Government injected into BA, the less the airline would have to spend on interest payments and the higher would be its net earnings figure. This, it could be argued, might mean a double benefit for the sale price. If the City clung to an unchanged price/earnings multiple as the basis for BA's valuation, the higher earnings would entail a higher price. More than that, though: the lower interest payments might be seen by the market as improving the quality of BA's earnings and justifying a higher price/earnings multiple into the bargain.

But as BA deliberated over its balance-sheet requirements through October, there were two rather meatier issues on its plate – both of them concerned with the airline's fleet.

Few areas of their subject give accountants more hours of harmless fun than the treatment of leases. There are two species of lease, either of which can apply to any asset whether it be a typewriter or a Boeing jet aircraft.

Species One is a financial lease: it requires a company to show its future lease obligations as liabilities on its balance sheet. BA in March 1984 had nearly £130m. in this category, contributing to its £900m. of total debt.

Species Two is an operating lease: future obligations under this heading, happily for some, are not required on the balance sheet. This was the vehicle of the compromise struck with the Transport Department in 1983 over the purchase of a new short-haul fleet: those fourteen Boeing 737s (plus two more ordered since, making sixteen in all) had been acquired via an operating lease so that their £270m. cost would not appear on BA's balance sheet. But – and this had been one of Whitehall's concerns the previous year – the £270m. was heading rapidly in the balance sheet's direction. For after three years, BA would have to return the 737s or switch them on to financial leases (which do not entail the lessor taking back his assets). BA's balance-sheet debt would then swell accordingly.

The third argument for pressing for the £400m. remittance was the most basic of all: BA would in all probability be spending far more on its capital investment needs than even its own stockbrokers were anticipating. The cash-flow projections in the Phillips & Drew/Wood, Mackenzie report, for example, showed surpluses of £200m. or more for 1986 and 1987. But as BA soon made

clear to Whitehall, rising expenditure on the new genera-
tion of wide-bodied aircraft and longer-range versions of
existing Rolls-Royce engines – specifically, the new D-4
engines for the fleet's existing Boeing 747 jumbos – could
soon leave these surplus expectations looking very
optimistic indeed.

Of course, when they got wind of this argument, many
of the civil servants smelt a rat immediately. The stockbrokers were supposed to have had every assistance
from the company in preparing their figures. So how
come the capital expenditure expectations had changed
so hugely in a matter of a few months (again)? The
suspicion began to grow amongst the civil servants that
BA's ample computer modelling facilities were whirring
overtime to produce whatever model the airline needed
to extract the maximum amount of money at each stage of
the talks.

There were other ulterior motives, too, which BA hardly
bothered to deny. It was always keen, for example,
to take any opportunity of reminding the Government
that Heathrow's expansion was A Good Thing. The
relevance of the point here was quickly apparent. If the
Government allowed Heathrow to take an expanded
volume of traffic as BA wanted, all would be well. If
the Government clamped down on the traffic, then BA
would have to invest immediately in new, wide-bodied
aircraft like the Boeing 767. And that would add to the
capital expenditure forecasts . . .

These and a score of similar issues carried the numbers
game between the Government and the airline far
beyond any simple talk of a 7:3 ratio.

There were plenty of sources of tension elsewhere,
too. The civil Laker litigation difficulty, for example, was
still lingering obstinately in the background. In September, Colin Marshall wrote to BA's Washington lawyers,
Paul, Weiss, asking the firm to begin discussions with
Linklaters & Paines, the London solicitors with primary
responsibility for the sale prospectus. BA, still assuming

no real likelihood of a settlement (not in the near term, at least), wanted the two firms to agree together how the litigation problem might best be referred to in the prospectus. But by early October, no obvious solution to this problem was forthcoming and both the Transport Department and Hill Samuel were becoming distinctly uneasy about it. BA was asked to secure the strongest possible protection in writing that Paul, Weiss thought itself able to provide.

The result was a note from Paul, Weiss, which was sent round by BA to David Holmes at the Department on 23 October. To the merchant bankers, at least, it did not look substantially different from earlier statements provided by BA: the Laker case, investors could still be told, was without foundation. Significantly, however, Paul, Weiss were troubled enough about the litigation to advise that it could offer no 'expertising' in the prospectus. This is legal jargon for a form of words from the lawyers which goes rather beyond loose reassurance and adds up to a formal opinion which offers some protection for the directors signing the prospectus. Paul, Weiss simply felt too unsure of the ground to step down this road.

At this point, the BA board got down to the serious business of finalising its balance-sheet demands and the financial plan for the next five years which it was about to submit to the Government. Both these matters were reviewed fully at a board meeting on 26 October. A week later, on 2 November, the board formally approved the move to request £400m. as an integral part of its five-year plan.

When the plan went in, the airline's chairman attached a mischievously worded covering letter to the Transport Secretary. He was 'glad', wrote King on 31 October, to be able to tell the Government that, as a result of all the hard work put in by BA's staff and employees, the Treasury could look forward to retaining over 50 per cent of the proceeds of selling the airline to the public.

To the Secretary and his advisers, the letter was salt

where they needed balm. Officials from Washington were due in London the very next day for critical talks over the Grand Jury's conclusions. Not only that, but Hill Samuel and the civil servants were still far from satisfied about the intentions of the US and English lawyers vis-à-vis the Laker suit. What were the implications of Paul, Weiss's cautious approach? Did the sale require a stronger go-ahead from the lawyers or not?

At the end of October, in a bid to clarify the legal options once and for all, the Government appointed a firm of US lawyers of its own to provide another opinion on the matter even at this late stage! So it was no wonder King's letter was received with something less than enthusiasm. BA was busy, as the rugby coaches put it, getting its retaliation in first to prepare for the financial scrum – while the civil servants were trying their utmost to protect the pitch against an invasion of troublemakers wielding multimillion-dollar suits and a criminal indictment against the airline!

BA's commercial story since 1979 and the tangled legal chronicle since 1982 were, in fact, about to become inseparable.

17

The Convergence of the Twain

Until this moment late in 1984, top executives at BA had invariably pursued their privatisation goal with hardly a thought for the relevance of the legal background. And the lawyers working on the action before Judge Greene's court had scarcely had reason, amidst all the other international legal implications of their case, to pause for contemplation of BA's commercial background.

King's letter of 31 October, the appointment of US lawyers to the Government and the arrival of the American officials at the start of November launched a month that was to change all that. The next few weeks were to see a crunching Convergence of the Twain.

First on the agenda was the bad news from the US Justice Department. The official bilateral talks at the start of November were proceeded by various delicate approaches by the Americans, designed to soften up Ministers inside and outside the Cabinet about what to expect. Their efforts were in vain. In fact, they only raised the temperature of the proceedings still higher. UK officials and even Sir Michael Havers, the Attorney-General, made hasty and unpublicised trips backwards and forwards across the Atlantic in a last-ditch attempt to pre-empt the DoJ's moves.

The British had already indicated their attitude by disallowing applications from the North Atlantic carriers for lower fares from 1 November. The fares had reluctantly to be rejected, said the Transport Department, because the US authorities had been unable to guarantee they would not lead to antitrust proceedings. It was a transparent and unpopular gambit (not least with BA, which reacted defiantly); but it made the UK position usefully clear. The Americans made theirs clear, too. The DoJ had evidence of price-fixing and market allocation conspiracies. Charges would be levelled against BA. It was unclear whether Laker Airways would be a co-defendant or whether it would be cited only as a 'non-indicted co-conspirator'. The DoJ was mindful of the possible impact on privatisation and had therefore made various concessions; but the case itself could not be dropped in view of all the precedents.

It was hoped, said the Americans, that the absence of any predatory pricing charges and the blatant incon-sistency between the planned indictment and the civil antitrust case might even be helpful to the defence against the Laker suit. In the criminal court, meanwhile, BA could always plead no contest and might reasonably expect to get away with a fine of less than £2m.

These tidings sparked off one of the most uncomfort-able episodes in Anglo-American relations for years. Mrs Thatcher would have none of the DoJ's feeble palliatives. The indictments had to be abandoned or else, the Americans were told. The suggestion that BA might plead guilty and still hope for a happy outcome to the civil suit was castigated as ludicrously naive. There was simply no room whatever for compromise. The Prime Minister stayed her hand over a counteroffensive just long enough for President Reagan to be re-elected in his landslide victory on 6 November. Then she tore into his Administration with a passion which left US officials – and occasionally her own – at a loss for words.

Charles Price, the American Ambassador in London, retreated quite shaken from a private audience at Number Ten. His reception caused dismay in Whitehall, too: the Prime Minister was 'becoming almost obsessive about the American government's attitude', as one adviser later told *The Times*. There were plans afoot for Mrs Thatcher to call on President Reagan just before Christmas, on her way back

back from an official visit to the Far East. The Ambassador warned the White House what to expect, if the case against BA were not dropped. The President's men jumped to exactly the conclusion that Whitehall had feared. Assuming the case were still outstanding – a reasonable presumption, given the history of Grand Jury dismissals – the Christmas meeting should be cancelled.

Then a remarkable thing happened. President Reagan gave in. There were, he said, more important fish to fry. Give the lady what she wants.

No charges were being brought against Pan Am or TWA. Perhaps this made the decision easier. But it made no difference to the DoJ's bitterness. Its officials felt badly let down. They had, after all, been working on the indictment since February 1983! But there was no question of any remonstration. 'The Reagan people played hardball over this,' said a senior Washington lawyer on the touchline. 'Any questioning by the Justice Department would have prompted instant dismissals in the antitrust division.'

A few months later, one of the officials most closely involved with the investigation left the Department to go into private industry. His colleagues gave him the customary leaving present at his farewell party . . . and he gave his chief a Union Jack flag.

In London, the President's veto was announced on 19 November. At first, an almost palpable sense of relief swept through Whitehall. At long last, there were hopes in the Transport Department of an unimpeded run at BA's privatisation. But this mood did not last long. The realisation quickly dawned that the President's action had done nothing to improve the outlook for the civil suit. Indeed, it may even have worsened it. Who knew how a civil jury might react to an impassioned plea from Beckman that it was the last refuge for Laker in its search for justice? And the DoJ's thwarted intention of serving indictments for price-fixing conspiracies was being openly acknowledged in the US press!

As for the progress of the civil suit itself, on 9 October Judge Greene had actually gone so far in his court as to issue an injunction enjoining BA and British Caledonian from seeking assistance from their own Government, never mind the English courts. It was the very sovereignty of the Mother of Parliaments which was now in question! But why, came the demand from Number Ten, was there any reason – now that the criminal case had been abandoned – to put up with the indignity of the Laker Airways civil suit at all?

As it happened, Wald Harkrader & Ross, the US law firm hired by the Government at the end of October, were about to play a most useful role in focusing everyone's mind on this very question. Hill Samuel had asked about it countless times since 1983. The civil servants had asked about it. The lawyers working on the prospectus had even asked about it. And the answer had always been the same. The BA board and its advisers were confident that when the right time arrived, it would be handled with minimum disruption.

Yes, but how? Paul, Weiss had thought a great deal in recent months about the chances of negotiating an out-of-court settlement. They appeared to have concluded, for the moment, that there were just too many obstacles. But a satisfactory explanation of the law suit for investors' purposes was proving no easy matter, either. Paul, Weiss is not primarily renowned as a law firm experienced in prospectus matters of this kind. Yet theirs was a tough job. No one had sought before to put together a satisfactory description of the suit for the purposes of the marketplace.

Other circumstances had apparently made less onerous demands. Even BA's own auditors, Ernst & Whinney, had been happy with a four-and-a-half-line summary of the litigation threat for the airline's 1983–4 accounts. (Note 28: 'On 24 November 1982, the liquidator of Laker Airways Limited brought legal proceedings in the United States District Court for the District of Columbia against certain airlines, including British Airways, claiming that they had conspired to drive Laker out of business in violation of the federal antitrust laws. The complaint seeks treble damages in excess of $1 billion. British Airways believes that the complaint is unfounded and has answered denying all material allegations and asserting various affirmative defences [sic].')

The Grand Jury's investigation had not even been mentioned in the last annual report. A Glossary of Terms at the back of the report contained Load Factor and Punctuality; definitions of Treble Damages and Pricing Conspiracy might have been more relevant. Nor had the stockbrokers really questioned BA's guidance on the subject. The October report from the airline's brokers had reassured its readers ('Appendix 4: Laker Airways litigation'): 'It may be noted that three other airlines (Pan Am, TWA and KLM) all raised new capital in 1983, despite the existence of the Laker litigation.'

Alas, the US law firm with the name like a composite character out of *Star Wars* was a mite less sanguine.

The Government had used Wald Harkrader & Ross on a number of occasions in the past. They were regarded as especially knowledgeable about US antitrust questions. Their opinion of the Laker civil suit was that it entailed very considerable uncertainties for any prospective investor in BA; these might well require the kind of 'health warning' which would give the bankers and brokers to the sale a tricky problem – to say the very least.

Wald Harkrader presented this gloomy view at a meeting with government officials on Friday 23 November. It was attended also by a representative from Linklaters & Paines, BA's City solicitors, who had done much of the work to date on the sale prospectus. What King and his senior colleagues said to each other when the lawyers' fresh doubts were conveyed to them later in the day, went unrecorded. But Sid Rosdeitcher and a senior colleague, Jay Topkis, were quickly summoned from the Paul, Weiss offices in Washington. Things were coming to a head.

Over the next few days, ironically, the Transport Department was already committed to a rush job to find and appoint an advertising agency in time for the February sale. (Outsiders construed the haste as a sign of panic now that British Telecom was almost away and the BA campaign was being focused on at last; but Whitehall insisted that the short time-scale helped sort the sheep from the goats.) The civil servants visited a number of agencies on 22 and 23 November, asking just three of them to work nonstop through the weekend in order to make a formal presentation to the Department on 27 November.

On Tuesday the 27th the presentations went ahead as planned, with Dorlands, the British Telecom agency, competing against Allen, Brady & Marsh and Boase Massimi Pollitt. But then: silence. None of the agencies heard a squeak out of Whitehall for more than three weeks.

For on Wednesday the 28th, with just five business days left until 3 December and the point-of-no-return, the irresistible momentum of BA's privatisation collided with the immovable object of Judge Greene's court.

It happened in a room in the Transport Department in Marsham Street, SW1, attended by the civil servants, BA, Hill Samuel, Lazard's and a host of lawyers including partners from Slaughter & May, Hill Samuel's City solicitors, as well as Paul, Weiss, Linklaters & Paines and Wald Harkrader & Ross. The outcome, as the lawyers saw it, was not to be seen in a negative light. The choice had always lain between finding an acceptable 'health warning' and going all out for a settlement before privatisation. Admittedly, it was a bit late in the day to be making the final choice. But it was Linklaters' belief at the meeting of the 28th that a settlement could be achieved. Coinciding with Wald Harkrader's pessimism, Linklaters' bold suggestion decided the matter. No one made the conclusion explicit that day; but it was now inescapable.

Some of the non-lawyers, perhaps understandably, took a less positive view of developments. At Hill

Samuel, where work on a US prospectus as well as the UK sales campaign was now fast approaching the critical 3 December date, the turn of events was received with dismay. Michael Gatenby, the head of the bank's BA team, went to see Peter Lazarus, the Permanent Secretary at Transport. (Lazarus had appeared in front of the Public Accounts Committee at the House of Commons on 2. November and had spoken warmly of BA's turnaround to the MPs who questioned him.) In view, Gatenby told the Permanent Secretary, of the less optimistic stance now being taken by all the lawyers – including Paul Weiss – Hill Samuel had no choice but to advise that BA would be unsaleable in the City so long as the civil suit was pending.

And on 29 November, King and Colin Marshall went to see Ridley. It was less than two months since Ridley's White Paper squashing the CAA Report. The object then had been to facilitate BA's sale as quickly and cleanly as possible. Now here were BA's top men, forced to admit that privatisation looked a doubtful starter at all, as things stood – for reasons that had applied with equal force since 1983 and earlier!

Not a word reached Fleet Street. Given the publicity accorded the 14 February sale date, this new setback for BA might easily have been presented as an utter debâcle – which in many ways it was. But there were no public recriminations. Nor was anyone, even privately, accusing BA of playing down the legal problem until after 3 December in the hope of forcing the Government into giving it an indemnity. King and his colleagues seemed at least as angered and disappointed by developments as anyone else.

An anxious BA board did now warn the Government, however, that settling the suit could cause interminable delays. Coming so soon after the CAA fracas, another halt might leave the airline looking dangerously accident prone to investors. The time for flotation looked ripe and who could tell how long the bull market would last? In short, BA fell back upon its earlier suggestion that the Government should grant it an indemnity against the Laker suit so that investors could simply ignore it.

The idea was a non-starter. Whitehall had already rehearsed the objections at length. Were government lawyers really going to spend years fighting the case – and on behalf of a private-sector BA at that? What would the House of Commons think about that kind of privatisation-with-reservations? And what were the chances of the Laker defendants escaping with less than the maximum damages, once the British Exchequer had its cheque-book open? As for the Treasury's reactions, they hardly needed stating. An indemnity would have landed the Public Spending Estimates with an unquantifiable future liability. And a critical principle of the privatisation programme – that any exit from the public to the private sector constituted a clean break – would have gone by the board with incalculable consequences.

The alternative approach raised a few eyebrows in the Treasury that the quest for a settlement was being launched at such an apparently late date. But the privatisation programme always required a thoroughly pragmatic approach, however much City advisers sometimes had to be convinced of the immutability of deadlines. And as things had worked out over the autumn, the proceeds of public asset sales were already well on their way to beating the budgeted target for 1984–5. Indeed, the success of the British Telecom sale, virtually assured by the last week of November, was another good reason for the Government to take the lawyers' advice that a settlement should be sought before privatisation. It really made little difference to the Treasury now if BA's sale had to be postponed as a result.

So that was that. BA accepted the decision promptly and without complaint. It was over to the gentlemen from the litigation department. Thus began one of the most extraordinary sagas in modern business history.

18

A Breakfast and a Lunch

The idea of an out-of-court settlement had actually
been circulating amongst the Washington law firms for
months. Even more remarkably, it had been colouring
Beckman's strategy towards the case for much of the
year. For as early as February 1984, BA's Washington
lawyers, Paul, Weiss, had put out the first real feelers
towards an out-of-court negotiation. The occasion was a
hearing in front of the English Appeal Court to decide
whether or not a BA employee working in the US could
be obliged to appear before Judge Greene. Sidney
Rosdeitcher arrived in London as the Paul, Weiss partner
on the Laker case and checked in for his stay at the
Connaught Hotel.

Rosdeitcher invited Beckman to breakfast. Beckman
turned up looking spruce as usual. Rosdeitcher – small,
balding, with round pebble glasses and turnups on his
trousers – cut an appropriately contrasting figure. He
had a few things he wanted to discuss. All terribly vague,
of course, and really hardly worth discussing, except that
here they were in London together and, well, it only
seemed sensible to mull things over with each other
while they had the chance. And, well . . . Would
Beckman's client be interested, the BA lawyer wanted to
know, in exploring the chances of a settlement?

It was not yet clear that privatisation would depend on
lifting BA off the Laker hook. So the two Americans
sitting over breakfast together at the Connaught at the

beginning of February 1984 were not wholly aware of the drama of their meeting. But its ultimate significance was not lost on Beckman. Calmly and deliberately, he chewed the cud with Rosdeitcher as though it were a run-of-the-mill case just like any other. Then he strode out of the Connaught and hopped, skipped and jumped all the way back to the Grosvenor House Hotel. Some day, somehow, for some huge amount – BA was going to buy him off! Beckman rang Morris with the news. Neither really had a clue how long it would take to arrive; but the settlement was on its way.

As it happened, that was the end of BA's contribution for rather longer than they had hoped. Perhaps Rosdeitcher had been discouraged by the response he had drawn. The overture, anyway, led to nothing more from his side. And the more Paul, Weiss looked into the settlement possibility in the ensuing months, the further it receded.

Rosdeitcher briefed Marshall and William Knighton together on the issue on 11 July at the Transport Department. Jay Topkis, his colleague, visited Speedbird House to discuss it in September. The tenor of their remarks was broadly the same on both occasions. An out-of-court settlement might seem the obvious solution. But given the sharply differing approaches of the various different nationalities on the defendants' side, it was hard to see how the Washington law firms could come to grips with the problem.

Beckman, though, took his cue to perfection. He had already decided to aim his depositions at the defendants' top men as part of the discovery wrangling. From February onwards, he knew his real audience was not the trial jury but the men who would advise in favour of a settlement. Long, tedious cross-examinations about overall policy rather than factual evidence might serve little practical use for the courtroom; but their theatrical effect would be invaluable. He would bore the defendants into submission. The strategy began to pay off within a matter of months. The American lawyers were growing rich defending their clients against Beckman; but even their patience with the interminable discovery requests and seemingly fatuous deposition hearings was running short by the middle of the summer.

One of the leading protagonists for some kind of settlement was Len Bebchick, the British Caledonian counsel. He had probably seen more of Beckman in action over the years than anyone else in Washington. What he was now witnessing looked familiar enough. As the second anniversary of the filing of the suit approached, Bebchick began to do some arithmetic.

Matters came to a head for the BCal lawyer in August 1984. He was in St Louis, Missouri, at the headquarters of McDonnell Douglas. Beckman was cross-examining both Sandy and John McDonnell, the two men at the head of the company whose offers of help to Laker were at the centre of the alleged refinancing conspiracy by the defendants in the winter of 1981–2. Bebchick considered the depositions a complete waste of everybody's time. It would be better sooner rather than later, he concluded, for the defendants to come up with an out-of-court settlement offer.

Then an idea occurred to Bebchick. Would not the shrewdest approach be to take care of all the small creditors fully and then to strike a bargain as cheaply as possible with the medium-sized and major creditors? On that basis, the defendants could then present a package to Christopher Morris that he might find difficult to refuse. With the liquidator's claim settled, the rest might fall into place reasonably quickly. Bebchick fancied that $30m. or so might do the trick.

On the evening of 9 August, he shared these views with Jim Murphy of Bryan, Cave, McPheeters & McRoberts, counsel to McDonnell itself, and Gary Wilson of Wilmer, Cutler & Pickering, the Lufthansa lawyers. Murphy, at least, was very sympathetic.

Three weeks later, Bebchick was over in the UK,

making one of his regular visits to the BCal offices in Crawley. On his own initiative, he travelled up to London to see two key men who would be able to help fix the exact position of all the creditors behind Morris. One was Robert Ayling, the senior lawyer at the DTI; the other was Tony Willis, a partner at City solicitors Coward, Chance which was acting for the Midland Bank. How much, Bebchick wanted to know, would Morris need to settle all the outstanding debts of Laker Airways so that Touche Ross could retire honourably from the fray? Neither man was hostile to his approach. But nor could they offer him their help. The position, they said, was simply too sensitive.

Bebchick was undeterred – and his sally left him with a better grasp than most lawyers in Washington of the Jersey dimension to the case. The bank lenders to Laker had recovered perhaps 70 per cent or more of their money . . . but only by exercising mortgage rights which were unrecognised under Jersey law. The liquidator was appealing against their mortgages as part of his general strategy on the case. If his appeal ever looked like succeeding, the banks might have more interest in a settlement than they thought.

Bebchick spoke to Willis again halfway through September: the Coward, Chance solicitor telephoned him with an update, as he had promised to do. It seemed that Morris was pressing the mortgage threat against the banks far more aggressively than people in Washington generally realised.

This only confirmed Bebchick's hunch that some room existed for settlement talks to start. Early in October, most of the defendants' US firms on the case were present when Beckman launched his long-awaited – and meticulously planned – deposition of Freddie in Washington. Bebchick asked all the defence lawyers to a confidential meeting at the offices of McDonnell's counsel on 15th Street and spelt out the situation as he saw it. It was the kind of session which invariably crops up eventually in every antitrust suit before the US courts. About 90 per cent of them are settled out-of-court, a process which has to start with one side or the other taking fresh stock of its position. Bebchick's ideas were given a good hearing. But then, it was easy to talk. The likelihood of any action looked remote. For these particular defendants had one problem which put their case a long way out of the ordinary. As everyone at the meeting acknowledged – though Beckman for his part never accepted for a moment – there was little point in spending time and money searching for an out-of-court deal so long as the Grand Jury's investigation was hanging over everything.

All this changed on 19 November. Suddenly, with the jury packing its bags to go home, there was at least the chance for a settlement to be explored. But with so many parties involved, a strong lead from someone was indispensable. Who should it be?

That was the question which BA answered in the last days of November 1984. And when the BA board realised that the whole of its privatisation policy now depended on the achievement of a settlement, there was no doubt at all who would be given the job.

Within the discreet world of City of London solicitors, no firm is rated more highly than Linklaters & Paines, the largest solicitors' partnership in the City. Linklaters still occupies the same building in Gresham Street that it moved into in 1956 – but it has had to turf out its tenants at a fairly rapid rate. For it has led the profession's astonishing growth over the last decade-and-a-half: today it has over eighty partners, against twenty-seven in 1970, and its total staff has grown about 6 per cent a year in that time. It has been a leader in more subtle ways, too – helping, appropriately perhaps, to push the City's legal partnerships closer to the US model of the international law firm. Linklaters was one of the first to specialise in bankers' documentation for the Euromarkets, one of the first (in 1983) to appoint an administrative director for its internal management and one of the first to welcome the influx of women solicitors in the late seventies (most unusually for the City, it already has five women partners).

King's chairmanship at BA had seen the airline change its accountants, advertising agents, insurance brokers and merchant bankers; it produced a switch on the legal front, too – and a lot of new business for Linklaters. By November 1984, the firm was already deeply involved in BA's privatisation process through its work on the prospectus. So on the 23rd, Linklaters sent one of its younger men, Graeme Brister, to attend the meeting at which Wald, Harkrader & Ross disclosed its view of the Laker threat. It was already clear at the end of the discussion that an unusual job was in the offing for any senior litigation lawyer ready to accept the challenge. Brister spent much of the weekend of 24/25 November persuading his older colleague, Bill Park, to pick up the gauntlet.

Over the ensuing months, Park's name was to become synonymous with the hunt for an end to BA's legal nightmare. It brought him more public attention in nine months than most City solicitors receive in a lifetime. This in itself is slightly ironic, for Park has always been something of an outsider compared with the Establishment run of City solicitors. He did his articles in the 1950s with a firm in the North of England and, most unusually, worked with another provincial firm for some years before joining Linklaters in London when he was thirty-two – the age at which successful City men are already looking for partnership status. And he has always been a litigation lawyer – traditionally considered by the City practices (though less and less so) to be distinctly down-market from commercial and banking law, rather as criminal work ranks below Chancery law at the bar. There were no litigation partners at Linklaters when he joined them and Park is fond of recalling that he was warned, until he was past forty, that he would never be made a partner.

But by the early eighties, Park had already had an interesting international career. Sheikh Zayed of Abu Dhabi, for example, was one of his more important clients and he travelled frequently to the Gulf. Before that, he had done work for BP during the row over Rhodesian sanctions and Lonrho's African activities. In the later seventies, he had represented RTZ in the US antitrust court battle with Westinghouse Corporation. Both these latter episodes were to find echoes in the new assignment which Brister pulled him into that November weekend.

Park was reluctant at first. He had just had a busy few months and was looking forward to winding down gradually towards a Christmas holiday in West Cumberland, as he still liked to refer to his favourite part of the world. But the mandate to find a settlement for BA was an offer no lawyer could refuse. Park did some homework on the papers, then went along with Brister to the 28 November meeting in Marsham Street. It was clear immediately from the mood of the meeting that a decision one way or the other over a settlement would have to be reached with no more delays.

Yes, said Park when he was asked, he thought it should be possible to negotiate a settlement. He was in no way implying that Paul, Weiss had erred. But he believed that a City solicitor might be able to succeed where a US law firm could not yet hope to do so.

For Park – and this was crucial from the very beginning – was going to steer as wide of the Washington legal net as possible. By going to the Laker creditors directly rather than their US lawyers and by presenting himself as BA's personal representative, as it were, Park was confident he would enjoy key advantages over the US firms which had been labouring on the case since 1982. Above all, he would strive as far as possible to make the negotiations a City of London affair. That way, he hoped a settlement might be helped along by some of the mutual trust and respect shared by the City professionals involved. All the cooks in Washington had been stirring the broth for two years: it was time for another approach.

He was given the brief. It was not an elaborate one. He was required to find the minimum possible sum which BA could persuade both the plaintiff and the defendants in the Laker suit to accept as the basis for an out-of-court settlement.

Approval for the size and timing of BA's own contribution would need to be sought at every critical stage from both the airline's board and the Transport Department. But in the process of negotiating the eventual deal, the Government would allow the BA directors and Park on their behalf to handle matters entirely at their own discretion. And speed was of the essence. There was, too, one further demand. The settlement had to be all-embracing. It had to include Freddie himself, even though he was not a plaintiff in the suit. The last thing anyone needed was a settlement followed by years of spin-off litigation from Freddie. Above all, perhaps, it had to include all the airline defendants.

The code-word here was Bermuda III. Everyone in the international airline industry could see the havoc wrought by the application of US antitrust laws to the Atlantic sector. The US and UK Governments had acknowledged to each other the need for some kind of remedial action, perhaps even a renegotiation of Bermuda II. (Pan Am's domestic market advantage over BA, Peter Lazarus told the Public Accounts Committee on 21 November, was 'something we have had to have in mind in discussions of various sorts with the Americans about the future relations between ourselves and the Americans on air services'.) Talks were planned for the near future. But none of this could happen before a total settlement of the Laker suit – for all the interested parties.

So much for the brief. The Linklaters men spent a few days preparing their strategy. It was virtually identical with Bebchick's, though they did not know it. While a united front was to be vital for the defendants, Park would attempt to deal separately with the various parties in the Laker camp. He would seek agreement with each of the major creditors directly; he would try to recruit Morris's cooperation as the liquidator and protector of the creditors' interests; he would chase a side bargain with Freddie himself and with Beckman as the link man between him and Morris.

Beckman, though, had other ideas. The clash was not long in coming.

Michael Crystal QC, a barrister who had taken silk whilst representing Morris on the case, was well liked and trusted by Linklaters, for whom he often acted. Park and Morris had met at dinner at Crystal's home about a year before: it was just the kind of City relationship Park needed. He arranged to meet Crystal on the morning of 2 December to launch the settlement process. Crystal urged that they should contact Morris directly – and the liquidator, leaving his Sunday lunch in the oven in Cobham, was soon on his way to lunch at the Savoy Hotel.

Park, Brister, Morris and Crystal got rather further over lunch than Rosdeitcher and Beckman had got over breakfast. No details were discussed; indeed, Park candidly admitted he really had very little idea as yet how he was going to proceed. But a general understanding was reached. It was Linklaters' intention to go to each of the Laker creditors in turn and offer them a direct payment from BA. Would Morris, as the liquidator, be prepared to let this happen and to help them on their way with the necessary names and telephone numbers? Yes, replied Morris, this looked a reasonable course. BA was free to explore a settlement directly with the creditors – though he, Morris, would want to be kept closely in touch with developments and he would need to see some reasonable offer made to Freddie, as well.

When Beckman heard about the meeting later that Sunday, he exploded with indignation. How could such a critical initiative have been taken without his participation? Still, he was quickly mollified. The important point, after all, was that BA had at long last broken cover. Beckman insisted they all meet again as soon as possible. He would leave the timing to Morris to arrange. But it was a hurried conversation: he was going to put the telephone down to start preparing for the evening flight to London . . .

Waiting at Washington's Dulles Airport for his plane, Beckman bumped into none other than Len Bebchick, who was waiting for the same flight. The two men sat and talked together on the mobile launch out to the aircraft. Beckman was wondering how he should play his hand with Linklaters; Bebchick was brooding more intensely than ever over the prospects for settling the Laker case out of court. But neither could disclose the faintest hint of their real thoughts to the other. Bebchick was relieved when the Laker lawyer talked instead about his approaching skiing holiday. Exclusive as ever, Beckman was off for Christmas to Deer Valley in Utah – a resort which caters amply even for tastes as expensive as Beckman's. (His high living had become a standing joke to all the lawyers who saw him travelling on the Grand Depositions Tour.) 'That's a wonderful place,' he told Bebchick, lyricising over Deer Valley. 'You come off the slope and there's a valet to meet you and take your skis back to the lodge!'

Beckman never got to Deer Valley, though. When he arrived in London the next morning, Morris had a message for him. Park could not see them until Wednesday . . . and the settlement, according to Linklaters, had to be reached by Friday.

Park and Brister spent much of Monday flying to a meeting at Charles de Gaulle Airport outside Paris. Park forgot his passport and BA had to make elaborate arrangements for the meeting to take place within the airport buildings. There they sat down with Lloyd Cutler, one of the founding partners of Wilmer, Cutler &

Pickering of Washington and White House counsel during the Carter presidency. Cutler was just returning to Washington from an international tribunal hearing in Paris. He and Dieter Lange, his colleague from the firm's London office, responded in a very noncommittal way to the English lawyers. But Cutler was later going to play an important role behind the scenes.

The next day, it was Len Bebchick's turn to be approached. He was telephoned at BCal's offices by Park and invited to a meeting at Linklaters' confidential West End flat in Beauchamp Street, near Harrods. There, Park disclosed his intentions – and Bebchick responded more enthusiastically than his host could possibly have expected. Park asked how much Bebchick thought it might be practical to extract from each of the defendants towards a settlement kitty. The figures Bebchick sketched out – leaving BCal's contribution suitably vague – were not so very different to those Park himself had in mind.

The following day, Wednesday 5 December, Park went along to the Touche Ross boardroom in Little New Street for the meeting Morris had requested. Seated at the table beside Morris and his immediate team were Freddie himself and a bevy of American lawyers, including Dick Shadyac and Carl Schwartz as well as Beckman himself. Clearly, Park's first aspiration – to keep the proceedings heavily English in tone and as pragmatic as possible – was already under threat. He responded with a lively display of the kind of histrionics available in the repertoire of every litigation lawyer worth his salt. The face that would do credit to an ex-boxer was lowered over the table and simply refused to notice Beckman's presence.

Park directed himself solely at Morris, all the time keeping his head bowed ferociously over his papers (''oovering the bloody floor with 'is 'ead', as Freddie succinctly put it). And the message from the BA boardroom was the same as before: the possibility of a settlement including some premium over and above the creditors' claims was open only until that Friday.

But this line never stood a chance. Beckman responded combatively. Any hope of grabbing a quick settlement, uncomplicated by US legal manoeuvring, was dead – if it had ever really existed – within the hour.

Beckman asserted his right, as the plaintiff's counsel, to be Park's chief negotiating adversary. And as soon as this had been established, Park's second aspiration – to deal separately with Morris, Laker and Beckman – was finished, too. For Beckman declined to negotiate details of any kind so long as Park had no firm offer to place on the table. The American told Park that everyone on the plaintiff's side was genuinely interested in discussing a settlement. Purchasing all the creditors' debts also appeared a sensible route. But where was the money coming from?

This, as Beckman shrewdly appreciated, was BA's dilemma.

The BA board had asked Linklaters to negotiate a comprehensive settlement; but the flag-carrier had no intention of paying the whole bill itself. Rather, it was assumed that the defendants could be persuaded in time to share it. Park had hoped to set up at least the bare bones of a settlement before turning his attention to this little problem. But Beckman was going to deny him this luxury. So Park and Brister set off without delay to meet the other defendants.

19

Ducks in a Row

Like a cartoon character, BA kept on treading the air furiously long after it had run over the edge of the Laker abyss. In private as well as public, the board seems to have continued to regard February as the flotation month for nearly three weeks after the decisive meetings of 29/30 November.

The balance-sheet talks with the Government had gone an important stage further in the last week of November, with a meeting between BA and the civil servants to discuss the new Financial Plan. The BA board was thanked for its efforts to maximise the proceeds to the Exchequer of the airline's sale; Whitehall for its part was happy to envisage helping BA into the private sector with a cash injection for its balance sheet of perhaps as much as . . . £100m. The board was asked to go away and work out the implications of that.

Back went the reply five days later: BA would have to dispose of an entire class of its aircraft and lay off another 5,000 jobs. More discussions were planned.

Meanwhile Colin Marshall, addressing the Industrial Society in London on 26 November, had thought the sale would 'most probably' be in the second half of February. As late as 13 December, when BA gave a champagne breakfast reception for forty unsuspecting journalists from the national press, February was still the target.

The launch of a new corporate livery for the airline in the first week of December was used quite deliberately to keep interest and enthusiasm bubbling along. It was the result of the new contract awarded back in the summer of 1983 and was accompanied by a predictable amount of razzmatazz at Heathrow. But the new paintwork designs for BA's aircraft and all its other capital equipment – involving expenditure of nearly £50m. – was less than a total triumph with Fleet Street. The work had been carried out by 'an American design firm well known for its work on cigarette packets', said one correspondent rather sniffily.

No doubt the BA management's thinking was as wishful as it was positive at this stage. Senior executives were desperately hoping the legal headache would prove short-lived. The stockmarket setting for a sale was well-nigh perfect. British Telecom, from BA's perspective anyway, had been a triumph. On Wall Street, airline stocks had been soaring in anticipation of excellent results for the year just ending: between August 1984 and mid-January 1985, US airline equities climbed 37 per cent, compared with a little under 11 per cent for the Standard & Poor's 500 Index. In short, it was frustrating beyond belief to think the Laker suit could possibly stand between BA and take-off into such sunny skies after so much preparation.

By the time the champagne was gushing on 13 December, though, there could really be no doubt about it. Park and Brister had by then returned from a journey round the defendants' offices – and the challenge they had accepted was looking formidable.

The Linklaters lawyers were taken on their whirlwind tour by BA's in-house legal director. This was Bernard Wood, a slight, snappily-dressed man in his fifties with a penchant for addressing others as 'old boy'. They saw Pan Am and TWA in their Manhattan offices on Monday the 10th; they were in Amsterdam, Cologne and Zurich on the Tuesday and they breakfasted with SAS executives in Stockholm on the Wednesday. The party was given at best a polite but cautious reception. If anyone had been dangling the Bermuda III carrot in front of the continental boardrooms, it seemed to Park and his assistant to have done very little good.

Typical was the meeting at the Balsberg, as it is known: Swissair's headquarters a couple of miles from Zurich Airport. The discussion with Andreas Hodel, the in-house counsel, was brief and to the point. Swissair was totally confident of success against the Laker camp and saw absolutely no reason to go running after a settlement. If BA had good reaons for wanting one, that was its own affair. It was perfectly at liberty to seek a comprehensive deal, naturally, and Swissair would look at any proposals put forward by Linklaters. But the lawyers were not to suppose they were acting on Swissair's behalf. Nor was Swissair in the least committed to the principle of settling out of court.

As for Lufthansa, the German carrier had always been an outspoken critic of Laker Airways. Dr Herbert Culmann, the chief executive until July 1982, had publicly attacked Freddie's notions about the 'forgotten man' – the potential passenger deterred by IATA's high fares – as half-baked nonsense. He and Reinhardt Abraham, Lufthansa's technical director and another powerfully influential figure in the international industry, had yielded nothing to David Kirstein, Beckman's partner, during a deposition in Bonn three months earlier. (A crowded room in Bonn's Steigenberg Hotel had been treated to one of the most barren cross-examinations of the whole series.) Following their example, Heinz Ruhnau, the new chief executive, and his in-house legal counsel, Professor Arnold Rudolph, were no less discouraging than Swissair.

(Some days later, on 21 December, Bernard Wood travelled alone to pay a visit to the glass skyscrapers of the Paris suburb of Puteaux and the headquarters of UTA. The French airline's legal director expressed sympathy for BA's predicament. But UTA, he warned, would have no interest in contributing any money at all to a settlement nor was it interested in joining talks about a settlement. It was possible the airline would attach its name to a settlement if one emerged. But as a member of BA's flying crew – as Gordon Dunlop later put it – UTA was determined to remain Tail-End Charlie.)

All this travelling left no illusions at BA about the antagonism felt by European airline executives towards Freddie personally; nor did Park return with much confidence in the support he could expect from them in the negotiations ahead. But at least the way was paved for a pre-Christmas conference at Speedbird House which Park was planning. Before that, though, there were one or two other items on the agenda. For a start, public expectations of a February flotation would have to be spiked as delicately as possible. The cat could not be kept in the bag much longer.

Out it jumped on 14 December. The full board of BA assembled at Cleveland House in St James's. A marathon meeting lasted through the morning and over a sandwich lunch into the afternoon. The airline's chairman listed all the obstacles remaining between BA and the private sector. Above all, though, he spelt out the implications of the legal barrier now firmly entrenched across the privatisation runway. Sid Rosdeitcher came over from Washington for the occasion and gave a thorough exposition of the problem. It was made clear to all that unless it could be removed, there might be no sale at all. The February date, as the press was told afterwards, was looking 'a bit optimistic'.

Park's next task was a trip to the US. In Washington on 17 December, he bought dinner for Beckman at the plush Four Seasons Hotel. It was now obvious that he would have to deal with Beckman – and would have to try dissuading him from the not unreasonable demand that a firm offer be presented as the basis for negotiating. In other words, he was looking for a favour from the Laker lawyer – and Beckman encountered a far more charming Park than he had seen in London.

Then Park went to call on Pan Am and TWA again. The

two US carriers had to be approached very differently from BA's seven European airline co-defendants and were in a class apart – quite literally, in some respects: Lufthansa had placed an injunction on its US lawyers to stop them talking to the US carriers' counsel. As on 10 December, Park found the US carriers at once more and less sympathetic to the search for a settlement.

On the negative side, Pan Am and TWA were answerable to private shareholders for everything they did; they were also companies with big cash headaches. TWA, which had only recently emerged from a major financial reorganisation, was coming to the end of a reasonably successful year, though its fourth quarter looked like being unprofitable. But it had suffered operating losses approaching $500m. since 1981 on its domestic US network. Pan Am, meanwhile, had been lurching from one financial crisis to another for years. Pre-tax losses of $75m. in 1983 were going to look enviable when the airline announced its losses for 1984.

So neither company was anxious to be seen spreading millions around unnecessarily on a settlement which hostile critics might present as crucial only to the fortunes of BA – an aspiring private sector competitor. The Grand Jury investigation had been an unwelcome source of worry; but the open secret that neither carrier had been lined up for price-fixing charges had given both a useful fillip.

On the other hand, TWA and Pan Am both had a much finer appreciation than the European airlines of the US legal system. They knew the unavoidable risks of putting any complex commercial issue before a US jury; neither of the airlines had any illusions about their unglamorous public image. (*Fortune* magazine in January 1985 listed the 250 Least Admired Companies in the US: TWA was No. 243 and Pan Am was No. 246.) Far more than the Europeans, they conducted regular reviews of the pros and cons of settling – known, inevitably, as risk/benefit analysis.

There was never any real doubt that they would be happy to pay an immediate cash sum equivalent to the foreseeable legal costs of continuing their defence – perhaps $3m. or so each. That was the easy part. The crux of the matter, though, was different: how much of a premium would they be prepared to pay over and above that amount in order to rid themselves of the uncertainty of the trial jury's verdict? But at least both they and Park knew very well that, at the end, it would come down to some straight horse-trading over the figures.

The European carriers, on the contrary, knew no such thing. Grudgingly, their in-house legal directors gathered at Speedbird House for their pre-Christmas conference on 19 December. KLM, Sabena, SAS, Lufthansa, Swissair and British Caledonian were represented at the meeting (only UTA stayed away). But BA and Linklaters won absolutely no tricks with their vague promises of a new start on the North Atlantic. The Europeans would not commit themselves. Far more than the Americans, they were affronted by the very principle of settling a case which they regarded as groundless. *Amour-propre*, it seemed, was going to be less susceptible to horse-trading than was American risk/benefit analysis.

Judge Harold Greene served up the very next day a timely reminder of the possible courtroom dramas they all might face if the horse-trading failed. In an opinion of 20 December, the judge responded to the protracted arguments since October over his action in proscribing the British defendants from talking to their own Government. He withdrew his order, grandly announcing the need to respect one or two past edicts, including the Magna Carta and the 1689 Bill of Rights. But he also read the Riot Act about the disruptive efforts by BA and BCal to abort the suit before his court – 'the tenacity of these defendants in seeking a resolution of this lawsuit everywhere but in the appropriate legal forum,' said the judge, 'is remarkable and probably unprecedented.'

What he had particularly in mind at that moment was the use which was being made of the Protection of Trading Interests Act (PTIA) by the British Government to stop the disclosure of documents held in the UK. On 18 and 19 December, Robert Ayling, the DTI legal adviser to the Trade and Industry Secretary, wrote to Paul, Weiss and to Pan Am's London lawyers conveying the Secretary's denial of requests for consent to hand over papers to Beckman. Both letters contained an interesting paragraph:

> The effect of the decision of the House of Lords, discharging the injunctions against Laker Airways, emphasises the need for the underlying dispute between the two Governments to be resolved as soon as possible. Her Majesty's Government is at present renewing its efforts to this end and is currently discussing the matter with the United States Government.

Those efforts – whether aimed at Bermuda III or something less ambitious – could be doomed unless the Laker suit was settled.

(Robert Ayling, it might be said, was spending a great deal of his time at the DTI on BA's affairs. On 1 November 1985 he did the most logical thing – and joined the airline. He has now replaced Bernard Wood as BA's legal director.)

This was where matters stood when Christmas arrived. Park took himself off to West Cumberland for a short break and a chance to contemplate the next move. (He was going to contemplate the purchase of a magnificent country house, too, in the Cumbrian village of High Lorton. The name of the house? Lorton Park, naturally.)

The essence of BA's problem was simple. Neither the plaintiff nor the co-defendants were prepared to adopt any identifiable position long enough for Linklaters to elicit a firm response from the other side. Park's answer to the problem was less simple. He would try to establish as clear an understanding as possible with the defendants about the outline structure of a settlement. Then he would just assume their ultimate complicity while he lined up the various creditors where he needed them, beginning with the most pliant and ending with the most intractable.

Once that was done and the basis was clearly established for a firm settlement, Park would go back to the defendants to coax the appropriate offer out of them. Meanwhile, still playing both ends against the middle, he would attempt to line up Beckman and Freddie in anticipation of the offer.

Of course, as one US lawyer put it, Park had 'an awful lot of ducks to get in a row'. There was always the danger that one or two might fall out of line before he had a chance to take pot-shots at them all – leaving Park with his targets still scattered in all directions by the end. But it was a danger BA was ready to accept. Park told the board he hoped a deal might be struck by the end of January.

Gordon Dunlop was in his office at Speedbird House at 8.00 a.m. on the day after Boxing Day. It was no time for festive over-indulgence; and nor was he there to write his Christmas thank-you letters. In the remaining days of 1984, the board had to agree the figures for Park's outline settlement.

With Whitehall's blessing but nothing half so firm from the co-defendants, BA adopted a 20:20:20 plan: that is, BA would pay $20m., the two US carriers would pay $20m. and BCal, together with the remaining six continental airlines, would pay $20m. The two other co-defendants – McDonnell Douglas and McDonnell Douglas Finance Corporation – would pay nothing to the settlement but would abandon their claims as creditors of Laker.

The last days of the year saw the end of a month of scurrying to and fro across Europe by BA board members and their advisers. The firmer the understanding with the continental airlines, the better the chances of Park affirming his settlement by 31 January 1985. That would make privatisation a possibility for the early summer. When the New Year arrived, it was decided the time had come to leave the co-defendants to their deliberations and move on to the next job: aligning the creditors.

In a sense, Christopher Morris had had an eventful December, too. For the legal ground under his suit had shifted abruptly. Nor was this just a reflection of the out-of-court manoeuvring. On 10 December, the John Jones memorandum and a record of his debriefing before the Grand Jury of 15–16 November 1983 was filed publicly in Civil Docket No. 82-3362 at the US Federal Court House. Morris was taken aback when he read their contents. Beckman made light of the implications. If Jones had had that impact in two days, said Beckman, imagine the changed complexion of the civil case after a week or more of detailed evidence from him before a civil jury! Morris was not so sure. It seemed to him the out-of-court talks had begun opportunely.

In the first week of 1985, Morris and Park finally agreed the mechanics of the putative settlement. Morris wanted to see the creditors satisfied. But it was not feasible simply for the defendants to pay them back their money. Removing Laker Airways' debts like that would have amounted to a magical source of income for the airline – with less magical consequences for its income tax returns. So BA set up a new subsidiary in Jersey: Ivanhoe Investments. It would purchase the debts owed to each and every creditor, leaving BA itself as Laker's sole remaining creditor.

How much BA would pay for those debts, of course, was the tricky question. Morris had to move carefully here. He was under no political pressure: William Knighton had had a general discussion with him the previous autumn about the case, but at no time had the Government shown any improper interest in it. Rather,

Morris was handicapped because under Jersey law there was no creditors' committee for him to consult. In this sense, he was flying solo – but he was getting invaluable ground control from his advisers in the City, solicitors Durrant Piesse, and his Washington lawyer, Mike Nussbaum of Nussbaum, Owen & Webster.

In the event, a surprising influence was wielded over the negotiations by Freddie himself. BA at first wanted to offer total reimbursement to all creditors owed £20,000 or less. It was Freddie, with Beckman's support, who pushed this up to £50,000. Park accepted these terms, which allowed him to set aside about 160,000 minor parties, including 2,300 Laker ex-employees and 14,000 dispossessed ticketholders. They would all be repaid in full, costing the defendants about $15m.

Minor creditors were those owed £50,000 to £200,000. There were some forty-five parties in this category, including one or two larger trade creditors, owed some £20m. in all. It was agreed that Linklaters would approach each of them on BA's behalf – a prodigious undertaking – and would offer £50,000 plus 20 per cent of what each was owed over that. This would cost about $8m. (The mix of dollar signs and pound sterling signs was going to cause everyone confusion by the end of the story.)

Finally, it was agreed that Park would approach the dozen or so major creditors – mostly banks – last of all. Laker's outstanding bank debt amounted in sterling terms to £264m. But BA knew the receivers had done a thorough job: in fact, the banks had realised about $350m. on the sale of Laker's assets. So Park and his men were not going to be offering them huge sums for their remaining dues. The BA board decided to try settling for a flat $250,000 to each of them, across the board: perhaps $3m. in all.

But Morris did not need to know the finer details at that level. They could be left to bilateral bargaining between BA and the creditors themselves. Morris was scrupulously careful to distance Touche Ross from all that. 'I have taken the view,' he wrote to creditors later in January, 'that it would not be right for me to give any advice, one way or the other, to any creditor or class of creditors.' So he just gave Linklaters the names and addresses they needed – and a green light to go ahead.

The finances at this stage looked reasonably encouraging: $15m. and $8m. and $3m. for all the creditors. But Park had one other critical consideration. The BA board had decided to offer $8m. to Freddie and $8m. to Beckman for the settlement of all the plaintiff's legal costs. The grand total, in dollar terms, came to around $42m. – enough to allow something for administration costs, a $10m. emergency reserve and still a useful bit of change out of the $60m. BA had warned the co-defendants to expect.

The BA board and its solicitors reviewed the whole package together on 7 January 1985 and approved it. Next day, the chairman had lunch with Nicholas Ridley at Mark's Club in Charles Street, W1. A great deal of water had passed under the bridge since their last meeting. Obviously February was out and a summer flotation was now the target. King outlined the plans for the settlement; he hoped it would leave the way clear very soon for work on the privatisation to go full-steam ahead. To that end, the two men determined to leave past disagreements behind them and to try conveying a new spirit of friendly cooperation to their subordinates. (The BA and Transport Department press relations people met for a good lunch together shortly afterwards.)

Meanwhile, the rush had begun to fix up the settlement by the end of the month. (Park was informed at this moment, as luck would have it, that Lorton Park was definitely up for sale. He rushed up to see it and paid the asking price all in one weekend. But he was not going to have a lot of spare time for any do-it-yourself conveyancing.)

On 7 January, a team of Linklaters solicitors began telephoning a list of fifty-nine minor creditors to offer them BA's terms. They were told they had until Friday 11 January to accept, otherwise the offer would most probably be withdrawn. The hurry made it quite impractical for Linklaters to start dealing with thousands of individual solicitors around the country. Breaking an egg or two for its omelette, the firm lent heavily on anyone who muttered about a need to think things over for a while. They had had nearly three years to think them over: now they had to jump.

Most did, and signed papers which handed their claims against Laker over to BA in return for a payment by 31 January. The ten who did not were pressured to do so on 14 January. They included Robin Flood and her husband – the lady who had taken that message for Freddie in the Flying Tigers hangar at Kennedy Airport in February 1982. Her company, Harrison Flood Ltd, had arranged Skytrain's publicity and promotion and was still owed £94,000. Linklaters offered £50,000 plus 20 per cent of the balance. Partly out of a sentimental loyalty to Freddie, whom she supposed was still holding out fiercely, Robin Flood refused to sign. She need not have worried for her old boss's interests: he was not being neglected. That weekend of 12/13 January, Freddie was holding court for all the professional negotiators near his home in Florida.

Park and Brister had broken the news to Beckman of the Double Eight proposal – $8m. for Freddie and $8m. for his 'expensive American lawyer' – over another Four Seasons Hotel dinner in Washington earlier in the month. Beckman himself had seemed to the Linklaters men to be relieved that a financial resolution of the case might at last be round the corner – he was still, after all, working on a contingency-fee basis. He had run up some big bills over the past two years and more. But Beckman had warned that Freddie would be looking for more than just a cash pay-off.

More than anything else, Freddie wanted to have his status restored to him as a man of consequence in the international airline industry. This did not have to mean hundreds of millions of dollars to buy another fleet of aircraft. But it did mean free travel passes, assurances of cooperation if he set up again in the holiday business – and a willingness by the industry to extend to any future Laker airline all the usual courtesies exchanged between the international carriers around the airports of the world. In the jargon that grew up amongst the lawyers, Freddie wanted 'warmth'. And he made this clear during the weekend of 12/13 January.

A couple of blocks from Freddie's condominium on the expensive Key Biscayne coastline near Miami is the Sonesta Beach Hotel. BA's lawyers checked in there for the two days. They did not have much time for swimming in the ocean off the hotel's private beach. Park turned up looking the quintessential Englishman, dressed in grey flannels, blue blazer, collar and old school tie. He was courteous and friendly throughout the long discussions which ensued in Suite 717, belonging to John Beveridge QC, Freddie's English counsel.

Indeed, for all their obvious differences, Park and Laker got on remarkably well together. Their repartee was going to become celebrated and it started with a colourful refrain this weekend. 'What authority have you got for your offer?' asked Freddie. 'F*** all,' replied Park, with all due honesty.

It was not the only stumbling block. All the 'warmth' assurances sought by Freddie took Park into as yet hopelessly unfamiliar areas of negotiation. On the $8m. payment, however, Freddie seemed ready to agree. Park and Brister felt that he was broadly behind the settlement. They left the Sonesta Beach feeling reasonably encouraged.

Next day, the popular press in London carried an interview with Freddie. 'They are not going to buy me off,' he was quoted as saying from Florida. 'As far as I am concerned, the case can go ahead tomorrow.'

And go ahead it did – with the continuing deposition

of Freddie himself. He flew up to Washington on the Monday and at 10.30 a.m. on Tuesday 15 January he was back under the lights in Beckman's offices, being cross-examined for the sixth time by Sid Rosdeitcher on behalf of BA. 'Happy New Year to you all,' said Freddie to the assembled lawyers. 'The last time we were here it was Guy Fawkes Day when they tried to blow up Parliament.' It was as though the weekend at the Sonesta Beach Hotel had never happened.

Undeterred in London, Linklaters stuck to its original plan. Park turned to the final category of ducks: the banks and other major lenders. But while it may have been necessary, for the momentum of the settlement effort, to pretend that the outlook appeared rosier than it really was, the pretence was about to be worn horribly thin.

Most of the big commercial lenders belonged to the thirteen-member syndicate of banks led by Beckman's old friend, the Midland. This was the group which had so intrepidly lent Laker $131m. in 1981 to purchase three A-300 Airbuses. They had managed to grab back all or most of their outstanding principal. But their claims for interest in arrears and penalty payments were complex beyond belief. Park was offering a quick, rough-and-ready solution. But the banks, it was rapidly evident, were going to lavish on the solution some of the attention for detail which might have served them better had it been applied before the problem loan was ever made.

Within days, the 31 January deadline was starting to look academic. And it still remained for Linklaters to approach the creditor they and BA had judged might be the most difficult of all. At least they got this right.

20

The Metropolitan Deal

Its street front in Washington DC is all grey granite, with the words Export-Import Bank of the United States posted on a small brass plate over the stone. If the BA camp thought it was going to be a soft touch for a settlement deal, they were wide of the mark. Just possibly Linklaters may have been encouraged by the bank's initial response to telephone and telex approaches around the turn of the year. Sure, said the Exim officials, they were willing to listen to any proposals. As Laker Airways' biggest creditor, Exim was still owed a tidy amount. The bankers would be keen to hear what the lawyers had to offer.

Linklaters also had good reason to hope Exim might welcome a neat resolution of the Laker mess. After all, the bank had already extricated itself to a remarkable degree. Freddie's repossessed DC-10 fleet had sat in the sun at Yuma, Arizona, long enough to cause them a few second thoughts back in Washington. But in the summer of 1984, the aircraft had at last been sold: three of them to United Airlines and the remaining two to SAS, one of Freddie's alleged predators. And the sale price had been a pretty good one: $125m., plus another $11m. for surplus engines and spare parts. Well, the outstanding loan principal at the time of the collapse had only been $147.2m. . . . and that had since been written down in Exim's books, Linklaters knew, to just $97.2m. So the sale had been enough to repay the loan with no further write-off, leaving a useful amount over to take care of some of the outstanding interest owed to Exim.

In the background, too, was another consideration. Exim is not a department of the US Government; rather, it is an independent agency of the Government, operating under a periodically renewed charter from Congress. Nevertheless, it seemed unlikely to the BA board that Exim would hold out against a settlement where the US Department of Justice had had to give way. And William H. Draper III, the bank's chairman, was a Californian Republican with close ties to the Reagan White House. Indeed, Draper had worked hard for the Reagan-Bush ticket in 1980 and had been on the White House staff for six months before shifting his office a few blocks across the street to Exim in July 1981.

Bill Park and Graeme Brister called there in person on 22 January. They were brought into Draper's office by Ray Albright. Albright had moved on since 1982 to become head of the Asia division of the bank but he still retained operating responsibility for the Laker file. After a brief preamble about the importance of the settlement for Anglo-American relations and a resumé of the progress so far, Park unveiled his offer. Exim, like all the rest of Laker's institutional creditors, could look forward to receiving a cash payment of $250,000. That was very interesting, said Draper. Then he asked for more information about the whole settlement package. Park obliged with various details, moving inexorably to the revelation that Sir Freddie and his Washington lawyer were to be offered $8m. apiece.

The two American bankers took a moment or two to digest this news. Then they had some news for Mr Park. To be blunt, the offer was not really worth discussing. Taken in isolation, the cash proposal might conceivably have been reasonable, though it was at least arguable that Laker's major creditors deserved a better break than some of the smaller parties. But set against the prospective $8m. payment to Freddie, it was simply out of the question. To treat the shareholder of a bankrupt company so much more preferentially than its outstanding creditors, said Draper, was unconscionable by any banking standards. Exim would be seen publicly to have been treated with gross unfairness. He agreed that a Laker settlement was obviously important to Anglo-American relations. But that only underlined his point. To settle on blatantly unfair grounds could only damage those relations. The $250,000 was a paltry offer. Nor was Exim at all happy about writing off Morris's suit as a non-starter. On balance, concluded the bankers, they would prefer to await its outcome in the courts.

And that was that. As Park and his colleague left the bank, freezing Arctic winds met them on the pavement: it was, appropriately, one of the coldest weeks in Washington for decades. They returned to London to adjust all the purchase agreements struck with the minor creditors: for the 31 January deadline, they should now read 28 February.

At BA, both Colin Marshall and Gordon Dunlop were looking forward to a bit of cold weather: both were planning family skiing holidays in Switzerland for early February – which they had originally hoped might crown their weeks of toil on the Laker business. (Dunlop, a hard-hitter by temperament in most respects, is a late convert to skiing and a keen downhiller; Marshall, equally characteristically, prefers the steadier pleasures of langlauf skiing.) But the uncompromising message from Exim, while not entirely unexpected, put the negotiations with the US bank in a different league from the rest of the settlement talks. BA would need to tackle the Exim problem head-on. As the two skiers left for the Swiss slopes, Draper was asked to make clear how much he believed his bank was owed. Back came the answer: well over $60m. Marshall and Dunlop made arrangements to interrupt their holidays and take a Sunday-night Concorde to Washington on 10 February.

The request from BA for a face-to-face meeting

left Draper and Albright in no doubt what to do next. They decided to take a tough line and see what would happen.

One of California's most successful venture capital businessmen in the seventies, Draper had always believed firmly that there was no substitute for meeting people at first hand in any bargaining encounter. More to the point, though, he and Albright knew the value of appearing ultra-casual about a settlement when they sat down to talk to the BA directors that Monday, 11 February. If it should emerge that BA genuinely had no more money to offer, there would be plenty of time for Exim to revise its stance.

On the other hand, all the pressure would be on BA's men. They needed to settle in a hurry. Draper and Albright knew Park was locked in two parallel negotiations, chasing agreement with the co-defendants as well as the creditors. It had to be possible that Park could still raise more for the kitty: they would wait patiently for clues as to the real financial position.

They did not need to wait very long. Colin Marshall opted to try for a quick understanding. No sooner had the two sides set out their preliminary positions on 11 February than he proposed a fresh compromise. It now looked possible, said BA's chief executive, for Exim to be offered a full $5m.

It was exactly the kind of signal Draper was looking for. A few weeks' stonewalling had turned $250,000 into $5m. There seemed less point than ever in cobbling together a hasty deal. Alas, said the Exim chairman, BA had still not appreciated Exim's dilemma . . . he had to doubt whether there was any real basis for a settlement. BA's lawyers reminded the meeting that a trial of the Morris suit might last years and years. The two bankers shrugged and set their figures out again.

Laker Airways had borrowed $228m. to buy its DC-10 fleet. Exim had provided – directly or through guarantees – just over $161m. of this. When the airline had

231

collapsed, it was still owed $147.2m. It was also owed some interest in arrears. On top of all this, a penalty interest payment had been accruing since the default and now amounted to $42m. Finally, Exim was seeking $4.5m. compensation for maintenance costs on the repossessed fleet. It all added up to nearly $194m. The bank was able to reduce this by $136m., representing the proceeds of selling the fleet. But that still left $58m. – which, as it happened, was roughly what Exim had lost on all its past loan defaults put together. And this was a sensitive time for Exim, with the politicians on Capitol Hill reviewing its status as a part of the current budget hearings. The $5m. offer from BA went nowhere near addressing the political flack Exim would face in swallowing such a huge loss. Meanwhile Freddie himself would be getting the same plus another $3m. . . .

Talks resumed the next day, the 12th. Linklaters pointed to some of the difficulties arising out of the application to Laker Airways of Jersey law. It was even possible, said Park, that Exim's mortgages over the Laker fleet might have to be challenged, as those of the Midland and Clydesdale banks already had been. But that cut little ice with the Americans. (In fact, Draper had had Exim's own lawyers look into the Jersey complication; but they ended up as confused at the end of the day as they had been at the beginning.) There was no getting around the figures. Marshall made a last valiant effort to persuade the bankers that $5m. was really as high as BA could possibly go. 'See you in court, then,' said Draper, 'but no hard feelings!'

The BA team left, trying not to look as dismayed as it felt. A vague willingness to compromise had been established more or less at the outset with all the other Laker creditors. Exim, easily the most important, had shown not the slightest inclination to settle. It was just a week past the third anniversary of Freddie's collapse. Could this really be the end of the road for the Laker settlement – and with it BA's privatisation?

Waiting at Dulles Airport for a shuttle flight to New York and a Concorde back to London, Marshall felt so anxious about the prospects that he telephoned Draper. He just wanted, he told the Exim chairman, to check that the bank's doors were still open to them for further exploratory talks in the future. Certainly, said Draper. And from that moment, he and Albright felt sure they would get what they wanted in the end.

Next day, Marshall and Dunlop rejoined their families in Switzerland and the lawyers went back to their drawing-board in Gresham Street. At the very least, the Exim problem had blown the 28 February deadline out of the water. All the creditors were contacted again and the offer terms adjusted for a second time: a third deadline was fixed for 31 March.

But the real task was to produce a fresh offer for Exim which might keep the talks alive. Both sides had noted there might be some room for compromise over the interest left in arrears at the date of the Laker collapse. Perhaps this could be made a plausible basis for pushing up the $5m. without losing too much credibility? Exim responded politely to the idea. So, a few days later, back went Park and Colin Marshall to Washington for another meeting on 20 February.

By this time, though, BA had taken a better measure of the opposition. If Exim was going to be successfully cajoled into taking the lowest possible amount of money – which had to be the goal – then some stronger cards were needed. En route for the US capital, Marshall stopped in New York with Gordon Dunlop for a couple of discreet business calls. In Pan Am's offices towering over Park Avenue, they sat down with chairman Ed Acker and explained their problem to him. What, if anything, could Pan Am's lobby in Washington do to help? Acker was sympathetic and promised to have his Government Affairs people look into it. The BA directors then met with TWA and drew the same response. Efforts would be made on BA's behalf. But no one seemed confident of making much impression upon Exim without help at the very highest levels.

That help was at hand. It was, in fact, the happiest of coincidences that brought Mrs Thatcher herself to Washington that very week. It was a visit most widely acclaimed for the Prime Minister's triumphant appearance before a joint session of Congress. But there in the audience listening to her speech was a smiling Lord King. (The BA chairman was a close friend of the British Ambassador in Washington.) And when Mrs Thatcher sat down for private talks with the President, BA's quandary was high on her agenda.

There was no mistaking Mrs Thatcher's exasperation during her meeting with the President – much to the consternation of government officials on both sides. They had to stand by while lofty matters of state were thrust aside so that precious moments could be devoted to the airline and its affairs. It was almost like a repeat of the previous autumn. The US officials tried to point out as gently as possible that she had never given President Reagan any credit in public for his help on that occasion; in fact, she hadn't even said thank you in private. The Prime Minister swept their prevarications aside: that episode was all water under the bridge. What mattered now was the civil suit – and Exim's obduracy was threatening to wreck an out-of-court settlement. Her point, said the President, was well taken.

Meanwhile, the 20 February meeting at Exim itself was very much a nuts-and-bolts affair. Bill Draper was away on a trip to Europe. But he and Albright had prepared their ground carefully. In the chairman's absence, agreement was at least reached on a cut-off date for the accrued interest owing on the Exim loan before the receivers had moved in. Not that that was much immediate help to BA's lawyers. Albright added a firm $6.2m. to the $147.2m. principal. After all the sums had been reworked, that meant a net claim by Exim of $64m. Marshall indicated that a revised offer was now possible: the interest plus the original cash terms – $6.45m. in all. It was still far from an acceptable package, said Albright. The BA team left hardly more encouraged than when they had arrived.

Meanwhile, word of the impasse was spreading fast amongst the Washington law firms. Both sides were regarded as engaging in some desperate brinkmanship. Many of the counsel involved in the wider litigation had met together in Bonn on 13 February for the deposition of Lufthansa's vice-chairman. In the consensus view, the chances of a successful settlement were waning fast.

Mrs Thatcher, however, had not spoken in vain. Her visit had actually prompted all kinds of activity behind the scenes. Her meeting with the President had been followed as usual by talks at Cabinet level between the Prime Minister and her team and senior members of the Reagan Administration. Voices had been raised in defence of Exim's legitimate interests as a creditor. But it had also emerged that the State Department's own lawyers were, not surprisingly, divided over the merits of the Morris suit.

Linklaters and the British Embassy in Washington had put together a legal brief demonstrating the futility of the suit and this was being circulated widely around government departments. (Exim had swiftly presented contrary opinions from its own lawyers in Jersey as well as Washington.) The British effort to recruit support for its views had certainly stimulated a lively debate. But the outcome of the meeting was mercifully clear-cut: the British Government would reconsider its position – and Exim was to be given its marching orders.

When Draper returned from Europe, he was telephoned by Don Regan, then Secretary of the Treasury. Exim's position was causing more trouble than it was worth in Anglo-American relations, said Regan, and it had to change. He asked Draper to make sure that a deal was struck before the date of the next meeting between the litigation defendants and Judge Greene. Draper agreed to meet this deadline. But he asked for – and was given – discretion to keep talking in the meantime as he thought appropriate. It was as good a recipe as could have been devised for a dramatic climax to the talks.

Marshall returned a third time on Thursday 28 February. Park was already in Washington and since their last meeting had been floating a few compromise ideas of his own. There was a board meeting at Exim which lasted from 9.00 a.m. until midday and the two visitors arrived after lunch on the 28th. A two-hour meeting with Draper was very friendly: indeed, Marshall and Draper were by now taking quite a liking to each other. The BA chief executive explained that he had been doing his best to persuade the British Government that more concessions would be needed on both sides. Mrs Thatcher's visit had helped matters along, he said, and he had a new proposal.

The British airline had itself arranged a loan of $257m. from Exim back in 1981. It had committed Exim to receiving an interest rate of 9.25 per cent; four years later, this was looking an expensive piece of business for the bank, which had to fund the loan with borrowings of its own at much higher rates in the marketplace. As luck would have it, BA had not drawn down all of this loan: about $120m. still remained on tap. Perhaps, suggested Marshall, there might be scope somewhere in all these details for BA to make an additional concession to Exim – putting, as it were, some gilt on the settlement gingerbread?

Draper welcomed the idea. (In fact, he had been forewarned of it by Park.) It looked a promising vehicle to carry the two sides' figures closer together. But it was soon apparent to Marshall that he was still fighting a losing battle. He had envisaged pushing his $6.45m. base number somewhere up into double figures. Draper, on the other hand, kept reiterating the $64m. claim and seemed to be indicating an area for compromise some-where around half that level. Eventually, there was no ducking the issue: both men agreed the gap was simply too wide to bridge.

To Marshall, it was all very puzzling. He knew there had been moves to exert some discreet political pressure on Exim. They did not appear to have had much effect. Exim was even still insisting that a full trial of the antitrust action might leave the bank better off! There seemed nothing to lose now by prompting a public reminder of BA's predicament. Next morning, while still in the US, Marshall made a number of phone calls to London. 'It's no good,' he told David Burnside, the press relations man at Speedbird House. 'We can't get an agreement with Exim. The whole thing looks as though it's fallen through.' Both the Government and the civil servants at the Department of Transport were given the news that the negotiations had ended.

The five-hour transatlantic time difference meant it was late afternoon in London and the story was comfortably in time to catch Fleet Street's first editions. Burnside let it be known that there were no plans for any further meetings in Washington. Next morning, most of the British Saturday press proclaimed the collapse of the Laker settlement.

In reality, the climax to the Exim chapter was just round the corner. Word of Marshall's despondency had got back from London to Washington late on the Friday. It took officials at the British Embassy rather by surprise – and caused quite a flutter at Exim, too. But that was nothing compared to the reactions of the Governments on either side of the Atlantic.

The Exim chairman had been playing a cool hand. Now the bank was inundated with telephone calls from the State Department and members of the White House staff. Back in London, the Fleet Street version of events had excited another storm of indignation. Lord King was in China, travelling with a very grand UK trade delegation. But Mrs Thatcher had again intervened personally.

On the following Monday, Draper was at a meeting

in the State Department when he was approached by W. Allen Wallis, the US Under-Secretary of State for Economic Affairs. Wallis showed the Exim chairman a cable that had been received from Charles Price, the US Ambassador in London, whom Albright had personally briefed on the whole situation two weeks earlier in Washington. The Exim stumbling-block for the Laker settlement was getting in the way of the two countries' good relations, reported the Ambassador from London. Mrs Thatcher, it should be clearly understood, was giving the matter a very high priority indeed.

And so the last round began. Albright called the London embassy to explain that Exim would welcome further talks. Then he rang BA. Marshall and Park were back in Washington the next day: Tuesday 5 March. The talks were doing wonders for Concorde's passenger payload.

Both men showed remarkable stamina over the following few days. On Tuesday, it was agreed that a bilateral deal over the terms of the BA loan should provide the solution. On Wednesday, over lunch in the bank, it was established that BA's maximum offer was around $17m. and Exim's minimum around $30m. The two sides parted to think things over for the afternoon. In the evening, they met together for drinks at the Metropolitan Club, two blocks away from the Exim building, a prestigious watering-hole for the great and the good of the Washington legal and political establishment. It was a suitable venue for striking a deal. Marshall and Park went straight from the Club to the airport and flew back to London to clear the details with Whitehall.

Then on Friday they were back again – seldom can the Atlantic's distance have been treated with such disdain – and the papers were signed. It had been a long haul. And the result, from Exim's point of view, was something of a coup. Or in less genteel poker parlance: the Americans had cleaned up.

The bank had never made parity with Freddie an

explicit condition of any deal, but Freddie's $8m. had hung over the talks from first to last. Exim had questioned the sense of paying Freddie anything at all at the outset. Eventually Draper softened this attitude and allowed Freddie's treatment to be left to one side. But it was not entirely a coincidence that Park and Marshall agreed there should be an immediate cash adjustment to the terms of the 1981 BA loan, worth $1.8m. to Exim. The accrued interest payment already agreed was $6.2.m. So, with the original $250,000 offer, Exim was to receive cash of $8.25m. from the settlement.

But that was not all – not by a long chalk. The subsidised interest rate on BA's 1981 loan would be adjusted for the next nine years, to yield Exim an additional $12m. in discounted present value. And BA would agree to the cancellation of $60m. of the $120m. remaining in the 1981 facility. The consequent reduction in its subsidy cost was worth $5m. to Exim – though this last amount, of course, was not hard cash. (It was also true that Exim agreed to extend the term of the remaining $60m. of the 1981 facility, which was worth $5m. to BA. So the two sides could take a different view of the final figures, which suited both admirably.)

Exim's $25.25m., to take the bank's own total, was to prove very nearly as much as the co-defendants paid to all the other parties to the settlement put together. Taken together with the $136m. made from the sale of Freddie's DC-10s, it left Exim's accountants looking at the original $147.2m. loan default with something like a smile. As one British Cabinet Minister complained to the US Ambassador during the long wrangle, 'The trouble with that man Draper is, he treats the money as though it were his own.'

21

Making Ends Meet

A perceptible chill had descended again over relations between BA and Whitehall. However sincere had been the rapprochement between King and Ridley in January, the strain of the battle with Exim and of two failed deadlines for the Laker settlement was quite evident by March 1985.

David Burnside, the Ulsterman with the Machiavellian touch, had duly been promoted to head of public affairs at the start of February. A fortnight later, he took a short fishing holiday in Scotland. It was the first time the River Dee froze over for twenty years. Burnside was anxious to stop the same thing happening to the privatisation process. Meetings were arranged with brokers, bankers and advertising agents to keep BA's own ideas warm. It was still thought possible at Speedbird House that a Laker deal might emerge in time for a July sale date. The airline's board wanted to be ready, just in case.

The civil servants, though, had watched the legal complications since December 1984 with mounting dismay. There were those who felt resentful at the political embarrassment incurred through BA's failure to foresee the disaster. At first, back before Christmas, what had seemed a short-lived slip-up had been a source of discreet chuckles in high places; King had got his comeuppance. Three months later, the joke was not so funny. Few people in Whitehall were prepared to speculate any more about the date of a BA sale; nor was anyone in the Transport Department much inclined to make excuses for the airline, as they had done so many times in the past.

King and his senior colleagues were in their turn disconcerted by this apparent change of mood. In the first year or so after the 1983 general election, they had been buoyed up by a widespread enthusiasm. Half-hearted proponents of privatisation in the Transport Department or elsewhere had been easily left behind. Now, the BA board was encountering an unmistakable scepticism, even hostility. Morris, Beckman and their friends had a lot to answer for.

As for the suit itself, the pre-trial proceedings and the search for a settlement seemed to be moving along on quite separate rails: there was no suggestion that the trial had just been pushed into the sidings indefinitely. Freddie's deposition was continuing into the spring (thanks to endless cross-examining by the defendants' counsel, to Beckman's intense irritation). Depositions had been held again of Lufthansa personnel in February and were scheduled for KLM in May.

And if anyone at BA still thought a mountain had been made out of a molehill over the whole affair, there were occasional reminders of the sort of money at stake in big US civil actions. Only in January, the US Supreme Court had upheld a claim against Northwest Airlines, one of the country's leading carriers, brought against it by 3,300 air hostesses. A suit launched by the female cabin attendants [sic] under the Civil Rights Act and the Equal Pay Act had won them an award of $59m.

That coincidentally was about the figure Bill Park was now looking at – but the settlement numbers had been refined since the start of the year. It was still hoped to settle the sub-£50,000 creditors group for about $15m., the minor creditors for about $8m. and the major creditors (excluding Exim Bank) for about $3m. With a $2m. administration allowance, the $10m. emergency fund and the Double Eight payment for Freddie and Beckman, that came to $54m. But the original 20:20:20 concept was now redrawn more exactly as 18:18:18 for the US carriers, the Europeans and BA respectively.

After Marshall and Park had finally settled the Metropolitan Deal on 8 March, the first task was to square the Exim pay-off with the emerging 18:18:18 structure. Of the $25m. conceded, $5m. was the non-cash item which BA and Exim could keep between themselves. That left about $20m. – or, to be precise, $8.25m. in immediate cash and $12m. stretched over the next nine years – which BA saw as a deal reached on behalf of all the defendants.

And their reaction? They did not want to know. The European carriers told Park bluntly that BA's relations with Exim were its own affair. The February/March crisis, they suggested, was a bilateral row. BA had a history of close relations with Exim and could expect a continuing relationship, in view of its allegiance to Boeing aircraft. Many of the continental executives had no such link with the Washington bank. Park was going to have a terrible time persuading them that even a fraction of the Exim bill should be shared around the settlement table. But this, anyway, was what he resolved to do. He would ascribe half of Exim's $20m. to the $10m. emergency reserve; the remaining $10m. would be provided by BA in addition to its $18m. So now the key formula was to be 18:18:18 + 10 . . . The settlement would be $64m.

In Whitehall, just for a change, BA was lucky with its timing. The new figures were taken along for scrutiny just as the Government's privatisation policy was being given a fresh impetus from the top. British Telecom's popular impact had been a glorious revelation: the share application queues outside banks all over the country in November, the intense media interest, the 2.5m. payment forms submitted by the public, the doubling of the share price since early December. Now, as the spring of 1985 arrived, the sale of the Government's remaining 48 per cent stake in British Aerospace showed every sign of repeating the success. Wider share ownership could be more than an empty slogan!

The enthusiasm of the privatised companies' own employees was as heartening as the general public's response. Shares in their own workplace had been acquired by 99 per cent of the workforce at Cable & Wireless, 72 per cent at Britoil, 90 per cent at Associated British Ports and 96 per cent at British Telecom . . .

In short, the motives for privatisation were about to undergo a dramatic change. It was a shift comparable, perhaps, with the policy's reappraisal in the aftermath of the 1983 election victory. Not only was privatisation going to reduce the relative size of the public sector, improve efficiency, help fund the PSBR and give employees more involvement in their work – even more important, it was going to be one of the principal midwives of the great property-owning, share-owning capitalist democracy which the Thatcher years were salvaging from the gloom of the corporatist sixties and seventies.

In the face of which, another $10m. for BA did not look too bad. So the airline won support for its $64m. settlement – but it was still, alas, just a plan.

Turning it into reality, especially with an end-of-March deadline, looked almost impossible. After broken deadlines at the end of January and the end of February, BA was making no firm promises. The 31 March deadlines in the minor creditors' debt reassignment papers were amended with no near replacement date. Nevertheless, it was indicated to Whitehall that there was reason to hope the settlement might be in place by the end of April. In the background (as always) the Treasury pencilled in BA's sale for a space in the privatisation calendar late in September 1985.

The basis of BA's guarded optimism was that Park's strategy was now back on course after the Exim episode. Virtually all the minor creditors were on board. Some, it is true, were openly sympathetic to the suit; they wanted Freddie to win as much as possible on the side though he had left them out of pocket themselves, and they were threatening to withdraw their cooperation unless Linklaters could deliver on its proposals very soon. But they were still in place.

The major creditors were being rather more of a problem. After Exim, not surprisingly, each began to watch jealously over the money being offered to the others. The Royal Bank of Canada accepted the $250,000 as a realistic figure. Of the others – the Midland Bank syndicate members, the Midland subsidiary, Clydesdale, Mitsui of Japan, General Electric of the US and Airbus Industrie – none seemed too happy about signing away their debts before all the rest, for fear they might lose out on subsequent revisions of the settlement. This entailed the circulation of lorry-loads of documents around dozens of lawyers' offices every time that fresh litigation complications emerged.

But Park had one consoling thought all the way through – the institutional creditors behind the plaintiff had a lot to lose by causing the defendants any lasting offence. The most anomalous position, of course, belonged to McDonnell Douglas and its subsidiary, McDonnell Douglas Finance Corporation. They were the only non-airline defendants. They were also leading creditors. Of the $228m. lent to Laker for its 1980 DC-10 purchases, MDFC had contributed just under $20m. directly. It had also guaranteed a large slice of the $42m. thrown into the loan by a group of banks including Marine Midland, Morgan Guaranty and International Westminster Bank. McDonnell had emerged three years after the collapse still owed $46m. in principal and $3m. interest. As the structure of the settlement implied, McDonnell was contributing nothing to the kitty – and was going to take nothing out of it, either.

Nor were the other industry manufacturers expecting much compensation. General Electric of the US had guaranteed a $4.9m. credit from J. P. Morgan as well as its share of the commercial banks' $42m. in 1980. Airbus

Industrie, the European consortium aircraft manufacturer based in Toulouse, had guaranteed the first 25 per cent of the $131m. lent in 1981 by the Midland-managed syndicate of banks. Both expected a minimal pay-off and that was exactly what they were hoping to get. With so much new business in the balance from the ten airline defendants, they had very little choice. (Airbus had signed a multibillion-dollar deal with Pan Am in September 1984 which could lead to the delivery of as many as ninety-one aircraft for Pan Am's fleet modernisation programme into the 1990s.)

As for the commercial banks themselves, there was little point in threatening long-term relationships in a gruesomely competitive business just for the sake of relatively small interest payments in arrears. In the Midland syndicate, even the German and Austrian banks which had been proved right by events back in 1981–2 – Dresdner Bank in Luxembourg, Creditanstalt in Vienna and Bayerische Vereinsbank in Munich – were content to leave matters up to the Midland manager in London. And the Midland of all parties had no particular reason to see the Laker suit prolonged. (It was still awaiting the full trial of its injunction to stop Morris dragging the bank itself into Judge Greene's court!)

If all the creditors could be removed from the scene, that would effectively leave only Beckman and Freddie himself. Negotiations with them had been rather stuck in a groove for some time (Q.: 'What authority do you have?'; A.: 'F*** all!'), but they seemed promising.

So by the beginning of April 1984, Park was hopeful that, with $64m., he could bring off the settlement in April. BA asked Judge Greene to call a conference of all the parties in the action for 10 April in Washington. In the meantime, Park set off to pass the hat around the co-defendants.

It came back empty.

Up to now, Park had played the ends against the middle with reasonable success (Mr Draper excepted).

But he could go on doing it no longer. As had been inevitable sooner or later, Park now had to make ends meet, in more ways than one. There were only two ways to do this. One was to secure a settlement bid from the plaintiff, which was just not conceivable. The other was to present a settlement offer from the defendants. They had to put their money on the table.

Park could hardly see the table for ifs and buts. He was unlucky, certainly, that both the US carriers had bigger problems of their own to worry about: with the US influence reduced, the Europeans were even more disposed to endless prevarication. Pan Am had had more than half its flights cancelled for most of March by the longest strike in its history. And at the beginning of April, the rumour broke on Wall Street that TWA was being lined up by one of the US market's most notorious corporate raiders, Carl Icahn, as his next takeover target. The two US airlines had very little time for arguing with Park about their own positions, let alone for taking a lead amongst BA's co-defendants. It was left to the US law firms to try persuading the continental carriers' executives that a $64m. settlement might well be their best bet. The US lawyers did not make much impression.

Since late January, the Europeans had resolved to stick closely together. They became known as the Group of Five – KLM, Lufthansa, Sabena, SAS and Swissair – which underlined the absence of the two remaining airline defendants: British Caledonian and UTA. BCal always navigated a solitary course, relying heavily on the advice of its US counsel, Len Bebchick, and keeping as low a profile as possible. The Frenchmen at UTA simply refused to have anything to do with the litigation. Park found himself presented with a joint rebuttal by the Group of Five. They had never committed themselves to making a firm offer, they said; BA was seeking their help prematurely. They were still sympathetic, of course. But as for the idea of contributing $18m. between them – with BCal's help – why, that was just too ridiculous.

None of this was disclosed to Judge Greene on 10 April. When the conference day came round, twenty-nine lawyers turned up at his chambers to review the position. (The English professionals travelling over on Concorde the day before had held a sweepstake bet about the number in attendance; Bill Park won it.) The parties filed into the more spacious courtroom next to the chambers and Judge Greene was brought (partially) up-to-date. The creditors were as good as agreed on a settlement, said BA's lawyers. This would be tied up very shortly. The defendants were going to be squared next and then they could all go home.

The judge was encouraged by this news: he gave his blessing to a moratorium on further action in the simmering row over jurisdiction between the US and English courts. (It was about to come to the boil again, otherwise.) Deposition notices and discovery requests were allowed to continue; but it was agreed on all sides that the settlement would be given urgent priority. Judge Greene invited everyone back to his court on 8 May to see if they could wrap things up. BA's board was determined to do just that – and the cooperation of all the airlines in the case was clearly the next essential ingredient.

By the purest coincidence, the legal committee of IATA was due to hold its 71st meeting in Geneva on 16–17 April. There was going to be a rousing performance of Hamlet without the Prince: a long agenda included numerous antitrust discussion items, but not the Laker case.

Colin Marshall personally telephoned his fellow chief executives and insisted they meet for a special, top-secret gathering to iron out their differences. In the meantime, all the creditors were given until 17 April to complete and sign the various papers which would give Ivanhoe a clean sweep of the Laker debts. BA, however, was sorely disappointed. The other chief executives refused to make themselves available. The best that could be managed was a conference of their in-house counsels, with a

247

scattering of the top US lawyers, including Lloyd Cutler. So BA sent Park along alone to lay down the terms in uncompromising fashion.

The meeting was postponed until the morning of 18 April, to allow Pan Am's deputy counsel, Greg Buhler, to be there. He had at first declined to attend: the stunning disclosure of the sale of all Pan Am's Pacific operations to United Airlines, the US industry leader, was only a few days away. But he came – it was that important. The only absentee, in fact, was Edmond Braure, the 57-year-old vice-president of legal affairs for UTA. (This in itself was slightly ironic: Braure was at the time chairman of the IATA legal committee!) Otherwise, it was the first and only time that all the defendant airlines met together in one place. It was a tense meeting.

The suitably gloomy venue was one of the windowless conference rooms in the basement of the Penta Hotel in Geneva. Outside, 18 April dawned a gloriously bright spring morning; inside, by just after 8.00 a.m., the sombrely dressed lawyers were hard at their wrangling. They broke a couple of times during the morning – returning once, just before lunch, to find the corridor outside their room packed with hundreds of raucous marketing executives enjoying a conference break for cocktails. Heads bowed, the lawyers traipsed back in single file through the revellers to resume their bitter confrontation.

It was chicken-and-egg time. Park insisted there was absolutely no point in him returning to Beckman, Laker and Morris until he had got a firm offer to show them ('What's your authority?' – 'F*** all!'). The Group of Five insisted there was no point in committing themselves to any position until Park was able to bring them a firm response from Beckman. Some of the Americans present took a robust line on behalf of their continental clients ('If it busts the deal, it busts the deal.') But most – including Greg Buhler from Pan Am and Rick Hoffmann from TWA – were astonished at the apparent lack of

248

realism shown by their European counterparts. At one point, the detailed bickering came down to differences over just $350,000 each!

The essence of the stand-off, however, was deeper than that. The Group of Five airlines were not prepared to accept the risk of underwriting a prospective settlement which might, if talks faltered, lead to the need for more money from them at a later stage. Lufthansa's Professor Rudolph spelt it out: they wanted an indemnity from BA that whatever they put into the kitty would be their final exposure.

TWA's Hoffmann – who had worked for twenty-five years in the general counsel's office at the Civil Aviation Bureau in Washington and was always listened to with respect during the Laker case – told the professor and his allies that they had a cheek asking for an indemnity when they were offering so little money in the first place. But Park just shook his head gravely, sucked on his upper lip as he often did at such moments and said it could be the end of the road. The other carriers wanted BA to return to the fray without their firm backing – 'and that we are just not prepared to do'.

Late that night, Len Bebchick flew back to Heathrow to catch the Concorde connection for Washington. He seemed to have an aptitude for meeting people at airports. This time it was Graeme Brister, Park's assistant who had impressed everyone who had dealt with him during the talks so far and who was about to be made a partner of Linklaters. Bebchick approached him during the flight with a Concorde menu. On the back was Bebchick's arithmetic for a settlement excluding the Group of Five. Why should BA, BCal, TWA and Pan Am not go for a separate deal, he asked? At least it might be a useful negotiating card to play.

The BA board knew differently. It had to consider the longer-term future, the chances of a Bermuda III deal and its future relations with the other defendants. The idea of them struggling on for another four years or so against

Beckman and the Laker camp did not bear thinking about.

Colin Marshall had yet again to turn his diary upside down and begin a tiring campaign to resolve the crisis. He spent hours on the telephone to his counterparts in Europe. Conferences of the Association of European Airlines and of IATA had already allowed him to get to know most of the other airline chiefs a little since January 1983. But he was still very much a new boy in a notoriously closed world: it was tough going.

Park flew backwards and forwards across Europe impressing BA's case upon the boards of the Group of Five. In Amsterdam, for example, he pointed to the impending series of depositions which were hanging over KLM for the second half of May. If this case ever came to trial, it was going to be a public relations disaster for all the defendants, regardless of the jury's eventual decision. The mass of details built up by the depositions was bound to contain endless opportunities for damaging misrepresentation! As if to underline the threat posed by depositions, Beckman filed notices on 25 April for the deposition in May of three key members of BA's staff. More battles over the Protection of Trading Interests were looming, if Judge Greene's moratorium should expire.

BA was desperate to have the Group's cooperation. Marshall and Park made it clear to each chief executive in turn that they were ready to abandon the settlement and tell the judge it had failed, unless support was forthcoming immediately.

Finally it arrived. The allocation of their dues was vague. But the Group committed itself to a joint contribution of just over $14m. and BA received telexes from all the European offices confirming the offer. In the first couple of days of May, TWA and Pan Am did the same, chipping in with their $18m. And on 7 May, Len Bebchick left a note for Park at the Four Seasons Hotel, confirming that BCal would provide – on a take-it-or-leave-it basis – a fixed sum just under $4m. At last Park had the creditors and the defendants where he needed them. It had taken very nearly five months to the day.

Three individual offers went round to Beckman's offices in Washington on the afternoon of 7 May: there was $48m. for the creditors which Morris was asked to accept on their behalf; $8m. for Beckman and his fellow attorneys; and $8m. for Freddie. As Park had indicated would be the case at that first meeting in Little New Street back on 5 December, the financial terms of the offer were non-negotiable.

Beckman arrived back in Washington that same day from an International Aviation Law Seminar in Marbella on 'The New Regulation of International Air Transport in the Aftermath of Deregulation'. He had given a paper over the weekend in front of a distinguished audience which included Patrick Shovelton, the senior British civil servant who had been a key architect of the Bermuda II agreement in 1977. The international fracas over how that agreement should be interpreted was now promising to make Beckman a very rich man.

The Whitbread Brewery in the City of London was the unlikely venue the next morning, 8 May, for a press conference by the BA board to announce the airline's results for the year to 31 March 1985. Pre-tax profits were up from £185m. to £202m. In the beamed hall of the Chiswell Street brewery, King sat perched on a high dais behind a model of Concorde and handled the ceremonies with his usual pugnacity. ('As we have only one shareholder at this time, I think it might be in order if we start a little early.') Pressed to say whether a settlement was now agreed between the co-defendants – 'Yes, I suppose it is' – the chairman would not be drawn on the drama behind the scenes over the preceding weeks. All he would admit was that, within a few hours on the other side of the Atlantic, BA was to appear before Judge Greene to seek an extension of the 10 April moratorium.

That extension was granted by the judge, until 30 May.

It was not, however, the chief significance of the 8 May conference.

Judge Greene heard how the creditors had all been brought into an agreement, and the defendants too. The major part of the negotiations, it seemed, were accomplished. So much was quickly explained by BA's Sidney Rosdeitcher. But then Beckman had his turn to speak. 'Your Honor,' he said to Judge Greene, 'unfortunately what I have to report is that yesterday afternoon we did not receive what we would call an offer. We received an ultimatum . . .' For the best part of half an hour, Beckman listed his grievances. Freddie, who was present, added a few of his own: 'For reasons unknown to man,' said the world's least bashful advocate, 'they [the defendants] didn't want to give me the money as money and the proposal at the moment is . . . which particular sewer do you want it to come from?'

It was conspicuous to the judge that very few of their grievances actually focused on the amounts put forward in the threefold offer. But he seemed under no illusions about the seriousness of what he was hearing. 'To be entirely candid,' said Judge Greene to Beckman, 'I was not always happy in the past with the way the defendants have been running this lawsuit, but it seems to me at the moment you seem to be more of a stumbling-block than the defendants.'

It was going to take seven dramatic weeks for Christopher Morris to arrive at the same conclusion.

22

The Nussbaum Urn

Privatisation, BA's chairman told a UK lecture audience in the middle of May 1985, was 'a word that I have never really liked as I think it sounds like something unpleasant done to unmentionable parts of the body'. Looking at what was happening to his airline's corporate body in Washington over the ensuing weeks, King might almost have settled for that definition. The agony lay in the frustration of seemingly endless delays.

The creditors, more or less, were agreed on the $64m. settlement. All the defendants, more or less, were agreed on it as well. The plaintiff and the defendants could close the action in a day. All they had to do was file a 'Praecipe of Dismissal' with the court. And it could be as little as one line long – 'The parties to the dispute have agreed that it should be dismissed' – with all the details kept to a private arrangement.

Of course, no one expected the private arrangement to be settled in a day. In the aftermath of the 8 May conference, BA accepted that a few weeks would be required to tie things up. But at least, as Colin Marshall told the world's air correspondents on 23 May, they could now look forward to a real deadline on 30 May. (He disclosed many of the numbers, too, with $8m. for Freddie and all the freedom he wanted to start a new airline if he so wished.)

In the intervening days, time could be well spent in preparing the media world for BA's exuberant new image. Fleet Street editors, MPs and even civil servants were whisked down to Rio de Janeiro for a few days of intense study on the airline's newest route network. The fashion writers were wined and dined in Cannes for the launch of BA's new hostess uniforms. Some lavish functions were laid on as usual for the Paris Air Show on 30 May.

But that was the day, after a blissful interval, that the endless delays finally caught up with BA again. For the creditors and the defendants, it became suddenly and horribly clear, were not the only parties to the arrangement in prospect . . . And those that remained to be persuaded represented a highly inflammable mix of temperaments.

The portents on 8 May had been ominous enough. Freddie had hinted at further legal action on behalf of himself and other unnamed parties, as well as complaining that he needed more of that elusive 'warmth' to beat off any cold shoulders from the airline world in future. Beckman had worried about several aspects of the proposed settlement – future negligence suits brought by disgruntled creditors; the non-negotiability; the requirement (he said) that he should quit aviation law. But above all, he had given notice of one central grievance. 'I make clear to Your Honor and to all defendants,' Beckman had said, 'that they are nowhere near on the money . . .'

By 30 May, every extra day that passed diminished the chances of a September sale date for BA. The parties met in Judge Greene's Ceremonial Courtroom Conference Room just after 10.00 a.m. Within an hour, the chances of an autumn privatisation deadline were dead and buried. Or perhaps they were just buried – they had already died in the course of five meetings held between Beckman and the BA camp during May.

The Laker lawyer's formal response to the $64m. package of 7 May had taken BA rather by surprise a few days later. Beckman made a counteroffer of his own. If BA would hand over $25m. plus all the documents which the plaintiff needed to pursue the case against the other defendants, the airline could have its own, separate settlement. Then, as Beckman put it to Judge Greene on 30 May, 'they can get out, go about their business, enjoy their lives and go away'.

BA turned him down. It was Bermuda III casting its shadow again. Indeed, at the 30 May conference, Sidney Rosdeitcher referred to this factor as explicitly as anyone had done since December:

> The proposal to settle separately [he told the judge] would not bring peace which we think is a very valuable asset to everybody involved here, to the court and to the two governments that are involved here. We think more is at stake and so much is at stake in this settlement effort. We think every effort ought to be made to see if we can bring it to a satisfactory conclusion.

So BA was sticking to its guns. A comprehensive settlement was needed. But as the 30 May discussions proceeded, some intractable problems emerged. For example, there was the question of the fees for Beckman and his colleagues. The settlement offered them $8m. At a private meeting in May, Beckman had unveiled their demand. They wanted $65m. – just $1m. more than the $64m. package offered by the defendants to satisfy everyone. The English lawyers on the case did not know whether to laugh or cry.

Beckman had been quite brazen in defence of a figure which even took away the judge's breath when he first heard it. His position, however brass-necked, was obviously a negotiating stance and it was not without logic. The total estimated debts of Laker Airways added up to $300m. Beckman's contingency-fee contract provided for 20 per cent of the value of any settlement. He was chosing to identify the value not with the $64m. package but with the $300m. debts it would displace.

(The claim came out at $65m. rather than $60m. due to some front-end loading on the percentage calculations.) But Beckman was too canny a negotiator to disclose all his reasoning at the outset. He presented the claim with no frills and refused BA's requests to see a copy of his contract with Laker Airways.

In front of Judge Greene, both Rosdeitcher and Morris acknowledged the lawyers' fees as their biggest remaining problem. Morris, after all, was exposed to a real legal liability. Beckman's contract was with Laker; but under Jersey law, Morris was responsible for commitments entered into by Laker under his stewardship.

Beckman himself would not be drawn on the subject on 30 May. He spoke at length without referring to it. His real aim was to undermine the defendants' confidence that settlement was round the corner and he went about it ruthlessly. There were other problems, he said, and they were 'insuperable'. The judge asked why, if that was the case, the court was bothering to meet at all. 'Exactly,' replied Beckman. 'Because we think we are wasting an awful lot of time and money.' Of the other problems he referred to, two were critical. The first was Freddie – or more precisely, as he put it himself, Freddie's soul.

Most unusually, Freddie came along to the meeting clutching some written notes for the speech he was going to make. He even managed to keep to them for a few moments while he spelt out a message which he said the defendants had constantly ignored. ('It goes in one ear and out the other.') But his passion soon got the upper hand. The presence of so many serious-looking lawyers in one place together could hardly fail to draw a joke out of him. 'Without being facetious,' he obliged, 'if I had the money I am entitled to, I could probably buy British Airways.' The judge suggested drily that BA might have seen his offer coming. Well, replied Freddie, 'every disaster has to have a little humour in it.'

And that brief exchange opened the floodgates. He

was in favour of seeing the case settled, insisted Freddie, 'and I made it clear the last time [8 May] and make it clear again today that $8m. is not a problem to me.' But he was not going to sell his soul to the airlines. That was non-negotiable. So he had to be able to get back into the airline business. He had to have access to documents to help him write his memoirs ('my dearest wish, of course, is that the truth be told because I want that information myself and I want it for a young man seven years of age, Freddie Laker'). And he had to have 'warmth' that would restore him his self-esteem, free first-class tickets on the defendants' airplanes – and some recognition of the integrity of his position all along.

Finally, swept up in his own rhetoric, Freddie closed with a revealing plea that must have told the judge a good deal about the task in front of Park and his negotiators:

> . . . I am a simple person, all I want to do is go back into my trade [sic] and I want some undertakings from it. Please don't conspire against me again, please may I have access to the airport and fair and reasonable terms. Please do not make frivolous objections to route applications. After all, they ruled on my licences before, why can't I have them back without any problems? Why don't they just stand aside and let me make my applications? I had it before and Your Honor, that is it. Thank you. [Judge Greene: OK.]

The other problem was closely connected to Freddie's soul. If Freddie had once been aboard the settlement train but seemed now to be in the process of climbing off it, there was a ready and willing hand to help him down. Tiny Rowland, the chief executive of Lonrho, had played little or no visible role in the settlement negotiations up until this point. But the man who had stood by Freddie in his darkest hours during 1982 undoubtedly had a claim to some involvement. For he and Freddie had entered into 'deadlock partnerships' to set up People's Airline and Skytrain Holidays as 50:50 joint ventures – neither side could give undertakings about them without the consent of the other.

Essential to the $64m. settlement was a blanket undertaking from Freddie that he would pursue no further legal action in connection with any past events, dating from either before or after the Laker Airways collapse. In other words, they were asking him for assurances on behalf of Laker II – as the joint ventures were known – and therefore Lonrho, too.

No better negotiating card could possibly have been devised for Freddie, not even by Beckman himself. If Freddie was intent upon a spot of brinkmanship over a settlement worthy of his soul, the Lonrho factor could give him the perfect alibi.

The 30 May conference probably finished off BA's chances of privatisation in 1985 altogether; but it was not wholly discouraging for BA's lawyers. Judge Greene, for one thing, appeared to have shifted his attitude subtly towards the parties in his court. This was evident from a fractious exchange towards the end, when BA's lawyers asked for the conference to be struck off the public record.

Judge Greene:	How do you feel about that?
Mr Beckman:	I would like to have time to consider it and give my views.
Judge Greene:	No, no, tell me right now. I am not engaged in negotiations here. Either you agree or you don't agree.
Mr Beckman:	Well, the problem is the last time –
Judge Greene:	– Mr Beckman doesn't agree.

And by the time the parties broke up after an hour, Judge Greene had agreed to lend his help if they wanted it in seeking a way forward. The case was 'not an open and shut proposition by any means for either side', Judge Greene reminded them. Private negotiations, with the judge in the chair, were fixed to start the following week.

So June started out on an optimistic note. Within days, it was wavering badly. Then, quite suddenly, everything seemed to go haywire. This had little or nothing to do with Christopher Morris, the Laker creditors or their $48m. share of the proposed settlement. Poker had always been the real name of the settlement game. Now that most of the players – Morris the City gent, Park the English solicitor and many a leading name in the Washington legal establishment, among them – were looking ready to lay down their hands, those who were the most natural high-rollers stretched out to take over the table. Beckman and Freddie were in their element.

Many of the American lawyers on the case had always feared in private that Park had played the Double Eight card prematurely, back in January. A few had warned him at the time that both Freddie and Beckman would come back demanding more. As June wore on, that seemed exactly what was happening.

Backwards and forwards went the lawyers between Washington, London and Florida. There were interminable shared flights, shared hotels and shared meals – at fashionable Washington restaurants like Tiberios's or Mr K's on K Street. Occasionally they met in Judge Greene's chambers, with its book-lined walls and photographs of the judge and his family watching them in their struggle. Sometimes they met in the office of Mike Nussbaum, Morris's own sharp but very genial US lawyer, in Thomas Circle, Washington.

In a small alcove of Nussbaum's office stood a resplendent plinth – with nothing at all on it. 'On loan to the Getty Museum' read the permanent label on the plinth. As the early summer months began to slip by, the settlement was coming to appear as substantial as the Nussbaum urn.

259

And the parties met just once in the offices of Lonrho, halfway along Cheapside in the City of London. Park went there on the afternoon of 10 June, to meet with Beckman and Dick Shadyac in the company of Edward du Cann MP, Lonrho's chairman, and Tiny Rowland, its chief executive. Park needed to know whether BA could hope for Lonrho's help: would it consent to letting Freddie give the assurances which the airlines were seeking over Laker II?

It was some years since Park had last meet Rowland in person, during the Rhodesian sanctions business in the seventies. He was shocked to see how much Rowland had aged; the physical presence of the big man seemed to Park a shadow of its former self. But Rowland could still be formidable in argument, as he was about to find out. They talked politely about the airlines' dilemma for a while and the need to find some satisfactory answer to the Laker II problem. But there was no doubting that Lonrho, like Freddie, believed People's Airline and Skytrain Holidays had been the victims of predatory business practices.

In the background was a bitter, running feud between Lonrho and the UK Government over another matter entirely. Rowland had been enraged by the DTI's action three months earlier in allowing Harrods of Knightsbridge to be acquired by three hitherto little-known Egyptian brothers. Only five days had elapsed between the Egyptians' cash bid for the Harrods parent company and their clearance by Whitehall. Lonrho itself had been blocked from bidding for Harrods for the best part of seven years and was now counterattacking, chiefly by questioning publicly the sources of the Egyptians' apparently bottomless wealth.

Now here was a second source of friction between Lonrho and the Government (qua BA's shareholder). The Lonrho chairman made clear to Park that his company was extremely concerned at the treatment Laker II had received in the marketplace in 1982–3. Then

Tiny Rowland told Park he had a solution. Lonrho, he suggested, should be allowed to purchase 50 per cent of BA in the forthcoming sale, for a cash payment of £400m. Since Lonrho had 60,000 shareholders, would this not provide some measure of wider share ownership as well as a secure financial return?

Rowland asked if Park would report this, with his support, back to the Government. Well, said Park, he would report it back – but it would not have his support. The Lonrho chief executive boomed with rage. Park was just a City solicitor. Who was he to say he would or would not give his support? But Park retorted robustly. If his support was such a little thing, why had Rowland sought it in the first place?

There had been a day, thought Park to himself, when he would not have had the last word in such a brutal exchange with Rowland. That afternoon, though, the BA solicitor closed the meeting. On their way down in the lift, du Cann apologised to Park for not having been able to present a few more figures in connection with Laker II's possible claim.

Lonrho made good that omission just a few hours later, with the press. People's Airline had budgeted, apparently, to make profits of roughly $10m. a year for at least ten years. By putting it out of business, the ten Laker case defendants had therefore [sic] damaged it to the tune of $107m. There were also losses of $2m. to consider at Skytrain Holidays. That meant triple damages, under US antitrust law, of $327m. – and that was what Lonrho was going to claim in a suit to be filed shortly.

This was all for the birds, as far as its legal substance was concerned. All of the defendants' US lawyers were sure of it. But that was not the point. Here was a major British company announcing a wholly new departure in the Laker litigation. The impact was immediate.

It filled the airline boardrooms with gloom and despondency. The spectre of paying off Morris, only for

261

Beckman then to step in with another identical claim on Lonrho's behalf, petrified the continental carriers. It greatly alarmed BA, too. For a brief moment, the idea of a government indemnity was mooted once again. If Morris would settle for $48m. would the Treasury offer an indemnity against Lonrho?

Nicholas Ridley squashed that at the parliamentary lobby meeting on 20 June and in public appearances over that weekend. The Government was as opposed to indemnities as ever. But he also went out of his way to make it clear that privatisation would not be blocked by the 'Lonrho caper', as Whitehall was describing the latest setback. If necessary, BA would accept a partial settlement. But it would not be doing business with Lonrho in any form.

This was no doubt sound political sense; but it gave the co-defendants no comfort whatever. Were they really going to have to go on struggling for years after all? Some of the Washington lawyers honestly began to suspect so. Even Judge Greene appeared rather shaken by the sudden turn of events. At another private session on 14 June, he told Beckman his claim for $65m. was 'preposterous'. As for Lonrho's claim, nothing had been filed and he was not in a position to say what a jury might one day award or not award. But he did think the plaintiff's lawyers were 'behaving irresponsibly'. He was only prepared to make 'one last effort' at a settlement. After that, it was on to a full trial.

Nor was it just Lonrho's putative claim and the lawyers' fees which were threatening the end. Freddie himself was leading Park and Brister a merry dance. The very vagueness of the 'warmth' concept was presenting all sorts of difficulty. Park and Freddie liked each other. They had become quite a vaudeville act together over the months. (Park had a nice line in Freddie impersonations: 'Cairo, Cairo? I'd 'ave flown there if they'd 'ave let me!') But now it was all wearing very thin.

Perhaps Freddie was overly encouraged by developments in the English High Court during June. On the 10th, Mr Justice Leggatt finally ruled against the arguments put by Robert Alexander QC on behalf of Midland Bank for a permanent injunction against being joined into the Laker suit by Morris. (An appeal was fixed for 27 June.) Or perhaps Freddie just allowed himself to be overly enthused by those around him. Any combination of Freddie, Beckman and Tiny Rowland was certainly not going to be disposed to opting for a quiet life.

Whatever the explanation, Freddie had become unmistakably more difficult. Take, for example, the arguments he had with Park and Brister about future access to airline routes. If the defendants said he could go to Oslo, Freddie would say they were trying to bundle him off into insignificant markets. If the defendants said he could not go to Oslo, he would say they were blocking his re-entry into the international industry. On another occasion, Freddie insisted that he should be able to use the Laker Airways name again one day. Park said this could be arranged. Days later, Freddie said he wanted his company back in its entirety – as had been discussed!

The two Linklaters men began to despair of pulling it off. They flew to Florida for one last meeting at Freddie's invitation. The two of them, with Freddie, Beckman and Freddie's fiancée Jackie, went out to a local Miami nightspot called The Sand Bar for dinner. It was a ghastly evening. Freddie was too preoccupied with his fiancée for much of the time to bother with the lawyers. Park and Brister sat glumly at the table while Beckman harangued them for over an hour about the iniquities of his adversaries. The two City partners emerged shaken by the experience – and surer than ever of their eventual conclusion.

They reached it just days later.

At a private session in front of Judge Greene in Washington on Thursday, 27 June, Freddie was put on the spot. Did he or did he not accept the $8m. that was being offered to him? Yes, said Freddie, he did. But the next day, Park and Brister were in Beckman's offices and Beckman launched another offensive. Freddie's position cropped up again. On the Friday, it emerged, Freddie was not accepting the $8m. offer.

Park and his assistant left the building. It was a steamy Washington summer day, but they walked off past the girlie bars and jello wrestling parlours which face Beckman's offices and holed themselves up in the Four Seasons Hotel for a cool think. They exchanged long telephone calls with the BA board members in England over that weekend. Then they called Mike Nussbaum. By Sunday morning, they were ready for him to call Christopher Morris direct at his home in Cobham, Surrey.

Would the liquidator agree, they wanted to know, to a $48m. settlement, leaving Beckman and Freddie in the cold?

23

A Bold Gamble

Len Bebchick, British Caledonian's lawyer, went out with his wife late on the morning of Sunday 30 June for a day in downtown Washington. They had tickets for the capital's international Bach competition for violin and cello. At the end of the afternoon, Bebchick telephoned home to see if there had been any messages while they were away. Yes, there was just one: Bill Park had called. Would Len drop everything and get round to the Four Seasons Hotel as soon as possible? End of message.

It was only a few blocks from the concert hall. When Bebchick arrived, he went straight to the lift and met Park and Brister on their way out for a walk round the block. They went back up together to the Laker suite. Park invited Bebchick to order himself a Rubens sandwhich – cheese, sauerkraut and salami: a Bebchick favourite – and make himself comfortable for a journey over the Rubicon. About forty-five minutes later, Rosdeitcher and Rosenthal, BCal's other lawyer on the case, joined them for the crossing.

They had contacted Morris, said Park, and the liquidator was very sympathetic to the idea of breaking the link that had bound him to Freddie for two-and-a-half years. It had always been Park's impression that the main thrust of the Laker suit had been aimed at BA and BCal above all the others. So he and Graeme Brister had asked Rosdeitcher and Doug Rosenthal to join them to help make the critical decision.

Morris, it turned out, had been waiting for the chance to jump for a few weeks. Lonrho's arrival on the scene had been the last straw. But the logic of clinging to the idea of a comprehensive settlement had been dwindling for some time. Quite simply, Morris had no reason for believing he could win any more money for the Laker creditors than the $48m. on the table. He thought it would be unwarrantable to endanger that money in defence of Freddie's interests. Anyway, Freddie was not exactly being neglected. Morris had always accepted that he had some obligation to ensure that Freddie, as the 90 per cent owner of Laker, was not forgotten. Here he was with the Double Eight payment! Like winning the pools every morning, eight days in a row, Morris told his colleagues.

And he had good professional reasons for fearing that things were getting out of hand. It seemed to Morris that Beckman, Shadyac, Schwartz and all the rest were beginning to speak with less of a united voice than had earlier been the case. Again, he had his worries about the evidence they had gathered. It was not just the Jones debriefing. It was also the total absence of any testimony from airline industry economists prepared to stand by the conspiracy allegations. Finally and most immediately pressing, the plaintiff's camp was actually running out of money. Over $10m. had been spent on the case to date. That had exhausted all the limited funds put at Morris's disposal at the outset. And it was beginning to strain the two Washington firms acting for him.

So, early on the morning of 30 June, he and Nussbaum had given BA and its lawyers the green light they wanted. There were three conditions. One, $48m. had to be the settlement for the creditors: this was already agreed. Two, Beckman and Freddie had to be offered $8m. each for a reasonable period of time, to take it or leave it as they chose. Three, BA had to provide Morris with some indemnity against the possibility that Beckman might sue him for breach of contract over the contingency fee.

These were the terms Park wanted to discuss with the BCal lawyers. Were they sensible? If so, could they reasonably hope to carry all the other defendants with them in a partial settlement? The advice from Bebchick and Rosenthal was: you have no choice. BA must go for it.

Park and Brister started there and then, inviting one of the other defendants' US counsel out to a late-night dinner. Next morning, they began the rounds of all the continental airlines' lawyers. They started over breakfast and by the evening had completed the task.

Lloyd Cutler at Wilmer, Cutler & Pickering had not always endorsed BA's views to his Lufthansa clients. Nor had he always managed to represent the Group of Five's views with quite the unanimity which Park had hoped for in the early days. But on that Monday, he welcomed the BA initiative warmly. His support did much to reassure the European executives who had only come into the settlement at the end of April under some sufferance.

What BA was proposing now was manifestly more of a gamble than they had been asked to take in April. If both Laker and Beckman walked away, there was every chance they might come back to fight another day, perhaps with Lonrho in attendance. In a sense, the proposal made a nonsense of the rationale that the airlines were hardly paying much more into the $48m. part of the settlement than they would have to pay anyway in the defence costs of a full trial. They might end up paying a settlement and defence costs. It was this fear which had led them to reject suggestions made by Beckman and Freddie themselves in April and May that the airlines should 'break the linkage' and let Morris settle independently. BA as well as all the other defendants had been highly suspicious of the very idea.

But all the defendants had really gone too far to want to go back now. The persuasive efforts of Colin Marshall and the rest of the BA board had had their effect. And all of the defendants' boardrooms with the exception of Sabena – whose chairman, Carlos Van Rafelghem, had been injured in a car crash in the spring – had by now had a first-hand taste of depositions. (Van Rafelghem throughout these months was the most relaxed of all the continental executives: where was the problem, he would ask Park rhetorically.) That had brought home to them the ordeal threatened by a full trial. Greg Buhler and Rick Hoffmann at Pan Am and TWA had no doubt that part-settlement was the most realistic option. One by one, the Europeans reaffirmed their support for Park's amended strategy.

Ironing out the final details took nearly two weeks. But they were working now to a deadline: Judge Greene was leaving for his summer vacation on 12 July and they had to present their revised plan to him before he left – signed, sealed and delivered. There were several meetings between Park, Morris and Mike Nussbaum, who was by now very close to the liquidator and an important influence on events. Beckman soon learned of the meetings and demanded to be present. But they refused to admit him. They would present him with the details soon enough – and they were determined to hand them over as a fait accompli.

By 11 July they were ready to finalise the documents. Morris flew over to Washington. It was a Thursday and he landed early in the afternoon. By the time he joined Park and Nussbaum at Thomas Circle, they had virtually completed preparations for the $48m. deal. Morris and Park soon fell to negotiating the indemnities BA would give Morris, against the risk of disaffected creditors – and against the Laker lawyers.

Meanwhile, two letters were on their way round to Beckman's offices. One was an invitation to attend Judge Greene's court the next morning at 9.00 a.m. The other was addressed to Freddie. It was on Linklaters & Paines headed paper and it announced the end of the road for 'The Freddie and Park Show'.

'It was, and remains, my clear undestanding,' wrote Park, that Freddie had accepted the basic settlement deal, $8m. and all, on Thursday 27 June. Paragraph two followed the same wording: 'It was, and remains, my clear understanding' . . . that on Friday 28 June, Freddie had denied ever making such an acceptance. Under these circumstances, said the letter darkly, Park regretted that Freddie had to understand the co-defendants were unable to see any further point in trying to negotiate a deal with him. Accordingly, they were offering him an ultimatum. There would be $8m. on the table for him to take away at any time up to 20 August, provided – and the proviso was spelt out in detail – that he did not in the meantime institute or get involved in any way with legal proceedings against BA and the other defendants. The letter closed on a note of sadness. He regretted having to write to Freddie in this manner, concluded Park; but he had to say the defendants felt they had no choice in the light of the circumstances set out in paragraphs one and two.

Morris, Park and Nussbaum worked late into the night on their bilateral deal. In anticipation of it, BA had in fact already completed many of the financial transactions it was going to authorise. Of the forty-five minor creditors, for example, some thirty-six had already been paid (about £3.9m.) to reassign their debts to Ivanhoe Investments. But there were numerous i's to be dotted and t's to be crossed. It was not until 2.00 a.m. on the morning of 12 July that they finally set the seal on their bargain. Seven hours later, they joined Sid Rosdeitcher and Laker's US lawyers at Judge Greene's court.

Beckman was clearly astounded at the turn of events. He listened silently as the details of the bargain were explained to all the lawyers present, before the judge arrived. But his face was taut with anger. Beckman was visibly fizzing like a firework. If he went off, no one was sure quite which direction he would take – but it was clear that Morris would have to take cover. Beckman cut his client dead. Indeed, he spoke barely a word to anyone in the room, even when the judge arrived.

When the private talks began under Judge Greene's chairmanship, there was never any doubt of the central issue. The two law firms of Beckman & Kirstein and Metzger, Shadyac & Schwarz refused to accept their $8m. offer. Beckman consulted briefly with his colleague but it was Dick Shadyac who did the talking. The fact was, he said, that the time sheets kept by the plaintiff's lawyers since November 1982 recorded enough work to warrant payment of $7m. on an hourly basis alone. (Yes, that was seven million dollars. What the City professionals thought of the figure can be readily imagined.) Considering the gravity of the case, $1m. – split between two firms and several lawyers – seemed a meagre premium to offer for good will!

Round and round went the arguments. Lodged tightly under Bill Park's hat – had he been wearing one – was authority from the BA board to lift the Beckman party's fee to $12m. But there it stayed.

At last, the judge summoned the session to a formal hearing at 11.25 a.m. It was agreed to leave the Double Eight agreement, or non-agreement, to one side. The important thing was that it was no longer going to stand in the way of what followed. The terms and conditions of the $48m. settlement were then put on the record and agreed. Shadyac and Rosdeitcher did most of the talking. But the judge checked with all those present that the agreement met with their understanding and approval – 'out of an abundance of caution', as he put it, and who could blame him?

It took only twenty minutes to record. Judge Greene summed up the 'somewhat tortuous process':

> I want to congratulate the attorneys on both sides, or I should say on all sides since there are many more than two sides here, for their hard work on this case, particularly the strenuous settlement

talks . . . A settlement is normally to be preferred over protracted and extensive and complex litigation. In this particular case, the creditors will speedily obtain the repayment of their debt. For the defendant airlines, the settlement holds out some hope for peace in the international aviation scene. And I would suppose, from what I gathered from the discussions, that this may enable the British Government to carry out its plan to privatize British Airways.

Alas for BA, the judge was slightly jumping the gun . . .

The brouhaha about the lawyers' fees, at least, was settled quicker than most had feared. Beckman, Kirstein, Shadyac and Schwarz retreated at lunchtime to Beckman's offices in Eye Street. The deep pile blue velvet carpets, the elegant open-floor planning for their secretaries, the lines of bookcases with annual Civil Aviation Bureau reports stretching back to 1940 – Beckman was already surrounded with all the accoutrements of a successful career. The next few hours were going to crown the biggest case he, or any other aviation lawyer, would ever handle.

Since everyone had clearly been impressed by Beckman's genuine fury at Morris, it was agreed by Shadyac that he should negotiate in the afternoon using Beckman's total intransigence as his trump card. Beckman was still playing hardball, just as he had been on that first day in November 1982 when he filed the suit. Back they all went to Judge Greene, hard-faced men facing each other over the table to settle how many millions – how many expensive cars and country houses and skiing chalets and European holidays – the one side was going to surrender to the other. 'None of us,' as Shadyac later told the judge, 'are babes in the woods.'

It took scarcely more than an hour. Beckman delayed his entry and Shadyac insisted he had to have at least $15m. Park conceded the extra $4m. he had had in his hat

271

all along. And he was forced to commit BA to pay another $500,000 on top of that – plus a private $326,000 for Bob Beckman alone, for work done prior to November 1982. The main $12.5m. award would be split 50:50 between the two firms of Beckman & Kirstein and Metzger, Shadyac & Schwarz.

Then they all spent a short while persuading Beckman that, as the senior partner of his firm, he – and not Christopher Morris – would have to be answerable for any claims made by Beckman's former partner, Don Farmer, on the fees. Farmer had in fact just written to Nussbaum warning the liquidator not to pay the fees over to Beckman. Beckman himself was reluctant, as he put it, to be answerable for what was in Farmer's mind. Nussbaum said he was uncomfortable 'because I detect some slipping and sliding here'. But eventually Beckman agreed to take responsibility for Farmer's complaints – Farmer sued him shortly afterwards – and, to use Beckman's earlier phrase, they all went home.

So the die had been cast. Would BA's bold gamble pay off? Or were all the defendants going to find they had squandered $48m. – and spent it, at that – on a settlement that could even prejudice some future jury to suspect (what they strenuously denied) that more than just convenience lay behind their pay-off?

24

'Money, Judge, Money'

Christopher Morris gave a press conference in Washington on the Friday afternoon of 12 July to announce the $48m. deal. For the Laker liquidator, it was unambiguously a triumph. The conference itself was less of a triumph. Satellite time was booked for it to catch the BBC nine o'clock news at home; but the arguing over the lawyers' fees forced Morris to postpone everything by half an hour and he missed his chance to appear live on the nation's screens. But that was a trifle compared to the reality of what had happened. By winning $48m. for the Laker creditors, he had secured for Touche Ross probably the most successful liquidation in UK history.

Park had less cause for celebration. In fact, he was only too well aware of the risks that BA was taking. He and Morris flew back on the London flight together that night. Park had his usual mixed vermouth or two and the two men drank plenty of champagne with their dinner. But Park was less than elated with the terms of the settlement. BA had again had to lift its settlement costs. The extra $4.83m. icing on the Double Eight cake would be to its account. (That made 18 + 10 + 5 in round figures – $33m.) Nor was he yet confident of raising $18m. from British Caledonian and the Group of Five without endless allocation squabbles.

As for the details of all the 11/12 July talks, too much had been done in too little time. Park and Rosdeitcher had hardly left the courtroom on the Friday afternoon, for example, before they realised they had agreed to pay over the first $6m. of the lawyers' fees just a fortnight later. What would happen if they paid out and then found for some reason that the settlement could not go ahead? The prospect that it might somehow be blocked by Freddie was, of course, the biggest headache of all. This was the essence of the gamble. Would Freddie just take his money and go away? Or would he redouble his efforts to prove a conspiracy? Would Beckman's success in lifting his $8m. by half as much again spur Freddie, perhaps, into a similar last-ditch fight for more money?

And what was Beckman's own position to be? He had taken the money. Yet he semed almost as bitter about the outcome as if he had been left without a penny. BA had explored the possibility of trying to get a formal court constraint to prevent him using his knowledge of the Morris action on behalf of anyone else. But that was a non-starter. Under the rules of the Washington circuit, no attorney could be barred from acting for new clients.

Beckman had one particular 'new client' who was very eager to talk to him. Within twenty-four hours of the $48m. settlement's conclusion, Beckman and Lonrho's executives in London were in touch about the next step. Tiny Rowland's company had been saved the £700,000 which Rowland had promised publicly to return to Laker's dispossessed ticketholders back in 1982. But no one at the company's Cheapside headquarters seemed inclined to be very grateful to Morris.

On Sunday 14 July, Lonrho had an interesting message for the British press. 'We spoke to Mr Beckman yesterday and he confirmed to us that he was still free to act on behalf of Sir Freddie Laker and Lonrho Plc,' said their spokesman. Tiny Rowland and Freddie had already resolved to continue the struggle. As Rowland put it: 'There is no question of Sir Freddie or ourselves doing anything separately. We are together in this – and neither of us needs the $8m.'

In other words, Freddie and Lonrho together were

going to attempt to use the English and Jersey courts to demolish the 12 July settlement. They faced a dilemma, however. They wanted Beckman's help. But having accepted his contingency fee as a part of the Laker I settlement, Beckman was going to be in a delicate position – to put it no more strongly than that – if he began advising parties who were intent on killing the settlement as a preface to launching their own action on behalf of Laker II.

Beckman could and did argue on occasion that the two were wholly separate cases. Some of the other lawyers in the case had been at least sympathetic to this view during June, when both Park and Morris had asked Beckman to speak to Lonrho about the settlement. But distinguishing Laker I from Laker II now struck most people as transparent nonsense. Within weeks, BA's own lawyers would be complaining as much to Judge Greene. The Laker I negotiators, after all, had sought an assurance from Freddie that no future actions would be brought on behalf of Laker II. Freddie had refused to make any promises. How could he, came the reply, when he and Lonrho were legally required to act together or not at all over Laker II? It seemed a bit late to try drawing a rigid distinction between the two Laker cases, with the settlement of the one so heavily dependent on the progress of the other!

Back in June, Lonrho's chief executive had tacitly acknowledged the delicacy of the situation by seeking Morris's permission for his company to instruct Beckman. It was a Sunday and Morris needed time to consult his Touche Ross partners on the point. Then he rang Rowland back at his home in Bourne End, Berkshire, and gave the verdict to Rowland personally: while Beckman was acting for the Laker liquidator, he would not be allowed to act for Lonrho – or for Freddie either, come to that. And Beckman was going to be acting for Morris for some time yet, before the formalities of the $48m. deal were all completed.

So that was that.

Or was it? As Lonrho's unguarded enthusiasm on 14 July suggested, there was room for confusion.

Understandably, perhaps, Beckman himself seemed in two minds. His loyalty to Freddie and still passionate commitment to the justice of his conspiracy complaints pulled him in one direction; his obligations to Judge Greene and the US Federal Court pulled him in the other.

It was soon apparent that Beckman was ready to sail dangerously close to the wind. On 23 July, for example, BA's lawyers finally received a reply to Park's letter to Freddie of 11 July offering him his $8m. on certain conditions. The reply was written by Beckman! ('Sir Freddie has instructed me to respond to your letter to him of 11 July . . .') Park was amazed to see that copies of it had been sent to Freddie and Tiny Rowland, but not to Beckman's own client, Christopher Morris. (The reply, incidentally, refuted Park's claim that Freddie had agreed to accept the deal on 27 June. Freddie had accepted nothing, said Beckman. When Judge Greene saw this later, he described Beckman's alternative version of the 27 June meeting as 'totally false'.)

Again, there were rumours of Beckman being paid substantial fees by Lonrho for his advice on other matters – including the still-running battle over the ownership of Harrods – and it was no secret that he and Rowland saw each other socially. Beckman was invited to dine at Bourne End on 5 August, for example, on the eve of Freddie's wedding day (his marriage to his fiancée Jackie was Freddie's fourth). But as Beckman knew, the disciplinary rules of the Washington Bar meant that he could have serious problems if he was seen to be unambiguously acting for Laker II or undermining the settlement in any way. It was, whatever the complications, his own client's settlement.

As for Freddie, he had no such problems. His opposition was characteristically flamboyant from the start. He was having none of it, he announced to the world on the Sunday after the settlement was signed. 'There is certainly no question of my accepting any sum of money at this moment in time to be put out to grass.'

Ah yes, but how long exactly was that 'moment in time' going to last? Would it, for example, last well beyond midnight on 20 August, when the $8m. offer expired? Or would it just last a week or two, while Freddie made sure there was no more money where the $8m. came from?

No one knew – least of all BA. The airline's board was by now resigned to sitting out the weeks until 20 August as stoically as possible. Privatisation in 1985 was already a lost hope. If it emerged after 20 August that Freddie and Lonrho were indeed intent on a major antitrust action of their own – with new lawyers and all the rest – that would require serious reappraisal of the implications for privatisation in 1986. But the board and the Government would cross that bridge when they came to it . . . if they came to it.

In the middle of July, the shape of the proverbial bridge seemed to come and go through the legal fog which still clung around the settlement. Between 12 July and 20 August, Freddie saw that there were at least three opportunities for him to try turning events against the settlement.

There was the Appeal Court's hearing on the Midland Bank injunction against Laker, dismissed on 10 June. If the court confirmed Laker's ability to sue the Midland in the US, it was unclear where that might leave Morris and Beckman. But it would certainly be encouraging for Freddie and Lonrho. After that, there would be Morris's applications to the English High Court and to the Royal Court in Jersey to have the $48m. settlement formally accepted within their jurisdictions. Freddie resolved to oppose those applications – and Lonrho offered to help with the fees so that he could be represented by the QC who was already familiar with the case, John Beveridge.

These were typically brave tactics on Freddie's part. He had a lot to lose – $8m., in fact. There were plenty of powerful men on the defendants' side of the Double Eight offer who would be only too delighted to retract it the moment Freddie appeared in a courtroom to oppose the settlement. Bill Park's letter of 11 July had made it clear they would have that right. Freddie seemed marvellously unconcerned at the risk. He had just turned sixty-three years of age and was about to be remarried. Most men in his position would have been glad to put the courts behind them and retire to a distant beach with $8m. in the bank. Not Freddie. He was going to keep going.

It was impossible to read his true motives. Had he really decided to forego the money – as he publicly insisted – and to go on tilting at the airlines, like some latter-day Don Quixote, as a matter of personal honour? Was he undecided about the merits of his struggle and only anxious, as a matter for his own conscience, to pursue every last chance before giving up? Or was it all just an unscrupulous attempt to twist a last few million dollars out of BA's back pocket while his old adversary was still stretched over the privatisation barrel?

Mike Nussbaum had no doubts at all that it was the latter. In a remarkably cogent speech to Judge Greene a few weeks later, the Laker liquidator's US lawyer and adviser spelt it out in graphic terms:

> Here is what I predict is going to happen. Sir Freddie will take every possible step to challenge the approvals in the UK and in Jersey. The major aim will be to delay those proceedings to the maximum extent possible . . . Once those suits are on file, wherever they may be filed, and once the pot in England and the pot in Jersey is bubbling in terms of approvals, Sir Freddie can come to British Airways, and perhaps the other defendants and say this: 'You always wanted total peace. Now you

> can see that you cannot have it. We have you in
> trouble on the approvals in the UK and Jersey, at
> least to the extent that those matters are being
> delayed. We have you in trouble, because we will
> have another billion dollar claim against British
> Airways and hence the privatisation of British
> Airways will be in jeopardy. Now, if you really
> want total peace, you will do x for Sir Freddie . . .

Was this an unjustly harsh view of Freddie's motivation?
And if it was not, then what was 'x' going to be? The
appeal over the Midland injunction – which had kept the
bank successfully out of the airline defendants' company
ever since November 1982 – gave no answer to either
question.

The Washington lawyers for the airline defendants
became very excited over some of the Appeal Lords'
asides. (Lord Justice Lawton even remarked that there
was 'sufficient evidence, for the purpose of these
proceedings, of a primary conspiracy between British
Airways, Pan Am and possibly other carriers . . . to force
Laker out of business by unfair means and, in particular,
by charging "predatory" fares'! Did he realise the subtleties of conscious parallelism? Had he appreciated the
significance of Mr Weit's lost battle with Continental
Illinois and the other banks, asked the Americans?) But
the Appeal Courts reinstated the injunction and allowed
Midland finally to consign Attachment 7 to its remotest
archive vaults.

Six days later, though, Freddie's intentions were writ
large in the High Court. Nussbaum was proved at least
half-correct. For on 5 August, Freddie's counsel and
counsel for Christopher Morris at last appeared on
opposing sides of a court. Freddie was indeed going to
challenge the approvals for the settlement. And warnings went out to the English judges that a string of
emergency appeals might be about to interrupt their
summer holidays.

An unusual court hosted the first round: a private hearing in chambers before Mr Registrar Bradburn. Beckman turned up, an incongruous figure in his double-breasted suit and yellow silk tie under the crepuscular basement arches of the High Court. His precise role was unclear and Beckman was offering no explanations to the crowd of waiting journalists. ('Come on, I haven't talked to you people in three years – I'm not going to start now.')

But Freddie himself disappointed the press. He stayed away. Perhaps he was busy with his wedding arrangements for the following day. Mr Bradburn, anyway, gave him no wedding present. He listened to the arguments for rejecting the settlement and approved it just the same. Freddie immediately appealed and the case approached its climax in England: the Vice-Chancellor's court would hear it on 12 August.

The substance of Freddie's objection to the settlement was that he had not got nearly enough out of it. The liquidator could have won far more than $48m. plus the Double Eight, said Freddie. He had lost a vast fortune as the ultimate 90-per-cent shareholder in the Laker group, since the antitrust case was an excellent one: out of a billion or two of damages, his counsel argued, there would have been ample to pay off all the creditors and still send Freddie back into the world as rich as Croesus. Instead of which, he was being shuffled off with a measly $8m.

One remarkable thing about this argument, of course, was that it boiled down to Freddie seeking linkage with the main $48m. deal – yet it was Freddie who had been one of the earliest advocates of severing this linkage in the first place.

On Monday 12 August, the Vice-Chancellor, Sir Nicolas Browne-Wilkinson, broke off his summer holiday in Wales to sit in his court in the Strand and listen to Freddie's plea . . . Within an hour of starting, it was obvious the hearing was going to run for days.

It was already a full calendar month since the 12 July

agreement. Matters were coming to the boil in England much as Nussbaum had warned. Less conspicuously, they had warmed up quite a bit in Washington as well. For as Rosdeitcher and Park had feared on the evening of 12 July, they had made a terrible goof of the $12.5m. payment arrangements for Beckman, Shadyac and their colleagues. BA had agreed on behalf of the defendants to hand over $6m. within two weeks and the other $6.5m. ninety days after that. As 26 July loomed on the horizon, the BA lawyers realised some amendment would have to be agreed immediately or they could end up paying out the money regardless of events in England and Jersey.

Beckman and the rest of the Laker camp lawyers were giving nothing up easily. Beckman was on holiday in Arizona when Rosdeitcher asked, please could they forgive an oversight and admit that it was obviously a bit silly to have agreed to pay the fees before the settlement was approved? On the telephone from Arizona, Beckman threatened to sue. Lunches were exchanged and tempers cooled. On 26 July, they turned to Judge Greene again.

Afternoon teas were just being cleared away in the lounges of the North British Hotel in Edinburgh that day when Judge Greene went up to his room for a telephone call he would rather not have had. The judge was on holiday. He had had an enjoyable stay at Claridge's during the American Bar Association's 20,000-strong invasion of London for their annual conference. Now he was trying to get away from US lawyers for a few days. The half-dozen who crowded into his room over a conference telephone call on the 26th were a rude reminder of what he was missing.

The court record of that telephone conversation reads in parts like a Marx Brothers script ('Who is this talking?' . . . 'Can you speak louder?') but the issue was deadly serious. Tempers quickly grew frayed again ('I didn't say that, Sidney. You misunderstood me. Sidney, I never said that. I never said that you agreed to do that etc etc'). The Laker lawyers wanted their money and they wanted it as agreed.

Judge Greene was astounded that they could expect to get their fees even if the settlement was demolished in the English courts; but so it seemed to be. Dick Shadyac at least acknowledged the judge's surprise. 'I was shocked, I must confess to Your Honor, in negotiating,' said Shadyac. 'I was shocked they agreed to it, but they did, Your Honor. It's a contract. They now want to change the terms of it. All of a sudden somebody took a two-by-four and hit them in the head and made them wake up.'

But the judge was in no mood for all this, especially at a distance of 3,000 miles. So the money stayed in the court registry and he and Shadyac met again in Washington on 12 August, the same day as the English Vice-Chancellor began his hearing. There were a few matters to discuss in Judge Greene's court that day. Asked by the judge at one point what was the purpose of the session, Dick Shadyac replied with disarming candour: 'Money, Judge, money.'

But for once, money was not to be the only consideration. The US judge had been reflecting on the developments in England since 12 July. Freddie had made the mistake of asking a fresh US lawyer to attend the 12 August meeting and Judge Greene reacted angrily to the newcomer's views. It was the beginning of a session in which the judge, finally, made clear on the record his view of BA's courtroom opponents.

He was fed up with Freddie and his 'self-serving statements which do not correspond entirely to reality' – that was clear. Judge Greene was saying nothing about the merits or otherwise of the underlying case, since he had never seen the evidence. But he had seen quite a lot of the settlement procedure. And he was certainly going to say something about that:

> So far as I am concerned the liquidator has gone the extra mile by bringing [Freddie] in and having

him participate. And the reason why it ultimately became impossible to reach a settlement with Sir Freddie Laker is because he kept changing his mind from one negotiating session to the other. What he wanted one day wasn't what he wanted on another day. He agreed on certain terms of settlement on one day and then the next day he repudiated them . . . [and] now we have Sir Freddie in London making every effort to torpedo the settlement and, to some extent, with the assistance of Mr Beckman.

This last point raised the issue of Beckman and a conflict of interests, which had already been openly alleged by Mike Nussbaum in an earlier meeting on 9 August.

Beckman, forewarned that this issue would be tackled, had brought along his own lawyer (!) to advise him. The judge weighed into Beckman, nonetheless. He was mindful, said Judge Greene, of one occasion when he himself had asked Beckman during the negotiations whether he was representing Morris or Freddie – 'to which he took great offence that I could even suggest that he was representing Sir Freddie', recalled the judge.

Beckman made things worse for himself on 12 August by arguing the toss over whether or not the antitrust suit documents would have to be returned. Morris wanted the documents returned. Beckman seemed to be suggesting he should be allowed to keep his own copies. But if, protested Judge Greene, he was planning to store them 'in order that he may conceivably use them in his new capacity as counsel for Sir Freddie, that only increases the problem of conflict of interest that has already surfaced. And I think that is a very serious problem.'

Their exchanges rapidly developed into one of the most remarkable contretemps of the whole story:

The Judge: . . . I think you are becoming more and more unreasonable the more meetings we have.

Beckman:	Your Honor, this is only further reason why I should be relying on my counsel, because Your Honor has gotten an impression of me and I shouldn't be talking for me [sic]. I am very, very deeply distressed by what Your Honor is saying.
The Judge:	You should be distressed.
Beckman:	That's right, and I am distressed. But I also know that when I am distressed and acting emotionally I shouldn't respond. That is why I very much want to rely on the advice of counsel.
The Judge:	You are the attorney here asking for attorneys' fees and it's not unreasonable to expect you to give your opinion as to whether this proposed settlement on attorneys' fees is agreeable to you.

(A complicated rearrangement of the payment schedule had been proposed, with interest provisions to suit a variety of eventualities in England and Jersey.)

Beckman:	I have already said, Your Honor, that the kind of approach that has been put on the table is agreeable . . . [But] I have been attacked, I have been told there is a risk of disciplinary action, I have been told about conflicts [of interest]. I have been told about all sorts of things.
The Judge:	None of that has anything to do with the amount of the attorneys' fees or the interest that is to be drawn in the meantime. None of it has anything to do with it. Let's not play games. You can't play games with me. I have been around a long time.

Beckman:	Your Honor, Your Honor is being very hard on me. I just beg Your Honor to give me –
The Judge:	Whenever we have been close to agreeing on something, there has been some new thought that you have had, that had to be considered and another postponement. It's been the pattern throughout, almost. Not from the very beginning, but certainly the last half of the time that we have been negotiating and here it is again . . .
Beckman:	Can't we please go away and try to resolve this ourselves? I have to tell you I flew back over the weekend [from England] and I am still out of whack and my head is starting to wool up . . .

By this stage in the proceedings, though, it was Judge Greene who most wanted to escape. 'I have no desire to go through this torture day after day', as he put it. But the lawyers had to keep him there long enough to ensure that their new payment arrangements were entered on the court record. Alas, it was Marx Brothers-time again. Lawyers were now arriving in the chambers to represent the lawyers who were already there. 'This is getting to be a farce rather than a serious negotiation,' said Judge Greene. Beckman's counsel in particular seemed to be driving him to distraction. 'I don't propose to sit here and negotiate with lawyers for lawyers who, again, are going to be advised by other lawyers. It's getting to be a preposterous farce.'

And so matters were brought quickly to a close. Beckman, Shadyac and the rest had given up the idea of taking all the $12.5m. before the English and Jersey approvals. They had even given up the idea that they should immediately take $1m. each, just to keep them going. And they settled for a compromise over the accruing interest which looked complicated enough to be worth many more happy hours of torture.

Back in the English Vice-Chancellor's court, Freddie's battle was proceeding in serene secrecy before Sir Nicolas Browne-Wilkinson. It took all week. Morris explained why he was settling. Freddie, who attended every day while his new wife honeymooned alone on the island of Capri, said he could win billions. Morris said that two-thirds of any damages would go to the UK Exchequer anyway, under the terms of the Protection of Trading Interests Act. Freddie said this would not apply to damages paid by non-British defendants. And so on and so on. Not everyone thought the battle worth pursuing. Mrs Joan Laker surrendered her 10 per cent shareholding in the Laker group on the Friday morning. She sold it to BA's Ivanhoe for $50,000.

That evening, 16 August, the corridors filled with all those who had been excluded from the court. (This naturally included the defendants, since there would have been no justice letting them hear Morris's reasons for calling it a day.) At last, at about 6.00 p.m., the hour of the Vice-Chancellor's judgement arrived. The Linklaters men and distinguished counsel for BA, together with a good sprinkling of the world's press, stood outside the windows of the courtoom and looked on as Sir Nicolas silently mouthed his verdict to the crowded benches within. Finally, he invited everyone inside to hear a crisp summary of the judgement: Mr Bradburn had done the right thing.

Freddie strode off down the corridor to Jersey.

25

One Bitter Lemon

Jersey's main town, St Helier, is a commercial traveller's version of Hamilton, Bermuda. The two places have much in common: the same small island provinciality, the same air of being British yet somehow not British, the same incongruous mix of offshore bankers and on-beach holidaymakers, milling together on the seaside pavements. In St Helier, though, everything is much, much cheaper in every sense. And it rains in August.

It rained almost continually through the summer of 1985. But the lawyers who descended on the town on Sunday 18 August brought no buckets and spades – just bulging briefcases and an acute sense of the day's date. John Beveridge, Freddie's English QC, checked in at the Grand Hotel on the seafront at the end of the afternoon and sat outside – the rain had stopped for a couple of hours – watching the seagulls over St Aubin's Bay. Just after 6.00 p.m., a navy-blue BA staff estate car drew up to the hotel. A couple of hostesses jumped out to help with luggage and down stepped Freddie, his new wife and his seven-year-old son, Little Freddie. It was VIP treatment and BA was doing everything possible to keep the door open for Freddie.

There were now just two days left until the midnight deadline on Tuesday 20 August. Freddie had already done more than enough to forfeit his $8m., as more than one of the European airlines had carefully noted. But BA's board made quite sure that he knew the money – as far as BA was concerned, at least – was still on the table. Freddie, on the other hand, was giving every impression of a man intent on a war of legal attrition, much as Nussbaum had predicted. If he was bluffing, he was making a good job of it.

He applied to the Court of Appeal against the judgement of the Vice-Chancellor. (The appeal date was fixed for 4 September.) He filed a representation with the legal authorities in Jersey to have Morris dismissed as the Laker liquidator. And he gave notice to Jersey's Royal Court that he would be opposing Morris's application for its approval of the settlement on Monday 19 August. After the heavy defeat the previous Friday in the English High Court, Freddie's chances of blocking the $48m. settlement seemed to be diminishing fast. But adversity had not deterred him before: had it done so, Skytrain would never have left the ground at all.

Right in the middle of St Helier is a little, tree-lined square where a handful of British redcoats fought off the island's French invaders in 1781. There, today, stands the Royal Court – and Freddie was announcing his determination to mount a fierce rearguard action of his own with that court's help.

On the Sunday evening, Beveridge left a message for the Linklaters team at the Pomme d'Or, the hotel where they were staying just a few hundred yards along the seafront from the Grand. But Park and his men had already gone out for dinner, driving a couple of miles from St Helier to the infinitely more exclusive Longueville Manor Hotel. They met Morris and his assistant Malcolm Fillmore in the residents' lounge. But Morris's lawyers were not there: Christopher Grierson and Richard Hacker from City solicitors Durrant Piesse and Mike Nussbaum from Washington were toiling with their Jersey colleagues in St Helier to prepare the papers for next day.

The liquidator was certainly not expecting Freddie to throw in the towel and take his money – or, at least, not yet. (In fact, Morris rather suspected he might take it some time later than the deadline, just to show it was still the old defiant Freddie.) Nor was Morris confident that the Royal Court would necessarily adjourn matters until after the English Appeal Court hearing in September.

The two parties with Park and Morris sat carefully apart for dinner, as they thought propriety demanded. But it was not an unduly formal evening. There was much joking about the splendid decor of the thirteenth-century Longueville Manor and the emphatically less splendid decor of the Pomme d'Or. When the time came for the BA lawyers to leave and the minicab driver asked their destination, Park could be heard in the stillness of the night pronouncing mournfully, 'Well, I'm very sorry to have to tell you . . .'

Beveridge's message was still waiting for him when he returned. The QC wanted to know if Park could join him for lunch the next day. It was an intriguing invitation. Perhaps it was just a courtesy; but that seemed unlikely in the circumstances. So was Freddie really agonising over his decision?

Even if it was a touch sentimental – for the reasons Mike Nussbaum had already explained to Judge Greene – it was still possible (just) to feel sorry for Freddie. To the professionals lined up against him, it was all a job and a very lucrative, exciting one at that. To Freddie, always an emotional man, it was his whole life and work that was bound up in the events of the next couple of days. So as he sat in Suite 301 at the Grand Hotel with his wife and son, watching the Jersey rain through the windows, was Freddie actually contemplating a dramatic volte-face?

Park went off to bed, hardly able to bear the thought of having to ring up all the continental airline defendants on BA's behalf from his room at the Pomme d'Or.

In the Royal Court next morning, there was plenty to reassure Park that no last-minute changes of mind were likely. There were prayers for guidance in French. Then the local advocates stood up before the magnificently

carved wooden bench of the court to begin the arguments rehearsed a thousand times before. Tony Olsen,
one of the island's best-known lawyers, appeared for
Freddie and insisted on BA's exclusion before anyone
referred to the contents of the Vice-Chancellor's judgement: 'it could be catastrophic,' he said, 'if such information were made available to the public for general use.'
Jersey was a long way from Washington.

Park sipped a mixed vermouth before lunch and
exchanged pleasantries with Beveridge. Then they sat
down to talk seriously. Was the $8m. still really on the
table, asked Beveridge. His client needed to know. BA's
lawyer promised to look into it. As soon as they parted,
Park rang Colin Marshall in London. The BA chief
executive conferred with some of his colleagues and they
began to ring round the other defendants to sound out
their reactions. All those they reached, including Thomson
at British Caledonian, replied in the positive. They had
swallowed so much from Freddie after all these years.
They were not going to strain at a gnat now.

That evening, David Burnside, the BA public relations
man, left his office as usual at Speedbird House and
drove home into Central London. Along the Cromwell
Road, he thought he spotted Tiny Rowland going fast in
the opposite direction. Rowland, though Burnside did
not know it, was on his way to an important rendezvous.

Meanwhile in Jersey, the court had recessed until
the Tuesday morning. Morris, Nussbaum and the rest
worked into the late hours of the night. Next morning, it
was 20 August. But the hearing in the Royal Court went
on just the same.

Except that Freddie was not in court to hear it. With his
wife and son, he had slipped quietly out of St Helier the
previous evening and taken the 9.00 p.m. BCal flight to
London. As the Jersey advocates got into their stride,
Colin Marshall received a telephone call he had been
awaiting for quite some time.

It was Freddie. He had met with Rowland the night

before, he said, and the two men had discussed the prospects for Laker II's action at great length. The outcome was that Rowland had given Freddie clearance to speak on Lonrho's behalf. So he was now able to sit down with the BA board and talk about a deal. Would they meet him at Heathrow? That was too public, said Marshall. Freddie, Beveridge and John Rowney, Freddie's English solicitor, should come to BA's Enserch House headquarters in St James's at 6.00 p.m. sharp.

The spartan interior of Enserch House, with its functional, stripped-pine furniture and cold blue colour-scheme, was a suitable setting for the evening confrontation. Marshall and Park sat on one side of the long BA boardroom table, their three visitors on the other. At one end of the room was BA's coat-of-arms on the wall. At the other, a small glass cabinet containing four models of BA aircraft. Otherwise, there were just papers and more papers, nothing more. Out in the corridors, BA directors came and went with supporting documents for the men seated in the boardroom like signatories to some historic peace treaty – which perhaps, in a sense, they were.

Freddie indicated again what he had indicated to potential intermediaries in the preceding few days. Would not the simplest way to resolve their outstanding differences be for BA to offer just a small amount, say $2m. or $3m., over the $8m. on the table?

No, it most certainly would not, said Marshall. There was no more money. It was $8m.: take it or leave it. Marshall had found himself playing poker once or twice over the preceding months – most notably at Exim – with not a colour card in his hand. Now that he had a fistful of aces, he was not about to play things gently.

The $8m. alone took hours to settle. Then they turned for the last time to the matter of warmth. What did they need to do, to settle the wording of Freddie's compliance with the eighteen conditions which Park had attached to his offer letter of 11 July?

As the evening hours slipped by towards midnight, no

move was made to introduce hot food. And it was strictly a mineral-water occasion. Everyone there knew the gravity of what was happening. Quite possibly, if they agreed, it would appear in retrospect to have been only a matter of Freddie's personal wealth that had hung in the balance. But if they disagreed, there was no telling the consequences with any confidence. After the stormy session in front of Judge Greene on 12 August, no one could doubt that complications were crowding in on the Laker settlement at a rate which threatened its destruction any day. That would finish off Bermuda III and BA's privatisation with it . . .

As midnight drew close, Beveridge stuck patiently to his task of ensuring that Freddie did not impale himself on any negotiating hook. (Beckman, of course, was not there. He would always insist later that he had had no influence whatever over Freddie's decision in these closing weeks.) Marshall and Park waited just as patiently for Freddie to accept what small concessions they were able to make. (Three free trips each across the Atlantic, for example, were promised to Freddie, his wife and his small son.) But there was nothing more on offer.

Freddie signed the papers, without amendment, at 11.59 p.m.

There was no ceremony. Marshall summoned drinks from the BA directors' bar. Freddie was handed one bitter lemon. Then he was given a BA car to drive him home to Sussex. He talked to the chauffeur all the way. He never mentioned the money once. It was of less consequence to Freddie, to judge by his chatter, than his perfect recollection of all the aircraft types that he had flown as a tireless sky tramp during the Berlin Airlift in 1948–9.

Next day, 21 August, Marshall set about squaring what had happened with the few defendants unaware of the last-minute drama. Professor Rudolph, Lufthansa's in-house counsel, reacted angrily to the news and its financial implications. He was unable to reach his boss, Heinz Ruhnau, and he was unwilling to commit Lufthansa without doing so. A brief but heated row followed before Rudolph gave way. If it was less than a totally happy ending, at least all agreed it was final.

All except one, that is. Rene Lapautre, the chairman of UTA, was just coming to the end of a walking holiday in Scotland. He was left to read of the ending in his morning newspaper.

All that remained for BA to do on the 21st was to exchange with Lonrho and with Freddie the thirty-seven documents which would give effect to the contract signed on Tuesday night. BA signed them; Lonrho signed them. Then, in the early afternoon, Beveridge took them away to carry down to Freddie in Sussex. The QC missed his afternoon train. He caught another and Freddie drove over to Gatwick to meet him in a restaurant. While the BA board reacted with dismay to news that the two men had apparently disappeared, they were sitting down together for a last private session. They were a stone's throw from where Freddie had sat up most of the night in 1982 to keep his airline alive. After three-and-a-bit years of torment, it was finally being laid to rest in peace.

Freddie signed all the documents. Then – a few years too late for his adversaries at BA, but a good deal richer – he went fishing.

26

To Fly, To Serve

Turbulence, air pockets, loss of thrust, low cloud, fog on the runway – Fleet Street had run out of clichés for BA's mishaps by the autumn of 1985. The next big BA privatisation story was going to have to be The Sale, or else . . .

How would private investors regard this prospect, after all the false starts since 1979? As the advertising agents geared up for a 1986 sale and BA's executives prepared their presentations for the road, could they hope to stir the enthusiasm of the marketplace for a sale so often promised and so many times withdrawn?

Perhaps it was Professor Alfred Kahn, the US champion of deregulation under President Carter, who had provided the answer a few years before. 'Maybe it's sex appeal,' said the professor, 'but there's something about an airplane that drives investors crazy.'

The least the brokers could hope for was that BA would enrich their investing clients half as well as it had enriched half the lawyers in Washington . . . But the lawyers' feast, it seemed, still had a course or two to go.

The Government was keenly aware that it could not afford any more dramas. On 8 October 1985, it called a meeting at the Transport Department offices in Marsham Street for all those most directly involved in the privatisation effort. It was attended by thirty-two people. For the benefit of the bankers, brokers and civil servants, the lawyers were asked to recount slowly and patiently exactly what had happened to BA over the preceding ten months.

It was a long meeting. It was also slightly unsettling. For at least one legal time-bomb had still to be defused. Until this had been done, the Government understandably decreed that there should be no relaunching of preparations for the sale.

Jerry S. Cohen is widely regarded as one of the foremost contingency-fee lawyers in the US. He devotes much of his time to representing plaintiffs who have brought suits on behalf of a class of potential litigants – so-called class actions – and his livelihood depends on picking winners. (Cohen was one of the best-known of the many US lawyers who visited Bhopal in the aftermath of the disaster at Union Carbide's Indian chemical plant.) Earlier in the course of the main Laker legal battle, Cohen's Washington law firm – Kohn, Milstein, Cohen & Hausfeld – had agreed to act on behalf of plaintiffs in four class actions against BA, Pan Am and TWA.

The basis of all four actions was the same and they were consolidated into one suit. This alleged that the three defendant airlines had caused Laker's collapse – and consequently had inflicted financial damage on all those who flew the North Atlantic between March 1982 and March 1984. Had Laker still been there, according to the suit, a whole class of individuals could have travelled more cheaply.

Once the main antitrust suit had been settled out of court, Cohen was well-disposed to a settlement of his own action. But it was going to take time.

By November, BA was confident that it had established the size of the class and had agreed the basis of a settlement with its co-defendants (though TWA was now owned by Carl Icahn and he wanted to take another look at one or two of the points already agreed). They would together set aside ticket vouchers to an aggregate value of $25m., with an additional $5m. worth in the event of more than 1.25m. claims arising from the case. These vouchers would be made available to applicants who submitted correctly completed forms. They would be valid for five years.

The Government felt reasonably assured by the middle of November that it could expect a satisfactory outcome to all this. Judge Greene signed an order for the settlement arrangements to proceed on 14 November. But the terms of the settlement still had to be advertised for thirty days; a further sixty days, finally, would be needed to complete the implementation of the settlement. It was disappointing to have to wait so long before resuming the privatisation timetable – but after all the frustrations and near-disasters of the preceding months, Whitehall officials could be forgiven a little shyness in the face of US legal problems.

As for BA, the board seemed so relieved at being rid of the Morris suit that it was not going to lose too much sleep over a careful resolution – at no cash cost – of the class actions. Even less was it going to allow itself to be drawn into a continuing tussle of ill will and distrust between the twelve defendants' Washington law firms and the person of Bob Beckman – though there were plenty of pretexts for further squabbling.

No one with the slightest knowledge of the settlement negotiations could have been surprised at this aspect of the denouement. To a limited extent, BA could not avoid being involved. Beckman's former partner, Don Farmer, was claiming a share of the plaintiff's legal costs. He had asked Judge Greene for permission to intervene in the case. The judge had turned him down on 29 August, though not without some sympathy for his views:

> Farmer claims that Beckman, his former partner, had been guilty of questionable conduct during the settlement negotiations and otherwise, and that he has repeatedly made false representations to the Court and others . . . [The] Court has also had occasion to express itself adversely concerning the reliability of representations made by Beckman. . . . Moreover, although Beckman agreed at the July 12 1985 settlement discussions that he and his firm

296

> would be responsible for any claims by Farmer this
> concession came about only after considerable
> equivocation. In light of Beckman's attitude in
> general, this concession cannot be regarded as an
> iron-clad guarantee that Farmer will indeed receive
> what, if anything, he is due . . .

Judge Greene had accordingly required the defendants to leave a seven-day gap between the signing of all the settlement papers and the payment of the millions due to Beckman and his colleagues. This was for Farmer to seek legal remedies elsewhere if he could.

The papers were signed on 1 October, after a mock run-through the day before. Paul, Weiss had moved into palatial new Washington premises over the summer – the firm must have made several million pounds out of the Laker case alone – and the piles of relevant documents were dumped on a boardroom table there for all to see.

There was not much ceremony at the end. Two dozen or so lawyers traipsed in and out to sign and collect their papers. Some $56m. changed hands telegraphically the same day, via the good offices of the Riggs National Bank. Then everyone went home – except, as it were, Beckman who had a week to wait before he could collect his money.

At this point, Beckman informed Linklaters that he was intending to retain a selection of documents thrown up by the case. When the Washington lawyers of the other defendant airlines heard this, there was much furrowing of legal brows. Len Bebchick convened a meeting to discuss plans to sue Beckman: he had, in their view, contravened settlement terms requiring the return of all documents plus all copies ever taken.

BA and Linklaters walked away, leaving the Washington firms to their deliberations as somehow seemed fitting. The City solicitors saw no future in acrimonious exchanges with Beckman – and he himself was apparently keen to conclude matters with Linklaters on a happy note. (Visiting

England in mid-October for a stag-hunting weekend on
Exmoor, Beckman paid a courtesy visit on Bill Park in his
City office and presented him with a handsome pair of
cufflinks, engraved with foxes' heads.)

All that mattered to BA, for the moment anyway, was
that it had settled the 1982 antitrust suit with definite
figures which could now be fully accommodated in the
airline's accounts. Precise details of the settlement were
never released, partly at the European carriers' behest.
But the payments into the kitty and out again were
roughly as follows:

		$ m
IN – British Airways		33.0
British Caledonian		3.9
Pan American		9.0
TWA		9.0
KLM		2.8
Lufthansa		2.8
Sabena		2.8
SAS		2.8
Swissair		2.8
UTA		0.1
	Total	69.0

		$ m
OUT – Laker ticketholders, staff and minor trade creditors		15.0
Major trade creditors		8.6
Export-Import Bank		20.3
Other banks and industry manufacturers		2.9
Sir Freddie Laker		8.0
Robert Beckman and other plaintiff's counsel		12.8
Administration and misc		1.4
	Total	69.0

So much for the Laker settlement. But what were the rest of BA's accounts looking like, now that minds could concentrate again on the prospect of privatisation?

Results for 1984–5, announced the previous May, had presented a picture of something very like a healthy, commercial company. Operating profits of £303m. compared with £274m. the year before (and £169m. in 1982–3). Pre-tax profits of £202m. compared with £185m. and £74m. in the two preceding years. All of the £202m. and even a bit more – from extraordinary items – was transferred intact to the airline's reserves!

On the cash front, BA had generated all of £470m. – the kind of riches able to cope even with BA's ever-growing capital expenditure plans. And the billion-pound debt mountain was no more; debt at £647m. now stood at roughly 2¼ times the airline's net worth.

As they waited to receive the call yet again, the various advisers to the sale therefore had every reason to feel confident that the next big initiative – however cautiously approached by the Government – could finally lead to the market-place.

Members of the marketing committee set up under the chairmanship of Michael Spicer, the junior Transport Minister, were already busy by November planning the advertising for BA's sale. A three-month campaign was near completion for launching late in January 1986, designed by Saatchis and paid for by BA at a cost of well over £2m.

The committee – consisting of external public relations and advertising men as well as BA executives and civil servants – had more difficulty agreeing over the immediate pre-sale campaign. This was to be put together by Allen, Brady & Marsh and would concentrate more on the financial aspects of the sale. Officials from the Transport Department and the Treasury could not agree the budget for the campaign and it prompted many hours of wrangling through November.

The bankers had other things on their mind. Ridley

had summoned the Hill Samuel team – now without Michael Gatenby, who had moved to rival merchant bankers Charterhouse Japhet – and had made a few suggestions. BA's privatisation, said the Minister, was not necessarily going to be like all the others. There was no question of just sticking to a formula. He wondered, for example, might they not do without underwriters? Then again, might it be better to drop the idea of selling any of the shares overseas? (Perhaps Ridley thought BA's history to date had not been quite adventurous enough . . . Rumour had it that the bankers were dismayed.)

The City's stockbrokers, meanwhile were eagerly awaiting the simultaneous publication of BA's 1984/5 Annual Report and the corporation's results for the first half of 1985/6 which had ended on September 30. Indications of a delay soon escalated in the City into stories about friction between the airline's board and its auditors, Ernst & Whinney, over the proper treatment of all BA's legal misadventures. And when the accounts did eventually appear, on December 17, at least one possible explanation for the delay was immediately evident. For the cost of the October settlement – that is, BA's $33m. contribution to the aggregate sum plus $5m. for administrative costs and the running of Ivanhoe in Jersey – was included as a £33m. exceptional item in the profit and loss account for the previous rather than the current year.

Gordon Dunlop had never made any bones about the fact that he intended to cope with the Laker settlement in the 1984/5 accounts, regardless of any inconvenient timing niceties. It was also obvious from the airline's April–September performance that he had ample reason to stick to his plan. By deducting the £33m. from the 1984/5 accounts, BA could at least marginally flatter the 1985/6 performance in any yearly comparison. But even with a little help from the accountants, there was no disguising a drop in the airline's trading profits. The operating surplus for the latest half-year was £205m.

against £236m. in 1984. Pre-tax profits had only inched ahead from £189m. to £201m.

The explanation, though, was not alarming. It was a timely reminder, perhaps, of typical factors which would influence BA's profitability whatever its ownership.

Accidents had taken their toll. A TriStar had slithered off the runway at Leeds and cost the airline a staggering £4m. to repair. A terrible Boeing 737 crash with grievous loss of life at Manchester in August had so far cost rather more than £5m.

Foreign exchange had caused even more distortion of the profits than usual. Sterling's strength against the dollar had hurt. To see why, take an imaginary transaction. Back in March 1985, say, BA had been booking tickets out to US travel agents with $1.05 equivalent to £1.00. So 100 tickets each worth $1.05 were theoretically worth £100. By the time BA collected the money, however, it was August and the dollar was trading at $1.40 – so the $105 proceeds of the March sales were only brought into the 1985–6 income statement as £72 (a £28 fall in profits, supposing both ticket sales and the $1.05 rate had held level throughout the previous year).

There is only one currency trend which hurts BA more than a strong pound – and that is a strong dollar. The airline has a cash shortage of about $800m. annually at present. Its various other world currency tills have to be emptied and converted into dollars; but they never come anywhere near $800m. – and the stronger the dollar around the world, the bigger the shortfall. Since the exchange markets had contrived in the April-September 1985 period to produce a strong dollar (against most currencies) as well as a strong pound, BA's profits had suffered a double-blow.

Third and most fundamental, passenger traffic had slowed. From March to August 1985 it was recorded each month at about 10 per cent higher than the year-earlier period. After August, this slipped to about 5 per cent. Volatility, as prospective investors in BA were going to have to accept, was a conspicuous feature in the affairs of every airline.

But the stockbrokers were in no mood to be perturbed by minor fluctuations in passenger traffic or foreign exchange losses. Far more striking was the transformation in BA's balance sheet at September 30. Total debt was down to £464m., while the company's net worth had risen to £499m. The implied debt:equity gearing of 93 per cent was certainly still onerous – but at long last it was in the same league as that of private sector competitors. As for the airline's operations, many brokers were starting to acknowledge the basis of a strong Buy story. With its stranglehold on one of the world's biggest airports and so many of the globe's most profitable routes – the North Atlantic was now at its most lucrative ever and had actually contributed no less than half of BA's worldwide operating profits in the latest six months! – BA appeared increasingly attractive. Always assuming, that is, no replays of the OPEC 1974 and 1979 horrors.

They had a chance to test out the feelings of the big City institutions in November, too. Singapore Airlines obligingly offered the perfect pretext. It approached the City with plans for a mini-privatisation of its own: it wanted to place about 8 per cent of its shares privately, if this could be arranged. The professional fund managers' reactions were most encouraging. International aviation, it seemed, was perceived as an industry with a desperately tormented decade safely behind it. Oil costs had soared and traffic had slumped. Now the reverse was happening. For those airlines which had used the fading crisis to streamline their operations, the future might hold great things. (The subsequent impact on Singapore Airline's shares of the collapse in the local Singapore stock market did not affect this general view.)

There were few voices ready now to echo doubts expressed a year earlier in a report on BA by the Institute of Fiscal Studies. The IFS in November 1984 had been by no means pessimistic about BA's prospects. ('If British

Airways is able to improve its productivity substantially . . . its future looks good under most conditions.') But its authors – Mark Ashworth and Peter Forsyth, both academics – had departed significantly from the consensus wisdom about the airline's progress: 'The much-publicised view of a dramatic improvement in efficiency is not borne out by the evidence.'

BA reacted predictably. It castigated the report as 'highly academic, inadequately researched, statistically misleading and overall of little material worth to the debate on airline policy or to the privatisation of British Airways'. The IFS smartly thanked BA for judging its report highly academic and reiterated that 'a detailed comparison of BA and a number of other airlines showed that BA is an inefficient airline by international standards'.

A public slanging match with the IFS, a widely respected think-tank, would not have been an ideal precursor to a sale in early 1985. But by the end of the year, the row seemed forgotten and its substance less important. It was not the only respect in which the postponement forced by the Laker legal battle could be seen in a favourable light. A blessing in disguise would be putting it too strongly; but the delays of 1984–5 had certainly helped improve the background for a BA sale in several respects.

As with the IFS episode, so memories had begun to fade of an acrimonious controversy over the redesign of BA's corporate livery. The choice of a Californian company to create a new image had been unpopular enough – amongst British designers, anyway – back in the summer of 1983. When the new image itself was revealed, British designers' reactions were almost unanimously hostile. Sir Terence Conran called it 'a design that they should all be thoroughly ashamed of' in October 1984. As late as May 1985, Sir Hugh Casson remarked that he had great respect for King – 'but British Airways seem to have been caught with their undercarriage down over the new livery'.

So the new image – complete with BA's coat-of-arms on the tailplane (motto: To Fly, To Serve) – was not a universal success. But at least by the end of 1985 it seemed unlikely to be much of a headache for the sale's PR men.

Again, an extra year or more in the sale's gestation period meant some useful financial spin-offs. Investors' inflationary expectations were slowly dwindling all the time, which helped dispel any worries still lingering over the old index-linked pension fund. Most important of all, of course, the balance sheet was a year older and a year fitter.

So much, anyway, for the view from the City. But while investors may have been more favourably disposed towards BA than ever before, what was now the British Government's attitude?

The answer, for BA's board and the champions of the carrier's privatisation, was a good deal less encouraging – not to say downright worrying. The traumatic events of late 1984, which could so easily have ended in the monumental embarrassment of a cancelled flotation, had left both Whitehall and Mrs Thatcher's Cabinet feeling profoundly cautious about the next step.

This was not immediately obvious in November, 1985. Indeed, the gods for once seemed to be smiling on BA, even (indirectly) in the courts. A last-minute legal obstacle to the planned privatisation of Trustee Savings Bank that month was remarkably reminiscent of the Laker Airways hitch for BA a year earlier. (Too much so for some in the City: David Freud at broker Rowe & Pitman had to shelve a 30,000-word report on BA in the summer of 1985 . . . then published a 30,000-word report on TSB six months later, on the very day that the TSB sale postponement was announced.)

But TSB's setback was BA's good fortune, as the airline's management prepared for a promotional tour of eleven British cities in January and February 1986. A 25-minute video film of the BA story was launched at an informal party at the Ritz on December 4. It was warmly received by those present – including Ministers and MPs – and BA looked forward to showing it around the country as a preliminary to the main sales campaign. With no TSB sale to compete for the public's attention, the January effort could bang the drum for BA's sale loud and hard with no inhibitions.

Nor was the general political background any less favourable to BA's sale. Indeed, rather the opposite. The Thatcher Government's commitment to privatisation as a means to wider share ownership and political change had been growing steadily stronger and more explicit since the British Telecom success at the end of 1983. Jibes about the sale of the family silver were still heard from time to time – even the Earl of Stockton, the former Harold Macmillan, joined that chorus in November 1985 – but they were increasingly wide of the mark. By the time BA came to market, it seemed likely, the promotion of share ownership would be a key motive.

But when would that be?

As talks resumed in earnest through the weeks leading up to Christmas 1985, it was clear that events over the preceding twelve months had done little if anything to improve relations between the BA board and the Government. BA was specifically cited by Ministers as one of the priority candidates for privatisation in 1986. But if the board was hoping that this might strengthen its hand in negotiations over the pre-sale balance sheet, it was quickly disillusioned.

Gordon Dunlop had a bright idea, or so he thought. During 1985, both British Aerospace and Cable & Wireless had contrived to combine sales of the Government's remaining holdings in their equity with primary issues of new shares. Dunlop was keen that BA should emulate their success. Of course, it would have to be a slightly more complicated operation. BA would not be able to execute a rights issue until privatisation had been completed and a full share register compiled. But the technicalities looked easily surmountable. And fresh capital raised for BA in this way might surely cast all the familiar balance sheet arguments in an entirely new light?

Perhaps BA's finance director was even hoping that a delayed publication of the 1984/5 Annual Report and the September, 1985 results might allow him to set down some commitment to his idea in cold print?

If so, he must have been sorely disappointed. For the Government rejected the whole notion of a rights issue. Nor, though, was it any more prepared than it had been in 1984 to consider injecting a huge cash subsidy into BA's balance sheet. And as before, nervousness about the reaction of Sir Adam Thomson's BCal and the other independents appeared a powerful influence on the attitude of the Transport Department towards all BA's financial demands.

In short, by the time the Annual Report was published on December 17, much of the mutual distrust engendered by the CAA row was surfacing once again. Dunlop had had to abandon his rights issue scheme after an exchange of views which had become increasingly acrimonious. The weighty prospects for the New Year had to be summarised in just a single sentence of the Directors' Report for 1984/5: 'The Board looks forward to concluding with HM Government all the outstanding matters on privatisation so that the Company's shares can be offered for sale during 1986.'

But alas, it was not simply the (predictable) rows over the balance sheet which were causing Whitehall serious concern by Christmas. For even while BA was setting its stockbrokers to work again and putting the final touches to the January/February roadshow, reports were coming over from the US of yet more trouble on the Laker front.

The US Statute of Limitations lays down that claims for civil damages may not be filed later than four years after the date of the original injury. This gave February 5 1986 a certain piquancy in the New Year calendar for anyone

306

interested in the Laker story – and as the fourth anniversary of the Laker collapse drew nearer, none showed more interest than Messrs. Beckman and Kirstein. For by December 1985, they were almost ready to serve two entirely fresh anti-trust lawsuits against BA and some or all of the airline co-defendants to the Morris action!

One plaintiff was to be a West Coast travel agent who had worked closely with Skytrain throughout the 1977–82 period: Brian Clewer, owner of Ambassador Travel in Los Angeles, alleged that his business had suffered directly from Laker's demise, justifying damages running into millions of dollars. The second, potentially far more serious action would be filed on behalf of a group of more than 200 of Laker's former employees – and damages claimed in this suit were possibly going to run to as much as $50m . . .

Beckman approached the British embassy in Washington just before Christmas to notify the UK Government about his intentions. His firm was apparently anxious to explore the possibility of some out-of-court settlement – perhaps drawing on a surplus reportedly discovered in the Laker pension fund – but there was no doubt that Beckman & Kirstein meant business. The lawyers were offering their services to the new plaintiffs on the same kind of contingency fee basis as before. A full-blown antitrust challenge was being prepared . . . and it would be able to draw very substantially on transcript evidence already amassed, courtesy of the last Laker action.

The UK Government was appalled. No more dramas, it had been decreed in October. Yet here was potentially the most dramatic possible sequel to the October settlement. And just the kind of nightmare the continental airlines had been fearing all along! Of course, the transatlantic legal arguments began almost at once. There were debates about the status of past documents, both those surrendered by Beckman's firm and others still on the public record. There were conflicting opinions about the validity of the actions in prospect. Above all,

307

there were arguments about the real seriousness of their threat to privatisation.

All of which, for some officials in Whitehall, must have sounded horribly familiar. The Government had already made absolutely clear that no commitment could be made to a privatisation date until all legal problems had been settled once and for all. If this applied to the class action – apparently moving smoothly along in the background, for the moment anyway – then presumably it had also to apply to the Laker employees et al.

So out went the word from the Transport Department: BA should cancel its late January launch date for the pre-sale Saatchi campaign. And on January 6 – the same day, as it happened, that Ambassador Travel's lawyers filed its suit in the Central District Federal court of California – the Government moved to abort BA's promotional tour of the UK, due to start just three days later.

Thus began, almost incredibly, yet another period of speculation about the timing of BA's departure for the private sector.

This latest setback prompted at least as much anguish as any earlier episode, probably rather more. BA had included a broadly reassuring litigation note in its 1984/5 Annual Report, for what that was worth. (It had been another cause for delay and was notably more cautious than its predecessor). More to the point, King and his colleagues had set their minds on a July flotation. They knew that later dates in 1986 might be impractical if British Gas stuck to its own sale timetable. They were even nervous about the schedule for 1987, given the growing queue of companies heading down the privatisation road. (It must have been galling in January to see the British Airports Authority announcing its proposals for a £500m. sale, let alone to hear Roy Watts talking confidently of his plans for a privatised Thames Water Authority). Above all, the new complications were hardly to be compared in size with the main Laker case.

So BA pressed on, determined that it would in the end be able to persuade the Government to accept a July, 1986 sale, whatever the minor legal bugbears. While the Transport Department was understandably preoccupied with the Channel fixed link competition, BA went ahead and rearranged its pre-sale advertising campaign for April/May. After all, King and his board had not seen off the CAA and a billion dollar lawsuit, to be diverted now by a couple of relative sideshows . . .

But amidst all the uncertainty, the rumblings of a mighty quarrel and the prospects of a never-ending sequence of postponements, one reality stood out. On January 9, despite all the Government's misgivings, the airline's top men began their promotional tour. The presentation that day in Glasgow began an eleven-city roadshow around England, Scotland, Wales and Ulster. And the message of the event was unambiguous: BA, whatever its ownership status, was at last a truly commercial business with a distinct and successful image to sell. Whether it was privatised in July, 1986 or July, 1987 – or even not at all – the real achievement of the 1979–86 years surely lay in this transformation.

Of course, the achievement still needed privatisation to happen before BA's story could be held up as the total triumph that its board envisaged. The airline had endured too much in the name of privatisation for the goal to be easily abandoned at this late stage. July was still the firm target. Yet, with or without privatisation, all the material changes since 1979 were glaringly apparent. The airline had 71 fewer aircraft, 62 fewer routes and 22,000 fewer employees. It had replaced its accounting systems; remodelled its pension fund; changed its basic marketing strategy; overhauled its corporate advertising; modernised its fleet; sold off its London air terminals; restructured its middle and senior management and put its entire workforce through a reorientation of basic attitudes to the company and its business.

There was even a sense in which the board could feel

grateful to its adversaries of the last couple of years. It was profoundly irritating that the Laker saga should have instilled such caution in Whitehall about the legal dangers of pressing ahead. But there was no denying the value of both the Laker suite and the CAA battle as catalysts of change in the general outlook of BA's workforce. As two leading US business strategists have put it, '. . . the greater the threat, and the more widely it is known, the greater the likelihood that a culture can be successfully turned in another direction.'*

The long struggle in the US courts and against the CAA had played an unexpected role in rebuilding morale at BA and helping to bind its employees together into a successful company. Certainly King and his fellow directors believed that. It was in their view a key reason why the merger of BOAC and BEA, begun in 1972, could at last be described as complete. For many thousands at BA, the threat posed by the CAA in particular had undoubtedly heightened their identification with King's board. And this identification had accelerated the general acceptance of the changes which King and his colleagues engineered.

Naturally there was plenty of room for argument about BA's relative strengths and weaknesses as an airline. Surely one day – whether sooner or later – the market would have ample time to debate those. But what was really no longer at issue was the commercial nature of the enterprise. Whatever the immediate outcome of the sale plans, in fact, BA had already taken off.

* Terrence E. Deal & Allan A. Kennedy, *Corporate Cultures, The Rites and Rituals of Corporate Life* (1982).

Summary Chronology and Statistics

1979

Feb — BA writes off the £160m. cost of its five Concordes, reducing its Public Dividend Capital to £140m.

Mar — BA buys 19 Boeing 757s with Rolls-Royce RB-211 engines (Dash 535 version).

Apr — Tories disclose plans to sell off part of BA if they win the May general election.

    — Laker Airways orders ten A-300 Airbuses.

Jun — Stainton succeeds McFadzean as BA chairman and Watts becomes chief executive.

Jul — Nott, Trade Secretary, announces plan to privatise BA as soon as possible.

Sep — Watts warns employees of sliding profits.

Oct — Laker applies for 666 new routes.

Nov — Civil Aviation Bill published, to turn BA into a public company with limited liability and to provide statutory framework for the CAA.

1980

Mar — BA managers leak *Marketing Strategy: An Internal Appreciation* criticising 1978 Watts Plan.

Apr — Laker wins licence for Gatwick–Miami route and borrows $228m. to take delivery of five DC-10s.

May — Nott suggests September 1981 sale date.

Jun — BA launches £99 fare to Hong Kong.

Sep — BA launches £77 fare to New York (against Laker's £78).

    — King and Dibbs appointed chairman and deputy chairman of BA with effect from 1 February 1981.

Oct — Hill Samuel advises against any near-term privatisation: **sale date postponed until 1982**.

1981

Jan — BA cancels first-class service on many European flights.
— Laker borrows $131m. to take delivery of three A-300 European Airbuses.

Feb — King and Dibbs take up office; Henderson appointed to BA board.

Jul — Laker serves private warning to BA that it plans new first-class service on its North Atlantic routes.

Aug — The 'Moles' Report' and cash crisis at BA.
— Laker begins talks with bankers to reschedule long-term dollar debt.

Sep — BA launches Survival Plan: workforce to be cut from 52,000 to 43,000 and route network to be pruned back.

Oct — Atlantic fares cut by Pan Am, TWA and BA after meeting at CAA in London on 16 October. Laker objections overruled.
— Merchant bank Samuel Montagu appointed to assist Laker's financial reorganisation.

Dec — Talks between McDonnell Douglas, General Electric and Samuel Montagu to seek recapitalisation of Laker.

1982

Jan — IATA conference at Hollywood, Florida.

Feb — Laker rescue talks collapse; Morris of Touche Ross appointed liquidator of Laker's Jersey operating company.
— Price Waterhouse Report submitted to BA; **sale postponed from 1982 to late 1983 at the earliest**.

Apr — Mrs Thatcher approves King's plans.

May — BA restructured into intercontinental, European and charter divisions.

Jun — Dunlop appointed chief financial officer.
— Survival Plan revised: another 7,000 redundancies planned to reduce workforce from 42,000 to 35,000.

Aug — Draper and other senior executives fired.
— Expansionist commercial strategy formally abandoned.
Sep — BA switches its advertising from Foote Cone & Belding to Saatchi & Saatchi.
Oct — Dunlop submits his financial plan to Treasury.
Nov — Beckman files antitrust suit against BA and others.
— Attachment 7 handed to Midland Bank; Midland and Clydesdale gain temporary injunction against Laker.
— Britoil privatisation flops in the marketplace.

1983
Feb — Marshall appointed BA chief executive officer.
— Mr Justice Parker renews Midland injunction against Laker.
— BA central services staff set up under Jim Harris, marketing director.
Mar — Mr Justice Parker grants, then lifts, temporary injunction barring Laker liquidator from taking action against BA and others in US courts.
— US Justice Department launches Grand Jury investigation into antitrust on North Atlantic.
Apr — Saatchis launch *Manhattan Landing* campaign.
— **BA sale postponed from 1983 to late 1984**.
May — Judge Greene asserts his jurisdiction over BA et al.
— Mr Justice Parker rejects application of BA et al for permanent injunction against Laker suit.
Jun — King made a life peer in Birthday Honours List.
— Tories re-elected on 9 June.
— Trade Secretary uses Protection of Trading Interests Act (1980) to bar BA and BCal from giving evidence in Judge Greene's court.
— Aviation Division moves from Trade & Industry to Transport Department.
Jul — Mass exodus of BA senior managers, including heads of the three divisions established in 1982.
— BA restructured into eleven divisions based on eight geographical areas and three special product units.

July—*contd*
  — Court of Appeal reverses Mr Justice Parker's ruling and awards permanent injunctions to BA and BCal v. Laker.
Aug — Watts resigns from BA.
  — BA launches Heathrow/Scotland Super-Shuttle.
Sep — BA orders 14 Boeing 737s.
  — BCal hands Blue Book to the Government.
Oct — Ridley becomes Transport Secretary.
Nov — Moore's speech on Thatcherism and privatisation.
  — Law Lords' Appeal Committee allows Morris to appeal against permanent injunction served in July.
Dec — Ridley announces CAA inquiry.
  — BA staff begin 'Putting People First' courses

1984
Feb — Beckman and Rosdeitcher breakfast in London.
Mar — Stockbrokers for the sale appointed by BA.
Apr — Registration of British Airways Plc.
  — CAA Interim Report.
May — Government appoints stockbrokers for sale and commissions Stock Exchange Long Form.
  — US Justice Department drops conspiracy inquiry.
Jun — BA new pension fund fully operational.
Jul — CAA Final Report published.
  — House of Lords reach unanimous judgement in favour of Laker liquidator proceeding against BA et al.
Aug — **BA sale postponed until February 1985 at the earliest.**
Sep — UK Attorney-General in Washington for talks with White House legal counsel over Laker case.
Oct — Government White Paper published, '*Competition in Civil Aviation*'.
  — Advisers resume preparations for February 1985 sale.
  — Beckman begins deposition of Freddie in Washington.
Nov — Reagan orders dismissal of Grand Jury.
  — Lawyers advise in favour of Laker settlement ahead of any privatisation for BA. Linklaters & Paines given mandate to seek out-of-court deal. **BA sale postponed sine die.**

Dec — Park and Morris lunch at the Savoy.
— BA unveils new aircraft livery at Heathrow.
— First Speedbird House Conference of European co-defendants against Laker suit.
— Judge Greene equates antitrust law with Magna Carta.

1985
Jan — Sonesta Beach Hotel conference.
— Minor Laker creditors agree to sell their claims to Ivanhoe Investments, BA subsidiary in Jersey.
Mar — BA strikes deal with Exim Bank in Washington.
Apr — Geneva Conference of co-defendants.
May — Formal settlement offer worth $64m. presented.
Jun — Lonrho warns of independent suit.
Jul — Settlement agreed with Laker liquidator on behalf of all defendants: BA, BCal, KLM, Lufthansa, McDonnell Douglas, McDonnell Douglas Finance Corporation, Pan Am, Sabena, SAS, Swissair, TWA and UTA.
Aug — English High Court approves the settlement.
— Freddie appeals against High Court ruling and objects to approval by the Royal Court of Jersey.
— Freddie accepts $8m. pay-off.
— BA Flight Manchester/Corfu destroyed by fire during take-off.
Oct — Settlement completed for Laker suit.
Nov — Judge Greene approves proposed settlement of US class actions.
— Talks restart on BA's finances.
Dec — BA unveils new video promotion.

1986
Jan — BA roadshow begins tour of provincial cities.
— Fresh US anti-trust legal action launched against BA and others.
— BA board sets July target for sale.

1979–85 Results

Yr end 31 Mar	1979	1980	1981	1982	1983	1984	1985
Turnover (£bn.)	1.64	1.92	2.06	2.24	2.50	2.51	2.94
Operating profit (£m.)	76	17	(102)	5	169	274	303
Profit before interest and tax (£m.)	110	56	(69)	10	204	294	281
Interest payable (£m.)	(25)	(38)	(73)	(111)	(117)	(106)	(89)
Currency profits (£m.)	5	2	2	(13)	(13)	(3)	(24)
Pre-tax profit (£m.)	90	20	(140)	(114)	74	185	168
Taxation (£m.)	(13)	(9)	(4)	(5)	(11)	(3)	(2)
Extraordinary items (£m.)	—	—	—	(426)	26	33	10
Net profit (£m.)	77	11	(145)	(545)	89	215	176
Group capital & reserves (£m.)	436	451	350	(192)	(117)	127	287
Group long-term debt (£m.)	303	460	732	915	982	840	566
Operating return on net assets (%)	14.7	6.3	(6.6)	1.0	23.2	29.9	28.7
Revenue per passenger kilometre (pence)	3.28	3.35	3.74	4.20	4.89	5.57	5.87
Breakeven load factor (%)	58.2	64.0	64.5	62.7	58.0	55.2	58.2
Number (000) of employees	56.0	56.1	53.6	47.8	39.7	36.1	36.9
ATKs* (000) per employee	135	145	154	158	182	199	213

* Available tonne kilometres: the payload capacities of BA's aircraft multiplied by kms flown.

[Source: BA Annual Reports]

Bibliography

Ashworth, Mark and Forsyth, Peter, *Civil Aviation Policy and the Privatisation of British Airways*, The Institute of Fiscal Studies, London, 1984.

Banks, Howard, *The Rise and Fall of Freddie Laker*, Faber and Faber Ltd., London, 1982.

Boyfield, Keith, *The Right to Fly: Civil Aviation & Airports Policy Towards the 1990s*, The Faculties Partnership Limited, 1984.

Beesley, Michael and Littlechild, Stephen, 'Privatization: Principles, Problems and Priorities', *Lloyds Bank Review*, London, July 1983.

British Caledonian, *A Competitive Strategy for British Air Transport in Private Ownership*, The Caledonian Aviation Group Plc., Crawley, 1984.

Brittan, Samuel, 'The politics and economics of privatisation', *The Political Quarterly*, vol. 55, no. 2, London, 1984; *Jobs, Pay, Unions and the Ownership of Capital*, Financial Times, London, 1985.

Civil Aviation Authority, *Airline Competition Policy – Final Report*, CAA, London, 1984.

Deal, Terrence E. and Kennedy, Allan A., *Corporate Cultures: The Rites and Rituals of Corporate Life*, Addison-Wesley Publishing Company, Inc., London, 1982.

Dell, Edmund, 'Interdependence and the judges: civil aviation and antitrust', *International Affairs*, London, 1985.

Eglin, Roger and Ritchie, Berry, *Fly Me, I'm Freddie!*, Weidenfeld & Nicolson Limited, London, 1980.

Hermann, A. H., *Conflicts of National Laws with International Business Activity: Issues of Extraterritoriality*, The British-North American Committee, 1982.

House of Commons Transport Committee, *The Organisation, Financing and Control of Airports* (Evidence to the 1983–4 Session), HMSO, London, 1984.

House of Commons Public Accounts Committee, *Monitoring and Control of Nationalised Industries* (Departments of Energy, Trade & Industry and Transport – Report from the 1984–5 Session), HMSO, London, 1985.

National Audit Office, *Report by the Comptroller & Auditor General on Monitoring and Control of Nationalised Industries*, HMSO, London, 1984.

Osborne, Mike, Costello, Michael and Perraudin, William, *Prospects for Privatisation*, Grieveson Grant and Co. in association with *Public Money*, 1984.

Porter, Michael E., *Competitive Advantage: Creating and Sustaining Superior Performance*, The Free Press, New York, 1985.

Rosenthal, Douglas E. and Knighton, William M., *National Laws and International Commerce: The Problem of Extraterritoriality*, Chatham House Papers, No. 17, Routledge & Kegan Paul Ltd., London, 1982.

Sampson, Anthony, *Empires of the Sky: the Politics, Contests and Cartels of World Airlines*, Hodder & Stoughton, London, 1984.

Seward, Bill and Morrison, David, *British Airways*, Phillips & Drew and Wood, Mackenzie & Co., London, 1984.

Stevens, Mark, *The Big Eight: An Inside View of America's Most Powerful and Influential Accounting Firms*, Macmillan Publishing Co. Inc., 1981.

Vickers, John and Yarrow, George, *Privatisation and the Natural Monopolies*, Public Policy Centre, 1985.

Index

319

321

322

323